Sanctification

Sanctification

A User's Guide to Becoming More Like Jesus

Thomas D. Hawkes

Foreword by Sinclair Ferguson

WIPF & STOCK · Eugene, Oregon

SANCTIFICATION
A User's Guide to Becoming More Like Jesus

Copyright © 2020 Thomas D. Hawkes. All rights reserved. Except for brief quotations in critical publications or reviews, no part of this book may be reproduced in any manner without prior written permission from the publisher. Write: Permissions, Wipf and Stock Publishers, 199 W. 8th Ave., Suite 3, Eugene, OR 97401.

Wipf & Stock
An Imprint of Wipf and Stock Publishers
199 W. 8th Ave., Suite 3
Eugene, OR 97401

www.wipfandstock.com

PAPERBACK ISBN: 978-1-7252-6870-8
HARDCOVER ISBN: 978-1-7252-6869-2
EBOOK ISBN: 978-1-7252-6871-5

Manufactured in the U.S.A.   10/05/20

Scripture quotations are from the ESV® Bible (The Holy Bible, English Standard Version®), copyright © 2001 by Crossway, a publishing ministry of Good News Publishers. Used by permission. All rights reserved.

To Ann Carpenter Hawkes,
wife, mother, grandmother, mentor, educator, and
my faithful companion in the journey toward Christ and holiness.

"She opens her mouth with wisdom,
and the teaching of kindness is on her tongue."
—Prov 31:26

Christ loved the church and gave himself up for her,
that he might sanctify her.

—Eph 5:25–26

Contents

Foreword by Sinclair Ferguson | ix
Preface | xiii
Introduction | xv

1. Understand Holiness | 1
2. Desire Holiness | 21
3. Rely on God | 39
4. Seek the Twofold Knowledge of God and Self | 58
5. Engage God's Word | 79
6. Apprehend God's Love | 97
7. Struggle for Faith | 119
8. Repent Regularly | 135
9. Deny Yourself | 155
10. Bear the Cross | 172
11. Contemplate Heaven | 188
12. Properly Use This Life | 203
13. Engage the Church | 218

Bibliography | 239

Foreword

I STILL LOVE THE AV (King James) translation of Peter's words to the paralyzed Aeneas in Acts 9:34: *Jesus Christ maketh thee whole*. The apostle was speaking about physical restoration. But since the effect was a massive turning to faith in Christ, it seems that Aeneas was not only healed but his entire life was transformed. The power of the risen Christ pushed back the devastating effects of the fall in his life. He was not only made *physically well*; he was made *spiritually whole*. From now, from this dramatic beginning—indeed a conversion—the rest of his life would involve the progressive outworking of its implications. Paul's later words were certainly true for him: "If anyone is in Christ, he is a new creation" (2 Cor 5:17).

The wonderful truth that "Jesus Christ maketh thee whole," that he still pushes back the effects of sin in our lives, and transforms us into his image, is the conviction that lies behind these pages. *Sanctification: A User's Guide to Becoming More Like Jesus* is in fact a guidebook for the journey this involves and a manual to help us understand and indeed experience how the Holy Spirit effects this transformation. We need a guidebook because it is easy for us to lose the way and wander from the path. We also need a manual because this process involves an extended deconstruction and reconstruction. For that reason, it is vital that we understand what God is doing, or we may become confused and discouraged because the process is taking longer, and perhaps hurts more, than we had expected.

To change the metaphor, what we have here is a textbook on the anatomy of sanctification and an introduction to the medicine chest of the grace of Jesus Christ. Sin has complicated our lives—mentally, spiritually, emotionally, and morally. The gospel simplifies them. But paradoxically many of us prefer to remain complex and complicated and sometimes stubbornly resist going to the True Physician for help.

It is just here that these pages come to our help. Tom Hawkes, their author, is in fact a doctor—of philosophy—which means, literally, that he is a doctor who loves wisdom. In other words, he is a soul-physician. But more than that he writes out of long personal experience of Christ's whole-making-ministry, and also being an attending physician in the Savior's healing of others. As you work your way through *Sanctification: A User's Guide to Becoming More Like Jesus* you will find at times that he is probing and pushing, but all the while explaining and encouraging. And during your consultation you will discover, sometimes in moving ways, that he too has been where you are; he is not merely repeating the phraseology of the technical manuals he read in school.

Since I serve here in the capacity of a receptionist to welcome you to these pages, may I offer a few words of encouragement as you head for Dr. Hawkes' consulting room?

First, lest you be surprised by the number of references you will find in these pages to some weighty figures in the history of the church, let me assure you that the vast majority of them were themselves expert soul-physicians. As it happens, about two-thirds of these references are to the writings of the same man—John Calvin. But do not be surprised, for besides preaching on average five or six times a week, endless letter dictating, serving as a Professor of Old Testament Studies, writing great books, every Thursday he sat with a group of others to give spiritual counsel to people in the congregation, many of whom had gone astray. So, he well understood the sicknesses and dysfunctions of the spiritual life and he was well acquainted with the spiritual remedies Scripture provides.

But secondly, because you will be given spiritual medicine in these pages, there are some simple instructions you should follow:

"Keep taking the medicine." This book is not a one-off injection that promises to work on its own. It is not a book to be read at a single sitting—or, for that matter, at two or three sittings. Like the Scriptures (in the words of the Anglican Collect for the Second Sunday in Advent), it is a book you need to "read, mark, learn, and inwardly digest." So, take it a chapter at a time, let its teaching sink in, and meditate on it until it all becomes part of you.

"Finish the Course." Sin is stubborn; and what our forefathers called "remaining sin" can prove to be very stubborn indeed. In fact, the more we grow in holiness the more we discover just how deeply engrained, and indeed hidden, sin can be in our lives. The treatment we need is multiplex and manifold. Sin needs to be identified and dealt with, and at the same

time strength needs to be built up for future growth. So, *finish the course of medicine;* do not stop short of the end—otherwise you will mistakenly think you can be whole when you have taken only half the cure.

So, now, let me open the door into *Sanctification: A User's Guide to Becoming More Like Jesus.* Dr. Hawkes is ready to see you now. I hope your consultations and treatment go well!

Sinclair Ferguson

Preface

Thank you for your interest in becoming more like Jesus! In offering you this book it is my deep hope that you will find help here. Not that this book is anything, but that our Lord, and his Word, that these pages will point you to, are everything. I offer you these chapters as a fellow struggler who has met his own sins face to face in dark alleys at night, and sometimes gotten mugged! No sinner who writes about holiness can pretend to have attained it. But I hope that from years of personal struggle, marriage, parenting, pastoral ministry, and scholarship that here I may be of some help to you on your journey with Jesus.

This book is designed to be, as the title suggests, a user's manual. This means that, as Dr. Ferguson has mentioned, it will be most helpful if you take it up a chapter at a time and work through the concepts there, even practicing them. I have included reflection questions with each chapter, either for you to use individually or to discuss with others, perhaps in a small group setting. If one chapter is particularly helpful and you want to know more, I have added further resources on each topic which may prove beneficial. And like any manual, you may need to return again and again to those pages which address the particular issues you are then currently facing. Going through a new trial? Try working through "Bear the Cross" again. Feeling stale in your Bible reading? Spend some time in "Engage God's Word." Does God seem remote? The chapter on "Apprehend God's Love," may help warm your heart. Are you finding church boring? Revisit "Engage the Church."

May I ask this of you? In your pursuit of becoming more like Jesus, please, do not be discouraged and give up. The Christian life is not one of ease, nor is it one of steady progress with no setbacks. Our lives in this world are a type of war, and it will often feel as if we have lost great battles with our own sin. Just then, at that moment, turn afresh to your Savior, who died and lives that you might finally be victorious in every battle. For Jesus' victory on the cross secured not only the forgiveness of your sin, but your final and full sanctification as well. "Christ loved the church and gave himself up for her, that he might sanctify her" (Eph 5:25–26). Jesus means for you to find more life—which means more holiness—in him, so don't give up! "I came that they may have life, and have it abundantly" (John 10:10). Please, keep turning to him, and you will find his promises, and his power, all true.

Thomas D. Hawkes
Charlotte, North Carolina
June 3, 2020

Introduction

How can I help them? That is the question I ask about all those who have turned to me in over forty years of ministry—couples in marriage crises, parents wondering how to raise children, new elders trying to shepherd their flock, a widow whose husband had just taken his life, church planters trying to lead their churches. How can I help them? What can I offer that will help them know Christ, to find help from him, to become like him? This is the question that every Christian leader must answer: how, at this moment, with this person, can I help? How can I help them move forward, progress, becoming in this instance, more like Jesus?

This question has moved me over the decades to seek answers to how best help God's people grow in holiness. Why holiness? Because the answer to the question for all those different people is, broadly speaking, holiness. The couple in crises must learn to see their own sins, and repenting of them, come to Jesus for help. The young parents must learn to follow Jesus and lead their children to Jesus. The new elder must come to the Great Shepherd to learn how to shepherd others. The widow must learn to bear a terrible cross as she follows Jesus. The church planters must learn to lead like Jesus. All of these are holiness.

If we want to help people, then, when we ask, "How can I help?" we mean, "How can I help them grow in holiness?" That is, "How can I help them become more like Jesus?"

There are, of course, no lack of those pointing to various ways to grow in holiness. Follow this teaching, practice this discipline, pray this prayer, and you will grow in holiness—guaranteed. Not surprisingly with these many divergent spiritual directors there is more confusion over how to advance in sanctification in our day than in many periods of church history.

It would seem that other ages have understood far better than ours how to help Christians grow strong and more like Christ. Read Gregory's *Pastoral Care* from around 600 AD, or Martin Bucer's *The True Care of Souls* from around 1530, or Walter Marshall's *The Gospel Mystery of Sanctification* from around 1690, and you will realize that the answer to the question, "How can I help them grow in holiness?" has been well understood by our predecessors. It is a wonder that somehow we have forgotten, or ignored, much of what they have known.

Among the various ways to address the question "How do we help them grow more holy?" few traditions, if any, offers more biblical clarity than the Reformed. The Reformers were single-mindedly dedicated to helping Christians become more like Christ. Among the great Reformers there arose a general consensus, a best practices, of how to help people become like Christ. They scoured the Scripture, and the church fathers, looking for that wisdom that is from above. They were extremely successful. They came to understand all the various aspects of the Christian life, biblical teaching, and ministerial practice, and how they all were to be woven together to help the body of Christ grow up in the unity of the faith.

They understood, as too many in our day do not, that it was not just one key—memorize this, or meditate on that—but rather, they understood the entire system of holiness that God had designed. How God had intended the various aspects of ministry to be used in harmony—church membership, church discipline, preaching, Bible study, self-denial, suffering, admonition, encouragement, prayer, faith, repentance—to help those who appeared before them grow in holiness, that is, to become like Jesus. Today there is a crying need for Christian leaders to better understand how we can help others grow in holiness.

My Passion to Help Others Grow in Holiness

There has been a singular passion directing my work for years—to help develop the next generation of leaders for the next generation of churches. This single focus has abided with me through many ministry permutations—campus ministry, on staff with Billy Graham's *Amsterdam '86*, training and assessing church planters for the Presbyterian Church in America, designing and directing the *Arrow Leadership Program*, pastoring Uptown Church, and teaching at Reformed Theological Seminary.

Introduction xvii

Over the course of that time I have noticed a paradox in the church. We have gifted leaders, and we have godly leaders, but too rarely are they in the same person. We can send out men who will start churches that might quickly grow to a thousand members, but then through leadership conflicts, or moral failures, their ministry would fall apart. Self-confident to a fault they had gifts and charisma but their characters were often in tatters. They desperately needed help in holiness.

This singular passion to develop leaders for the next generation of churches, along with the clear problem that we have too few leaders who combine godliness with giftedness, led me to further study. I entered a PhD program with the question: "How do we help Christian leaders become more like Jesus?" After considering several historical options, I decided to focus on the Genevan Academy where we find a nexus of theological depth, understanding of holiness and its formation, ecclesiastical sophistication, mission focus, and proven effectiveness.

The result of that study, and a lifetime of ministry in trying to help develop leaders for the church, is contained in this book. While I share insights from several Reformers, Puritans, and other historical and modern theologians, the structure of my insights are primarily from Calvin. Coming to understand what the Reformers understood about sanctification and training in holiness has transformed me and my ministry. Not a day goes by where I am not indebted to them for making me more helpful as a pastor and as a leader-developer. My simple prayer is that their insights, brought forward here, however imperfectly, will help you as well.

The Structure of This Book

I hope to offer in this book a comprehensive explanation for how to grow in holiness along with practical steps to guide that growth. Hence the subtitle: A user's guide to becoming more like Jesus.

The chapters of this book fall into four parts. In the first part we will lay the conceptual and theological foundations for holiness. In chapter 1, "Understand Holiness," we will define holiness and discuss what roles God and we play in our quest for holiness. In chapter 2, "Desire Holiness," we will look at why God wants us to be holy and why we should too. "As the business of the soldier is to fight, so the business of the Christian is to be like Christ, to be holy as he is holy."[1] Chapter 3, "Rely on God,"

1. Edwards, *Charity and its Fruits*, 249.

will discuss the great work of our triune God to make us holy, encouraging us to look to him, and explaining precisely how we are to rely on God to become holy. Chapter 4, "Seek Knowledge of God and Self," lays out the central paradigm which the Reformers used, showing that holiness moves forward with our growth in the understanding of God and ourselves. "The true knowledge of God is that which regenerates and renews us, so that we become new creatures; and that hence it cannot be but that it must conform us to the image of God."[2]

The second part, chapters 5–8, covers the broad methods of sanctification which are universally applicable: how to engage the Bible to grow in holiness (5), how best to apprehend God's love to become holy (6), how to struggle for faith (7), and how to repent (8).

The third part, chapters 9–12, cover Calvin's particular focus in his chapters on the Life of the Christian Man, where he relates four dynamic sanctification practices: self-denial (9), cross bearing (10), meditation on the future life (11), and the proper use of this present life (12). When embracing the cross we do well to keep in mind the sentiment of Thomas à Kempis, from whom Calvin had learned of the importance of cross bearing. "In the cross is salvation, in the cross is life, in the cross is protection from enemies, in the cross is infusion of heavenly sweetness, in the cross is strength of mind, in the cross is joy of spirit, in the cross is highest virtue, in the cross is perfect holiness."[3]

In the final part, chapter 13, we will address the more corporate aspects of holiness, life in the church. Our age must come to see that holiness is not an individual pursuit but was designed by God to be communal. Few have understood this with more clarity and passion than Martin Bucer. "The healing of wounded sheep is a work of Christ himself which he wishes to carry out through the agency of *all* Christians"[4] (emphasis added).

There you have it, our plan for the book, as well as our rationale for writing it. I only want to add this, I hope—sincerely I do—that this book, or at least something in it, will help you onward as you seek to follow Christ and become more like him. Our pursuit of holiness, of becoming more like Jesus, is not just a minor part of our life, it is the whole thing. It is in fact why Jesus came, that he might make us into his holy bride. May he do so increasingly for us all!

2. Calvin, *Commentaries*, 1 John 4:7. Hereafter: Calvin, *Com*.
3. Thomas á Kempis, *The Imitation of Christ*, 2:12.
4. Bucer, *True Care of Souls*, 100–101.

"Christ loved the church and gave himself up for her, that he might sanctify her, having cleansed her by the washing of water with the word, so that he might present the church to himself in splendor, without spot or wrinkle or any such thing, that she might be holy and without blemish" (Eph 5:25–27).[5]

---

5. English Standard Version. This translation will be used throughout.

1

Understand Holiness

What Is Holiness?

HOLINESS HAS A BAD reputation in our day. Many view holiness as either a stiff discipline—that always eats its vegetables first—or as simply being nice, like Barney, the purple dinosaur. But biblical holiness is much more than these.

For several years I had the joy of teaching a church revitalization seminar with Dr. Jack Miller.[1] Jack went to be with the Lord before our final seminar, so I was obliged to teach it alone. After the first night I felt as though I were missing something, and asked my wife: "What would Jack be doing differently?" Without hesitation she replied: "Laughing more!" Jack was one of the most holy men I have known. He loved Jesus

---

1. Jack Miller is perhaps best known for his work establishing the New Life congregations in Philadelphia, founding World Harvest Mission (now Serge), and creating the *Sonship* training program. *Sonship* has had many fans, as well as some critics. As a former mentee to Jack Miller, and past board member for World Harvest, I am both a fan of *Sonship* and, at points, a friendly critic. *Sonship* is intentionally a focused course on justification and adoption. It is not a book on sanctification, or a systematic theology textbook. It was aimed originally at a very orthodox Presbyterian audience, intending to help them find balance by understanding the freedom of knowing God's fatherly love. It was the right message for many, myself included. However, to an antinomian generation, such as we often find today, that at points believes they should merely be accepted for who they are, without any expectation of change toward holiness, the teachings of those original materials could potentially be dangerous. Happily, the leadership of Serge recognized this very issue and modified the original materials to encourage the obedience of faith by offering a helpful understanding of the third use of the Law, that is, where the Law serves as a guide for believers in their life with God.

and preached the gospel fearlessly, with winsome laughter at his own self-deprecating humor.

Holiness is far more than being either disciplined or nice, although holy people may well be both. Holiness is powerful and humble, true and loving, strong and beautiful. "As a general rule, in the long run of life, it will be found true that "sanctified" people are the happiest people on earth."[2] There is a new image: holy is happy.

Holiness is being like Jesus. His anger rose at hypocrisy, his compassion swelled facing brokenness, his passion drew him toward time with his Father, hurting women trusted him, and evil men feared him. He was the most fully human person to walk the planet since humanity had fallen.

Holiness makes us neither stiffly formal nor sickly sweet. Holiness makes us into the men and women God had intended us to be, men and women like Jesus. "Genuine holiness is genuine Christlikeness, and genuine Christlikeness is genuine humanness—the only genuine humanness there is."[3] Holiness is to be like Christ, fully and completely human. Who would not want that?

Who would not want be more like Jesus, who was wholly devoted to God? "To be holy . . . is . . . to be *devoted to God*."[4] This is a wonderful definition, intentionally simple and accurate. I offer an expanded definition only to allow a more technical understanding of holiness, used throughout this book.

> Holiness is relational wholeness with God where we are set apart from sin and wholly devoted to God so that, loving God and others, we are restored to the true image of Christ, and so render the obedience of faith to the Law of God.

Three Aspects of Holiness Explained

Before we explain our definition of holiness it would be helpful to differentiate three aspects of holiness: positional, definitive, and progressive sanctification.

---

2. Ryle, *Holiness*, 34.
3. Packer, *Rediscovering Holiness*, 27.
4. Ferguson, *Devoted to God*, 4.

Positional sanctification. The Bible makes it clear that when God saves a person he changes their position in regard to himself: they are set apart from the world to be included among his people, this is positional sanctification. We see this being set apart for God, positional sanctification, throughout Scripture. "You shall be holy to me, for I the LORD am holy and have separated you from the peoples, that you should be mine" (Lev 20:26). The same concept is found in the New Testament. "But you are a chosen race, a royal priesthood, a holy nation, a people for his own possession" (1 Pet 2:9).

In choosing us to be his, God changes our status in the world. When a woman is chosen to be a wife it changes her: her name changes, her status changes, her self-concept changes. In a similar way our status is transformed by the very act of God setting us apart as his. We are transformed from "not a people" into the children of God.

This positional holiness arises from God's choosing love for us and not by our own doing. "It was not because you were more in number than any other people that the LORD set his love on you and chose you, for you were the fewest of all peoples, but it is because the LORD loves you" (Deut 7:6–8). As we consider making progress in holiness we do well to remember that because we have been chosen in Christ we are already positionally holy.

Definitive sanctification. In definitive holiness our nature is distinctly changed by the work of redemption such that we are a new holy creation, dead to sin and alive to righteousness. "The Scripture's representations of conversion strongly imply and signify a change of nature: such as being born again; becoming new creatures; rising from the dead; being renewed in the spirit of the mind; dying to sin and living to righteousness."[5]

Passages such as 2 Cor 5:17 describe the definitive nature of this change. "Therefore, if anyone is in Christ, he is a new creation. The old has passed away; behold, the new has come." When we are saved we become *in Christ* and this essentially changes our nature by uniting us to him, freeing us from sin's dominion and implanting Christ's living righteousness within us. "Every believer is a new man . . . the old man has been crucified."[6]

Notice the force of the words of Rom 6 as it describes our definitive sanctification: our old self was crucified and we have been set free from

---

5. Ortlund, *Edwards on the Christian Life*, 42.
6. Murray, "Definitive Sanctification," 21.

sin. These are not hypothetical assertions of what we might be one day. These are all couched as the definitive sanctification that has already been wrought in us. "We know that our old self was crucified with him in order that the body of sin might be brought to nothing, so that we would no longer be enslaved to sin. For one who has died has been set free from sin" (Rom 6:5–7). We are essentially changed.

Augustine taught that human nature exists in four distinct states: the states of innocence, sin, grace, and glory. In the state of innocence, which only lasted through the first two chapters of Genesis, the human will was able to sin and able to not sin (*posse peccare, posse non peccare*). Sadly, our first parents chose to sin. This plunged us into a state of sin where human nature was not able to not sin (*non posse non peccare*). When the Holy Spirit regenerates us in Christ as new creations we enter the state of grace, where we are able to not sin, or to sin (*posse non peccare, posse peccare*). This fundamental change in our natures is definitive sanctification. We await the final state of glory where we will be unable to sin (*non posse peccare*), an entirely new state.

It is helpful in our battle with remaining sin to understand what is definitively new about us. Our will is changed: from a bad will to a good will, from a will that cannot resist sin to one that can, from a will that opposes God to one which submits to him. Our reason is changed. Before Christ our reason was twisted by our sin, but now our minds are set free to process information more accurately. Our heart is changed. Before, we would naturally hate God and love ourselves, now we naturally love God and hate our sin. In Christ, we really are new creations!

Progressive sanctification. Set apart positionally, changed definitively, we are also being changed day by day. This gradual changing of our lives where sin is put to death and righteousness is more and more lived out is progressive sanctification. We are to actively participate in our progressive sanctification.

> Put to death therefore what is earthly in you: sexual immorality, impurity, passion, evil desire, and covetousness, which is idolatry. . . . Do not lie to one another, seeing that you have put off the old self with its practices and have put on the new self, which is being renewed in knowledge after the image of its creator (Col 3:5–10).

Daily we are to make gains in holiness by the power of Christ and by our right use of the means of grace.

We will primarily focus in this book on the ways in which progressive sanctification takes place. Yet each aspect of sanctification has important implications for us in our restored relationship with God, which is holiness. Positional holiness means that God has set us apart to be his people that we might be in relationship to him. Definitive sanctification means that God has changed our nature such that we will desire relationship with him. Progressive sanctification cleanses us so that we are increasingly suited for relationship with a holy God.

Holiness Expounded

Holiness is relational wholeness with God. Holiness is relational. That relationship, one of devotion to God, leads to behaviors, but it starts in the heart. This is why Jesus could summarize the Law in relational terms. "You shall love the Lord your God with all your heart. . . . You shall love your neighbor as yourself" (Matt 22:37–39). God's aim in redeeming a people for himself is that we might be in relationship with him, which is holiness.

A common image used throughout Scripture to communicate this relational wholeness is marriage. "I will betroth you to me forever. . . . I will betroth you to me in faithfulness" (Hos 2:19–20). We hear similar language in Ephesians. "Husbands, love your wives, as Christ loved the church and gave himself up for her" (Eph 5:25). Christ's aim in giving himself up for the church was to sanctify her so she might become his holy bride. Restoring us to relationship to him *is* holiness.

The Pharisees misunderstood this relational aspect of holiness, thinking instead that holiness was mere outward conformity to the Law. Jesus rebuked them. "Well did Isaiah prophesy of you, when he said: 'This people honors me with their lips, but their heart is far from me'" (Matt 15:7–9). God wants our hearts first, a restored relationship, we dare not offer simple external compliance.

Holiness is first relational wholeness with God. Hearts that were distant from him are brought close to him. Wills that resented his power, now bend compliantly before him. Minds that refused to acknowledge him as good, praise his goodness. We who were estranged from God are now God's people (Hos 2:23). We who were the enemies of God are now God's friends. "I have called you friends" (John 15:15). We who were aliens and foreigners are now God's children (1 John 3:1). Holiness is, first and foremost, relational wholeness with God.

Where we are set apart from sin. Holiness is sinlessness. Because we are being redeemed as sinners out of a sinful world then all progress toward holiness is progress away from sin. Here is the negative aspect of sanctification—mortification—putting to death remaining sin. "Put to death therefore what is earthly in you: sexual immorality, impurity, passion, evil desire, and covetousness, which is idolatry" (Col 3:5). God means for us to be daily fighting against sin, to show it no quarter, to give it no space in our hearts or minds.

There is a strain of thought today that suggests that, since we are yet sinful, we should simply make peace with our sin. The Bible knows no such thought. "If by the Spirit you put to death the deeds of the body, you will live" (Rom 8:13). Yes, during the whole of this life we will sin, but we are never therefore to declare a truce with our sin, but rather we are to battle it constantly. John Owen said: "Be killing sin or it will be killing you."[7] To yield to sin, to accept sin as part of who we are, is to discount the grace and mercy of God for us. "Not to be daily mortifying sin, is to sin against the goodness, kindness, wisdom, grace, and love of God, who hath furnished us with a principle of doing it."[8]

We are called to cleanse ourselves from all sin. "Since we have these promises, beloved, let us cleanse ourselves from every defilement of body and spirit, bringing holiness to completion in the fear of God" (2 Cor 7:1). This cleansing we cannot do by our own power but only by the Holy Spirit-applied cleansing blood of Christ. Yet we are to strive toward this cleansing, confessing and coming to Christ again and again for cleansing. "If we confess our sins, he is faithful and just to forgive us our sins and to cleanse us from all unrighteousness" (1 John 1:9).

Though we will battle sin all of our lives on Earth, we are never to befriend sin, for Christ came to eliminate it from us and wants our complete cooperation in this endeavor. "Hence, as we are redeemed by the grace of God, it is befitting that we keep ourselves undefiled in respect of all uncleanness, that we may not pollute the sanctuary of God."[9] Holiness is sinlessness and we are to daily use all the means of grace to rid ourselves of all sin, every spot, wrinkle, and stain of it.

Wholly devoted to God. Here is the positive aspect of sanctification—vivification—where we are increasingly made righteous in all aspects of

---

7. Owen, *Mortification of Sin*, 9.
8. Owen, *Mortification of Sin*, 11.
9. Calvin, *Com.*, 2 Cor 7:1.

our lives: mind, will, heart, body, possessions, etc. Holiness is not just the absence of sin, but the positive, overflowing presence of righteousness. Having been justified by Christ, he continues to work in us such that we actually grow in righteousness.

Growing in holiness our minds are increasingly devoted to God. "Set your minds on things that are above, not on things that are on earth" (Col 3:2). All aspects of our minds—our knowledge and reason—are renewed in Christ. "Put on the new self, which is being renewed in knowledge after the image of its creator" (Col 3:10).

Sin is a kind of insanity which prevented us from seeing God as God and ourselves as his indebted creatures. When we are redeemed our reason returns. "Be transformed by the renewal of your mind" (Rom 12:2). We gain a true knowledge of God and of ourselves, the double-knowledge that is needed to restore us to a right view of reality that we might live in line with it. "The true knowledge of God is that which regenerates and renews us, so that we become new creatures."[10]

The renewed Christian mind is to be filled with "whatever is true, whatever is honorable, whatever is just, whatever is pure, whatever is lovely" (Phil 4:8), so that our minds work well in devoted submission to God who is truth and beauty. Our thoughts are of God, our dreams and hopes as well. We are entirely devoted to God in our renewed minds.

When we were in sin our wills were bound fast by sin. "No one can claim that anything else is responsible for his sinning except an evil will."[11] Freed by Christ our wills can will what God wills, submitting to and cooperating with him to bring about his will rather than resisting it. "Unless the will itself is liberated by the grace of God from the bondage that made it the slave of sin and is helped to overcome its faults, it is impossible to live an upright and godly life."[12] Our renewed will is increasingly devoted to God.

Our hearts must be renewed so that we can be lovingly devoted to God. "You shall love the Lord your God with all your heart" (Matt 22:37). As God pours his love into our hearts they are transformed so that hatred melts away and love flows for God and others. Our hearts are made whole toward God, purely devoted to God, eager to serve him. "As bondservants of Christ, doing the will of God from the heart" (Eph 6:6).

---

10. Calvin, *Com.*, 1 John 4:7.
11. Calvin, *Bondage and Liberation*, 169.
12. Calvin, *Bondage and Liberation*, 92; Calvin cites Augustine, *Retractions* 1.9.4.

Our bodies are devoted to God, so are increasingly used to serve him. "Present your bodies as a living sacrifice, holy and acceptable to God, which is your spiritual worship" (Rom 12:1). We stop using our bodies for sin and start using them for the Lord (1 Cor 6:13). We are no longer controlled by our sexual appetites but by the Spirit (1 Thess 4:4). Our tongues are no longer used for complaining or boasting but to bring Christ honor (Jas 3:2). Our physical devotion to Christ culminates when our bodies become like his body in glory (Phil 3:21). We are physical creatures so it is essential that our bodies be devoted to God: that our lips praise him, our hands serve him, and our feet walk in his ways. "So glorify God in your body" (1 Cor 6:20).

Our possessions and material wealth are devoted to God. Previously they had been used to serve our twisted will ("For the love of money is a root of all kinds of evils" [1 Tim 6:10]). Redeemed by Christ we no longer love money, but increasingly our wealth is given and invested for the forward movement of God's kingdom. "Their abundance of joy and their extreme poverty have overflowed in a wealth of generosity on their part" (2 Cor 8:2). Devoted to God we find our joy in giving our wealth for him.

Holiness is devotion to God. All we have and all we are is used to honor and glorify God. Calvin's personal motto captured this desire for total devotion to God. "My heart I offer as though slain in sacrifice to God."[13] That is whole devotion; that is holiness.

Loving God and others. Before we knew God's love, we were filled with enmity for God, but when we believe on Christ, we live with the constant shower of God's love poured out to our hearts (Rom 5:5). In response to being loved so powerfully we love God in return. "We love because he first loved us" (1 John 4:19). Filled with God's love, we naturally love those around us as well (1 John 4:11). Growing in love for God and others we grow in holiness. "Sanctification is growing in holy-love; love is growing in holiness."[14]

We are restored to true order of the image of Christ. When God originally created us he made us in his very own image (Gen 1:26). Then, we loved God and our neighbor, and we served God with thankful hearts. This true and right order of humanity was effaced, although not destroyed, with our fall into sin: we loved ourselves, hated God and our neighbors, and we rebelled against God.

---

13. Calvin, *Ioannis Calvini Opera*, 11:100.
14. Ferguson, *Devoted to God*, 18.

The grace of Christ moves us in a single direction: toward the restoration of that true order as we are recreated into the image of Christ. "Just as we have borne the image of the man of dust, we shall also bear the image of the man of heaven" (1 Cor 15:49). This is sanctification.[15] Christ, the second Adam, contains in himself the blueprint for a renewed humanity which will be restored to the true order that God had always intended for them.[16] "For those whom he foreknew he also predestined to be conformed to the image of his Son" (Rom 8:29). Holiness for us is restoration to the perfect humaneness which is the image of Christ. "Now we see how Christ is the most perfect image of God; if we are conformed to it, we are so restored that with true piety, righteousness, purity, and intelligence we bear God's image."[17]

Looking on Christ in Scripture with the eyes of faith is transformative. To see him is to become like him. "And we all, with unveiled face, beholding the glory of the Lord, are being transformed into the same image from one degree of glory to another" (2 Cor 3:18). This process of reshaping us into the true order, the image of Christ, continues throughout our lives and is completed when we finally look on him in heaven and see him fully. "When he appears we shall be like him, because we shall see him as he is" (1 John 3:2). Holiness is Christlikeness, which is the restoration of the true order, the original design for humanity.

We render the obedience of faith (to the Law of God). There is much confusion about the role of obedience to the Law in modern evangelicalism. The confusion is so extreme that some believe that every attempt at obedience to the Law is legalism. However, Christ wants us to render the obedience of faith for his glory. "Jesus Christ our Lord, through whom we have received grace and apostleship to bring about the obedience of faith for the sake of his name among all the nations" (Rom 1:4–5).

Apart from grace, some may attempt to offer God the "obedience of the law," that is, perfect conformity to his Law in order to be judged righteous. The chief problem with the obedience of the Law is that it cannot make us right with God. "By works of the law no one will be justified" (Gal 2:16). Also, the Law is powerless to produce our obedience. That power only comes to us through faith in Christ, for those "who walk not according to the flesh but according to the Spirit" (Rom 8:4).

---

15. Calvin, *Com.*, Eph 4:24.
16. Calvin, *Com.*, 2 Cor 3:18.
17. Calvin, *Institutes*, 1.15.4.

Indeed, the obedience of faith is only possible for those who know they have already been declared righteous. The obedience of faith flows in the midst of loving covenant relationship where God as our Father instructs, corrects, and guides, and we joyfully follow the instruction of his Word. "When then the Lord goes before us with his instruction and shows the way, and we become teachable and obedient, and look up to him, and turn not aside, either to the right or to the left hand, but bring our whole life to the obedience of faith,—this is really to follow the Lord."[18]

God means for us to grow in this obedience of faith. "Now to him who is able to strengthen you according to my gospel . . . to bring about the obedience of faith" (Rom 16:25–26). The end of God's entire plan of redemption is that we might become a people who absolutely delight to obey their Father in love and faith. Walking in the obedience of faith we know even more love from God. "If you keep my commandments, you will abide in my love" (John 15:10). Abiding in love and obeying commandments are not opposites, but all part of the true order to which we are restored. Holiness is rendering to God the obedience of faith.

(We render the obedience of faith) to the Law of God. There is much confusion around the role of the Law in the life of the Christian in our day, as there has often been. Hearing the Scripture say, "If you are led by the Spirit, you are not under the law" (Gal 5:18), and "For Christ is the end of the law for righteousness to everyone who believes" (Rom 10:4), makes it sound as if we can ignore the Law. Therefore, we need to rightly understand in what ways we are set free from the Law, and in what respects the Law is still to aid the Christian. We are set free from the Law in many ways.

1. We are free from the Law's power to condemn us before God. We will not be judged by the Law, since through Christ's perfect obedience imputed to us, we have fulfilled it all. "There is therefore now no condemnation for those who are in Christ Jesus. For the law of the Spirit of life has set you free in Christ Jesus from the law of sin and death" (Rom 8:1–2).

2. We are free from trying to find our righteousness by fulfilling the Law. Instead of a righteousness which comes from perfect obedience—impossible for us—we are made righteous by faith in Christ, who did obey perfectly (Phil 3:9). Since we look to Christ for our righteousness and not the Law, this explains Rom 10:4, "Christ is the end of the law for righteousness to everyone who believes."

---

18. Calvin, *Com.*, Hos 1:2.

3. We are free from the Law's power to condemn our consciences. While the Law does serve to condemn the consciences of those outside of Christ who will be judged by it, the Christian conscience is free from the Law's condemnation. Since Christ perfectly obeyed the Law, even when we fail, our consciences may turn to Christ to find their righteousness. "How much more will the blood of Christ . . . purify our conscience" (Heb 9:14).

4. We are free from the Law's demand of perfect obedience in order to be rewarded by God. Within the covenant of grace, God accepts and rewards our always imperfect obedience as though it were perfect, since Christ's perfect obedience is imputed to us. Calvin brings out this point as he comments on Gal 5:18, "If you are led by the Spirit, you are not under the law." "The performance of their duties is not rejected on account of their present defects, but is accepted in the sight of God, as if it had been in every respect perfect and complete."[19]

5. We are set free from the Law's inability to produce obedience and its tendency to produce rebellion. Before knowing Christ, our sin nature was aroused against the Law (Rom 7:5). But in Christ, our new nature, with a heart for God, delights in the Law as a path of life. "I delight to do your will, O my God; your law is within my heart" (Ps 40:8).

6. We are set free from the ceremonial requirements of the Law. Since we are in the new administration of the covenant of grace, the Old Testament ceremonies—which were always intended to serve as signs pointing to Christ—are fulfilled in him and made obsolete. "In speaking of a new covenant, he makes the first one obsolete" (Heb 8:13).

Set free from the Law we walk in the paths of its commands by the Spirit. Set free from the Law's negative powers, we have a new relationship with the Law. The Law is no longer an enemy who condemns our failures and whips us with guilt, but our friend who, fueled by the Spirit and the righteousness of Christ, lights the way to follow Christ. We are not free, therefore, to ignore the Law as our guide for holy living.

---

19. Calvin, *Com.*, Gal 5:18.

> For truly, I say to you, until heaven and earth pass away, not an iota, not a dot, will pass from the Law until all is accomplished. Therefore whoever relaxes one of the least of these commandments and teaches others to do the same will be called least in the kingdom of heaven, but whoever does them and teaches them will be called great in the kingdom of heaven (Matt 5:18–19).

Nor does freedom from the Law mean that we are free to sin. "How can we who died to sin still live in it?" (Rom 6:1–2). Sin is well defined as "any lack of conformity to, or transgression of, the Law of God." (Westminster Shorter Catechism, answer 14.) Since sinning is breaking the Law, and we are not free to sin, we must walk in faithful obedience to the Law.

From beginning to end the Bible instructs us to walk in obedience to the Law of God. "Keep the commandments of the LORD your God that I command you" (Deut 4:2). "If anyone loves me, he will keep my word. . . . Whoever does not love me does not keep my words" (John 14:23–24). Both Old and New Testaments affirm a very positive relationship between the believer and the Law which leads to blessing from our Father. "But the one who looks into the perfect law, the law of liberty, and perseveres, being no hearer who forgets but a doer who acts, he will be blessed in his doing" (Jas 1:25).

In summary, while we are set free from the Law's power to condemn, we are not set free to disobey the Law, but rather, set free that we might walk in grace-enabled, faith-filled, Spirit-led obedience to God's Law. "But now we are released from the law, having died to that which held us captive, so that we serve in the new way of the Spirit and not in the old way of the written code" (Rom 7:6). That is, the Holy Spirit now leads us to walk in paths of righteousness, convicting us of sin, turning our hearts to the truth of the Word.

The Law is relational and so involves the heart. The Law, misunderstood by many as outward conformity to rules, was always about a loving relationship with God as Father. Jesus explained that obeying the Law was never simply a matter of outward conformity to the Law; it always required a heart set free by God. "This people honors me with their lips, but their heart is far from me" (Matt 15:8).

Although in our churches today there is often a tension in our understanding between obedience and love, Jesus did not see it that way. "If you love me, you will keep my commandments" (John 14:15). Jesus can join the two seamlessly: love me, keep my commandments. Our obedience to the Law was always meant to be internal, a matter of the heart, and not just external compliance. When we are commanded to love God and love our neighbor it is clear that our affections, not just our actions, are required. Following the Law always requires a heart filled with God's love and God's grace.

It helps us to understand that the very act of giving us the Law was motivated by God's love for us, that we might know him and his will for us. We see that the Law serves as the loving household rules that a father designs for his children to show them how to live in covenant with himself and the rest of the family. When we come to appreciate that the Law itself is covenant love from God to us, it is seen as an invitation to relationship, not the end of one.

The Law is the image of Christ, the true order of humanity. To become holy is to become like Christ. But what is Christ like? How may we describe his character, his deeds, and his attitudes? Properly understood, the Law describes in detail for us who Jesus is, since he came to perfectly fulfill the Law. He fully loved God and his neighbor; he did not lie, covet, blaspheme, steal, or kill. All the moral Law was embodied in him.

Just as we find the perfect picture of human life in Jesus, so too, we find the same perfect image of humanity embodied in the Law. "So the law is holy, and the commandment is holy and righteous and good" (Rom 7:12). Since the Law describes perfect humanity in Christ, it is not meant to be useless in our sanctification, but is *extremely* useful. In what is usually known as the third use of the Law, that is the normative use, the Law is given to guide us in walking with God, to show us a very specific picture of what redeemed humanity, humanity restored to the image of Christ, should look like.[20] The Law is the exact picture of the true order that Jesus restores in us.

Because the Law is still for Christians today, a mark of God's loving Fatherhood, because the Law is a picture of Christlikeness and as well the picture of perfect humanity, because the Law reveals the loving desire of our Father for how we may walk in covenant relationship to him, we should walk in accordance with it. "And by this we know that we have come to know him, if we keep his commandments" (1 John 2:3).

---

20. Calvin, *Institutes*, 3.6.1.

What Parts Do God and We Play in Our Sanctification?

God Is the Primary Mover in Making Us Holy

There are two extremes that we should avoid in understanding God's role and ours in our sanctification: either thinking we do nothing (license), or everything (legalism). The first error leaves us passive, the second anxious. However, when we understand that God is powerful to make us holy and that we are dependent upon him in all our efforts toward holiness, then we are both secure and earnest.

Scripture is clear that God is the primary agent of our holiness. "I, the LORD, sanctify you" (Exod 31:13). God is holy and is the only source of holiness in the universe. So only he can make anyone holy. It is the Father's election that destines us to be holy. "He chose us in him before the foundation of the world, that we should be holy and blameless before him" (Eph 1:4). It is the Son's atonement which sanctifies us. "For by a single offering he has perfected for all time those who are being sanctified" (Heb 10:14). It is the Holy Spirit's work which produces vital holiness within us (Titus 3:5–6).

Calvin comments on 1 Thess 5:23, "Now may the God of peace himself sanctify you completely." "For if it had been our part to cooperate with God, Paul would have spoken thus—'May God aid or promote your sanctification.' But when he says, *sanctify you wholly*, he makes him the sole Author of the entire work."[21] God is the author of our holiness.

Because God is the prime mover in sanctification, all of our effort is done in response to his work and dependent upon his grace. The biblical plan for sanctification follows a "because . . . therefore" pattern. Because God has sanctified you, therefore be sanctified. Because Christ has died to sin therefore, "you also must consider yourselves dead to sin" (Rom 6:11). Because God is our Father, "let us cleanse ourselves from every" sin (2 Cor 7:1). Because we are raised to new life in Christ therefore, "seek the things that are above" (Col 3:1).

This pattern is not incidental but essential to our sanctification. Because God is the Holy One who makes us holy, our efforts all respond to and rely upon him. "If people were able on their own strength to fulfill the Law, He would have said to them, 'Work!' But on the contrary He said: 'Rest in order that God might work.' Thus from our perspective the Law may well be impossible to do, but it is possible for God to engrave it

---

21. Calvin, *Com.*, 1 Thess 5:23.

upon our hearts and to govern us by His Holy Spirit."[22] We must come to rest in this reality, God sanctifies us.

While God Is the Author and Enabler of Our Salvation We Are Yet Called to Work

The biblical call to strive for holiness is clear. "Let us therefore strive to enter that rest" (Heb 4:11). "Work out your own salvation with fear and trembling" (Phil 2:12). "Fight the good fight of the faith" (1 Tim 6:12). "Consecrate yourselves therefore, and be holy, for I am holy" (Lev 11:44).

We strive for holiness by following the biblical pattern of putting off and putting on, of mortification and vivification. We put off sin. "Put off your old self, which belongs to your former manner of life and is corrupt through deceitful desires" (Eph 4:22). And we put on righteousness. "Put on then, as God's chosen ones, holy and beloved, compassionate hearts, kindness, humility, meekness, and patience" (Col 3:12).

We are to strive for holiness, but always our effort comes in response to God's grace and with reliance upon it.

Grace enabled effort. Our effort is a response to God's prior grace to us, in the "because God . . . therefore we" pattern. "Work out your own salvation with fear and trembling, for it is God who works in you, both to will and to work for his good pleasure" (Phil 2:12–13). Although the language is reversed, the logic is the same: Because God works in you, therefore work out your salvation.

By depending on God's grace we are kept from the two evils of either trying to gain holiness in our own strength (legalism) or giving up on holiness (license). "The remedy for both evils is, when, distrusting ourselves, we depend entirely on God alone. And assuredly, that man has made decided progress in the knowledge, both of the grace of God, and of his own weakness, who, aroused from carelessness, diligently seeks God's help."[23]

Whenever we put out effort in sanctification it must always be done in reliance upon the work of God.

> We are to commit ourselves to being acted upon by God. Yet clearly the New Testament does not mean by this that we divide the field of sanctification up into sections and say, "This here is

---

22. Calvin, *Sermons on the Ten Commandments*, 118.
23. Calvin, *Com.*, Phil 2:12–13.

my part, and that over there is God's part," as though we were each responsible for, say, fifty percent of the task . . . No! Rather we are to work out our salvation into our lives because the Spirit is working "to will and to work for his good pleasure."[24]

We respond to God's *prior grace* and actively rely on God's *present grace*, for we cannot accomplish our sanctification by our own power. Romans 8:13 makes this clear: "If by the Spirit you put to death the deeds of the body you will live." Our flesh cannot make progress against our flesh, but the Spirit of God can, and on him we must rely moment by moment to advance in holiness.

Even the regenerated person does not autonomously possess the power to do good on their own. We can strive for holiness, because the person in a state of grace is enabled to depend upon God's grace. That is, our new will is "inclined to follow the action of grace,"[25] however, without that help, "it will straightway fall."[26] Relying on and resting in God's grace, we are enabled to grow in holiness.

Because our effort depends upon God's, Calvin will characterize our effort as "passive." "Believers act passively, so to speak, seeing that the capacity is supplied from heaven."[27] He explains: "We must rest entirely, in order that God may work in us; we must resign our own will, yield up our heart . . . that God working in us, we may rest in him."[28]

This moment by moment reliance on the grace of God is often described as walking by the Spirit. "But I say, walk by the Spirit, and you will not gratify the desires of the flesh" (Gal 5:16). It is a common error among Christians to think that after God has initially saved us, it us up to us—by force of human effort—to sanctify ourselves. It was the mistake that the Galatians made. "Are you so foolish? Having begun by the Spirit, are you now being perfected by the flesh?" (Gal 3:3). Paul's argument is simple: By the Spirit, not our flesh, we are enabled to put sin to death and live. "If we live by the Spirit, let us also keep in step with the Spirit" (Gal 5:25).

In the Christian life, we are—to use an analogy—piloting a sailboat, not a motor boat. The motorboat contains within itself the power to get to its destination. The sailboat is entirely dependent upon the wind. God

---

24. Ferguson, *Devoted to God*, 213.
25. Calvin, *Institutes*, 2.3.11.
26. Calvin, *Institutes*, 2.3.14.
27. Calvin, *Institutes*, 2.5.11.
28. Calvin, *Institutes*, 2.8.29.

retrieved a sunken sailboat, repaired the hull, gave it sails, and installed a compass. This was God's prior grace that enables our sanctification. Then God blows the wind of the Spirit to carry the boat by present grace toward holiness. The sailboat is entirely dependent upon the wind to make any progress, ask any sailor ever caught without wind! Similarly, the Christian is enabled, by the power of the divine wind to make progress toward holiness.

We are active, but our efforts are only effective because God is at work and upholds us and energizes the regenerated heart *moment by moment*. John Murray says: "God works in us and we also work. But the relation is that because God works we work. All working out of salvation on our part is the effect of God's working in us."[29]

Summarizing the relationship between God's work and ours in sanctification, we have seen that 1) God is the author of our sanctification, 2) we are to strive for our sanctification, and 3) all of our effort in sanctification is dependent, moment by moment, upon God's grace. God works our salvation as we respond in grace-fueled obedience to him. We are not to be lazy, or indolent, but apply ourselves diligently to take hold of the grace offered to us by God. This requires that we earnestly see his grace, using all the ordinary means of grace.

What Are the Common Errors Today Regarding Sanctification and Holiness?

There are two perennial errors that have plagued the church: legalism and license.

Legalism

This takes many forms but usually combines two errors: 1) the belief that *external* conformity to the Law is actual obedience and, 2) the belief that we can *earn* right standing with God by our external obedience.

Evangelicals tend to have a good theology of justification but a poor theology of sanctification. They understand God's work in justifying them, but then tend to think that the actual work of sanctification is largely left to us. Setting about to become more holy by human effort,

---

29. Murray, *Redemption*, 157.

they of necessity lower the biblical standards of holiness to be more attainable, by focusing on external conformity to the Law.

For example, when I was teaching this subject, one of our church members rebutted: "Well no matter what is in my heart, if I cut my neighbor's yard, as long as I do the right thing, I still get credit for it." Notice the presence of the two aspects of legalism. He thought that the work was good based upon external compliance—without regard for his heart—and he thought his good works earned right standing with God.

There is a reason that legalism is so popular. It is the natural human religion. Once we fell from grace we began busily trying to earn our right standing before God. Every human religion since then is an effort to perform well enough so that God (or gods, or the universe) will be obliged to accept and reward us, without any dependence upon grace.

Islam is a convenient example, but any man-made religion will do. In Islam there are five practice and five core beliefs. If one performs the five practices well enough, praying five times daily, for example, then at the judgment the good will outweigh the bad and heaven is given. These were the errors of the Pharisees as well. They thought that simple external obedience would merit God's benevolence. "God, I thank you that I am not like other men, extortioners, unjust, adulterers, or even like this tax collector. I fast twice a week; I give tithes of all that I get" (Luke 18:11–12).

As it did for the Pharisee in Jesus' illustration, legalism leads to self-righteousness. It is indeed the goal of legalism to be self-justifying so not to need grace. This self-justifying legalism infects the church today. We declare ourselves righteous because we are better than others at theology or mercy or being multicultural or giving or evangelism or, even, most ironically, understanding grace.

The cure for legalism is simply biblical sanctification. We must understand that God works our sanctification, we must depend upon his grace, and see that all reward comes to us from the merit of Christ's perfect obedience, not ours.

License

Two errors combine here as well: 1) there is no need to try to grow in holiness, since we are sinners who cannot really change, and 2) our continued sinning does not matter to God, since we are justified by faith.

Unfortunately, many who emphasize "grace" today teach that Christians are totally depraved, consequently, real change is not possible. They conclude that it is better to just accept one's current struggle with particular sins, seeking forgiveness, perhaps, but not change. But describing Christians as totally depraved is wrong. Total depravity describes humanity in a state of sin, not a state of grace. While it is true that we battle with sin all our earthly lives, Christ has given us a new nature that is holy, a new heart that delights in him, and a new will that can obey by grace. "Therefore, if anyone is in Christ, he is a new creation" (2 Cor 5:17). It is unhelpful to Christians who are called to strive for holiness—and demeaning to the glory of Christ—to teach that the work of Christ has left Christians totally depraved and unable to grow in holiness.

The other error of license, that we can sin and not displease God because we are forgiven, accompanies the first. We had a seminary intern who had fallen into this error. He said publically: "If you are thinking about committing adultery just go ahead and do it! It does not matter, it's all the same and God will forgive you." In reality God is very opposed to our committing adultery and our sins can displease him. David's adultery with Bathsheba did. "But the thing that David had done displeased the LORD" (2 Sam 11:27).

It is helpful to understand holiness within the covenant framework. Certainly, we are forgiven and accepted into the covenant of grace. But the covenant of grace has covenant expectations which lead to blessing or to discipline. If a child hits his sister, it does not mean that he will lose his standing as a member of the family, or that the dad stops loving him, but it does mean that displeasure and discipline will come his way. The family of God works in a similar manner. God still loved David, and because he loved him he disciplined him. "Because by this deed you have utterly scorned the LORD, the child who is born to you shall die" (2 Sam 12:14).

The cure for license is biblical sanctification. Christ did not justify us to leave us clinging to our sins, but rather gave himself to remove every spot and wrinkle from his holy bride. Growth in holiness is possible and it does matter to Christ.

Both legalism and license fail the biblical tests for truth about sanctification. Legalism fails to produce real holiness because it encourages one to rely on their own ability to obey the Law, which it reduces to external obedience. License fails because it denies holiness as a goal for the Christian life, substituting acceptance of sin instead of a battle against it. Neither legalism nor license produces holiness, indeed, they both indulge the flesh.

To make progress in holiness we do well to understand both what holiness is—a heart relationship with God leading to loving obedience—and how it comes—from God, who works through grace-enabled effort.

Further Resources

Study Questions

1. What is holiness? Define it in your own words?
2. In what way is holiness simply being human?
3. Distinguish positional, definitive, and progressive sanctification.
4. How does the double-knowledge of God and ourselves help us in sanctification?
5. In what ways have we truly been set free from the Law? In what ways are we still obliged to the Law?
6. Why must the Christian always rely on God's power and grace to advance in holiness?
7. Do you tend toward legalism or license in your efforts at holiness? What could you do to find a more biblical balance in pursuing holiness?

For Further Study

Sinclair Ferguson, *Devoted to God: Blueprints for Sanctification* (Edinburgh: Banner of Truth, 2016).

Mark Jones, *Antinomianism: Reformed Theology's Unwelcome Guest?* (Phillipsburg, NJ: P&R, 2013).

John Murray, *Redemption Accomplished and Applied* (Grand Rapids: Eerdmans, 2015).

John Owen, *The Mortification Of Sin* (Edinburgh: Banner of Truth, 2009).

J. I. Packer, *Rediscovering Holiness: Know the Fullness of Life with God* (Grand Rapids: Baker, 2009).

2

Desire Holiness

A LARGE PART OF growing in holiness is the very desire for holiness. "The highest perfection of the godly in this life is an earnest desire to make progress."[1] We are, therefore, urged to seek growth in holiness. "Seek first the kingdom of God and his righteousness" (Matt 6:33). Walter Marshall asserts that the first thing we need to grow in holiness is the desire for it. "We must love [holiness] . . . as the sick man health . . . as the captive liberty."[2] Ferguson concurs. "Commit yourself unreservedly to holiness in every aspect of your life."[3] To help increase our desire for holiness in this chapter we will explore: why God wants us to be holy, why we should desire holiness, and how we can increase our desire for holiness.

Why Does God Want Us to Be Holy?

God Wants Us to Be Holy Because He Is Holy and Will Only Dwell with the Holy

God is holy. It is arguably his leading attribute. "Exalt the LORD our God . . . for the LORD our God is holy!" (Ps 99:9). Because God is holy he hates sin and cannot look on it passively, he must do something about it: judge it, destroy it, or atone for it. "You who are of purer eyes than to see evil and cannot look at wrong" (Hab 1:13). He will not tolerate sin in his

---

1. Calvin, *Com.*, Eph 3:16.
2. Marshall, *Gospel Mystery*, 15.
3. Ferguson, *Devoted to God*, 155.

presence. "For you are not a God who delights in wickedness; evil may not dwell with you" (Ps 5:4).

God will not dwell with evil. This is the essential tension in the universe: God is holy, humanity is not. God's solution was to redeem out of sinful humanity a people for himself, making them holy, through the atoning blood of his Son, in order that he may dwell with them.

Therefore, one of the most essential commands of Scripture is founded upon God's desire for our holiness: "You shall be holy, for I the LORD your God am holy" (Lev 19:2). This is echoed in the New Testament. "But as he who called you is holy, you also be holy in all your conduct, since it is written, 'You shall be holy, for I am holy'" (1 Pet 1:15–16). Our holiness is essential to our ongoing relationship with God. "Strive for . . . the holiness without which no one will see the Lord" (Heb 12:14).

While we do not have perfect holiness in this life, once justified, we do have positional and definitive holiness, which make it possible to dwell with God. Moreover, we have progressive holiness and the promise of perfect holiness in heaven. God-the-holy passionately desires a holy people that he might dwell with them, this is the great accomplishment of redemption. "Behold, the dwelling place of God is with man" (Rev 21:3). We should desire holiness for God desires it for us, that we might dwell with him at peace.

God Wants Us to Be Holy Because He Created Us for Holiness

God's original design for us in creation was holiness. "God created man in his own image" (Gen 1:27). We were made holy like God that we "might be happy in enjoying God."[4] We were designed to love one another, to love and serve God in this world, and so even the "the individual parts of [the] soul were formed to uprightness."[5] We saw ourselves rightly, humbly, before the greatness of God and returned thanks to him for all his good gifts and his own holiness.

Since we were created holy after the likeness of God, he wishes to restore us to that holiness. "Put on the new self, created after the likeness of God in true righteousness and holiness" (Eph 4:24). After some natural disaster, when survivors, standing amidst the rubble of their home, are asked by reporters what they will do now, they naturally respond,

---

4. Anselm, *Cur Deus Homo*, 82.
5. Calvin, *Institutes*, 1.15.8.

"Rebuild it!" It is natural to restore what is broken to its original splendor. Why does God want us to be holy? Because God created us to be holy and delights in restoring us to our original created splendor.

God Wants Us to Be Holy Because He Redeemed Us for Holiness

Since God is holy, and he created us to be holy, his restoration of us has one simple and ultimate goal: our holiness. "He chose us in him before the foundation of the world, that we should be holy and blameless before him" (Eph 1:4). The great act of God's redemption, the cross of Christ, was to make us his holy people. "Christ loved the church and gave himself up for her . . . that she might be holy and without blemish" (Eph 5:25–27).

Christ's ultimate intentions are clear, not just our justification, but our complete holiness. "And you, who once were alienated and hostile in mind, doing evil deeds, he has now reconciled in his body of flesh by his death, in order to present you holy and blameless and above reproach before him" (Col 1:21–23). God's purpose in redemption is to make us holy that we might dwell with him in real peace. This leads us to consider more closely why *we* should desire holiness.

Why Should We Desire Holiness?

We Should Desire Holiness Because God Desires Our Holiness

God's purpose in creating and redeeming us points to his single desire, to have a holy people for himself. "For this is the will of God, your sanctification" (1 Thess 4:3). He has called us for holiness and we dare not disregard his plan of salvation. "For God has not called us for impurity, but in holiness. Therefore whoever disregards this, disregards not man but God, who gives his Holy Spirit to you" (1 Thess 4:7–8). We should desire to be holy because God desires and delights in our holiness.

We Should Desire Holiness Because Holiness Is to Be Like Christ

It is God's decreed intention for us to become like Christ, which is to be holy. "For those whom he foreknew he also predestined to be conformed to the image of his Son" (Rom 8:29). Even now we are in the process of "being transformed into the same image," of Christ (2 Cor

3:18). One day we will be like him fully. "When he appears we shall be like him" (1 John 3:2).

Because God intends for us to become holy we are commanded to strive to be like Christ. "Whoever says he abides in him ought to walk in the same way in which he walked" (1 John 2:6). We should be pure as Christ is pure (1 John 3:3). We should suffer as Christ suffered for God's glory (1 Pet 2:21). We should be servants of one another as was Christ (John 13:15). We are repeatedly enjoined to become like Christ, who is holy.

Why should we want to be holy? Because Jesus is holy. If we want to become more like Jesus there is only one way to do so—become more holy.

We Should Desire Holiness Because Holiness Is to Be Truly Human

As we saw earlier, holiness for us is simply perfected humanness. Sin is a departure from humanness. This sounds odd to us because we are so accustomed to sin. But every sin is not only a failure to conform to the Law of God, it is also a failure at being truly human. When Cain murdered Abel it was a shocking affront not only to Abel's value as a human, but Cain's as well. Cain precipitously descended by sin from what a person should be, "love your neighbor as yourself," and became something grotesque, something bestial.

It is this way with every sin. Certainly it is easier to see this with the more heinous sins. The child molesters and terrorists who murder the innocent show they have departed from God's design for humanity. But even with more acceptable sins—coveting, gossiping, lying, and lusting—we descend from God's plan for humanity.

Growing in holiness then is to regain our humanity. We are created to be content with what God has given us, to speak the truth in love, and to be faithful to one spouse until death—this is simply humanity as it was meant to be. The return to humanness, to holiness, is intrinsically good and it is the best way to live. "Blessed are those whose way is blameless, who walk in the law of the LORD" (Ps 119:1). We should desire to be holy to become more fully human.

We Should Desire Holiness Because This Allows Us to Enjoy God's Presence

When we sin it hinders the free flowing relationship we have with God. Sinning against our wives may hinder our prayers to God (1 Pet 3:7). Sinning can rob us of the joy of our salvation (Ps 51:12). Sinning leaves us polluted and in need of cleansing (1 John 1:9). When we sin we invite God's painful discipline (Heb 12:10–11).

Consider the relational tension between God and the believer hiding sin. Perhaps a believer has a secret affair, or has pilfered money from work, or harbors bitter hatred for another. Their faith grows weak, their worship flaccid, Bible reading and prayer fall by the wayside, doubt becomes their constant companion, God who once seemed close feels distant. God too is disturbed by our sin. He is described as afflicted and grieved over our sin (Isa 63:9–10). Our sin impacts our relationship with God.

In sharp contrast we see that the more we grow in holiness the less we experience these relational tensions with God. Holiness transports us, by grace, readily into the presence of God. "Holiness befits your house, O LORD, forevermore" (Ps 93:5). The more holy we are, the more naturally we live in the presence of the Lord, delight in God's Word, and enjoy the fellowship of the saints. "He declares, that without holiness no man shall see the Lord; for with no other eyes shall we see God than those which have been renewed after his image."[6] We should desire to grow in holiness for it allows us to more fully enjoy the presence of God.

We Should Desire Holiness Because This Avoids the Destructiveness of Sin

Our sin does harm. When Achan sinned secretly in Joshua 7, by stealing things devoted to God, he assumed that he had gotten away with it. But Israel was defeated and thirty-six Israelites were killed in battle. This led to an investigation and then the destruction of Achan's entire household. We must understand that our sin has consequences. There is a misunderstanding among many Christians today who believe that since Christ has taken away the eternal penalty of sin, that there are no temporal problems which result. While we may be forgiven, our sin does damage to those around us, even when we do not see it.

---

6. Calvin, *Com.*, Heb 12:14.

It was in fact a sermon on Joshua 7 about the impact of our sin on those around us which led me, as a young father, to finally put away pornography. I had considered it a shameful sin, which I hid, and confessed, but returned to, thinking that I was only hurting myself. But when I understood that my sin would be destructive to my children, as was Achan's to his, I was moved to hate my sin, for their sakes. When we understand that all sin, no matter how secret or slight, carries in its DNA the seeds of destruction for those around us, we learn to hate our sin and desire holiness, for the sake of others.

Not only does our sin injure those around us but it grieves the Lord. "And do not grieve the Holy Spirit of God" (Eph 4:30). Our sin is not just a legal affront to God's righteous Law, it is a deep personal disappointment to him. "And the LORD regretted that he had made man on the earth, and it grieved him to his heart" (Gen 6:6). The Lord grieved over the rebellion of his people (Isa 63:10). Christ was grieved over the unbelief of the people (Mark 3:5). As a father is grieved when his children sin, so does our heavenly Father grieve when we sin. We should desire holiness to avoid grieving our beloved Lord by our sin.

Our sin also hurts us. While justification removes the eternal penalty for sin, there are temporal consequences, which our Father may allow us to experience—not as judicial punishment, but as corrective discipline—in order to train us in righteousness for the future. "The Lord disciplines the one he loves, and chastises every son whom he receives" (Heb 12:6). God's discipline for sin may be as simple as allowing natural consequences; for example, when a man commits adultery and loses his family. Or God may work directly to discipline us by removing our joy and replacing it with pain. "Let me hear joy and gladness; let the bones that you have broken rejoice" (Ps 51:8).

James warns all Christians against the destructive power of sin. "Sin when it is fully grown brings forth death" (Jas 1:15). We should desire holiness because sin injures those around us, grieves our Lord, and harms ourselves.

We Should Desire Holiness for It Leads to Blessings for Us and Others

As we grow in holiness we are a greater blessing to all around. Sin destroys but holiness heals and creates *shalom*. "A harvest of righteousness is sown in peace by those who make peace" (Jas 3:18). As we reap what we sow in the flesh, so too we reap what we sow in the Spirit, "a harvest of righteousness."

My wife's grandmother, Annie Carpenter, is a wonderful example of this harvest of righteousness from a holy life. She lived to be ninety-nine and each year her holiness glowed more radiantly. Although largely housebound for her final forty years, she had a ministry that touched the lives of hundreds worldwide through letter writing. Because of her holy love and caring, those relatives and friends would regularly make journeys to visit her cottage in New Hampshire. To visit "Grandma" was a sure joy. To bask in the warm glow of her love, to respond to her caring questions, to receive her godly advice, was always a joy. Her holy life sowed and reaped a harvest of righteousness, cascading down the generations. We should desire holiness because it is a blessing to others!

Our growing holiness blesses us as well. Within the covenant of grace God not only warns of covenant discipline, but promises covenant blessings for obedience. "All these blessings shall come upon you and overtake you, if you obey the voice of the LORD your God" (Deut 28:2). This passage goes on to describe the blessings of children, finances, and victory. Because of Christ, God's benevolence runs to lavishly bless our always imperfect obedience, far beyond what we deserve. This lead Calvin to declare: "We must remember this principle—that the basis of true religion is obedience."[7]

Our obedience is promised the blessing of increased relationship with the Lord. "Whoever has my commandments and keeps them, he it is who loves me. And he who loves me will be loved by my Father, and I will love him and manifest myself to him" (John 14:21).

Our obedience in holiness brings the blessing of further usefulness to the Lord. "Therefore, if anyone cleanses himself from what is dishonorable, he will be a vessel for honorable use, set apart as holy, useful to the master of the house, ready for every good work" (2 Tim 2:21). The more we cleanse ourselves from sin, the more useful we are to God, the more he delights to employ us in his service. One of the great blessings of obedience is watching God work through us to advance his kingdom in other people.

Our obedience brings blessings upon our efforts: "he will be blessed in his doing" (Jas 1:25). Psalm 1 affirms God's external blessings upon

---

7. Calvin, *Com.*, Jer 7:23.

obedience. "He is like a tree planted by streams of water that yields its fruit in its season, and its leaf does not wither. In all that he does, he prospers" (Ps 1:3). We should desire holiness for it leads to great blessings from God.

Our growing holiness is a blessing to God as well. As disobedience grieves the Lord, so too does the obedience of faith delight him. "Has the LORD as great delight in burnt offerings and sacrifices, as in obeying the voice of the LORD? Behold, to obey is better than sacrifice, and to listen than the fat of rams" (1 Sam 15:22). God delights in our heartfelt obedience. When we lovingly want to please God in following his Word, he delights, just as a human father would delight in such obedience from his children. "The LORD takes pleasure in those who fear him, in those who hope in his steadfast love" (Ps 147:11).

God takes pleasure in many aspects of our growing holiness. When we pray faithfully, "it is pleasing in the sight of God our Savior" (1 Tim 2:3). When we care for widows, "this is pleasing in the sight of God" (1 Tim 5:4). When children obey their parents, "this pleases the Lord" (Col 3:20). When we share with others, "Such sacrifices are pleasing to the Lord" (Heb 13:16). God takes pleasure in our obedience. Thus it was Christ's goal in life to always obey and please his Father. "I always do the things that are pleasing to him" (John 8:29).

We should want to grow in holiness, for through our holiness we bless others, we are blessed by God, and God himself is blessed.

Having seen why God wants us to be holy and why we should desire holiness, we will now discuss *how* we can grow in our desire for holiness.

How Can We Grow in Our Desire for Holiness?

We Can Grow in Our Desire for Holiness by Making Holiness Our Aim

While we have many goals in such areas as education, finances, relationships, work, and athletics, few Christians set growth in holiness as an actual goal. But think of how naturally our goals are tied to our desires. A young couple might set the goal of paying off their home mortgage in five years. They are motivated by the goal. They deny themselves luxuries, they make sacrifices, watching excitedly as their debt shrinks. Having the goal of paying off the mortgage increases their desire. When we make holiness a principal life goal, our desire to become holy increases.

Desire Holiness

Not surprisingly, the Apostle Paul set holiness as one of his chief life goals. "I press on toward the goal for the prize of the upward call of God in Christ Jesus" (Phil 3:14).

Paul compares the Christian life to warfare and athletic competition, both of which require aiming toward the goal of victory. We are to run with all our might toward holiness, toward Christ (1 Cor 9:24). Paul calls us to fight powerfully to win the battle over sin. "Fight the good fight of the faith" (1 Tim 6:12).

Scripture repeatedly makes it clear that holiness should be the aim of the Christian life. "Let us cleanse ourselves from every defilement of body and spirit, bringing holiness to completion in the fear of God" (2 Cor 7:1). We are to put off the old and put on the new self, "created after the likeness of God in true righteousness and holiness" (Eph 4:24). We are to aim for holiness with our bodies. "So glorify God in your body" (1 Cor 6:20). Most pointedly, we are commanded to be holy—"You shall be holy, for I am holy" (1 Pet 1:16)—therefore we must aim to be holy.

Godly leaders down the ages have seen that holiness should be the Christian's goal. Pierre Viret exhorts us: "Remember always that you are called to sanctification and holiness and purity and not to vileness and pollution and filth and that you are for the Lord and Master who said: be holy, for I am holy."[8] Calvin warns those who do not aim for holiness. "It then follows, that those who do not strive for a pure and holy life, do not understand even the first rudiments of faith."[9] Walter Marshall wonders at the Christian who, satisfied with his justification, does not strive toward holiness.

> What a strange kind of salvation do they desire, that do not care for holiness? They would be saved, and yet be altogether dead in sin, aliens from the life of God, bereft of the image of God, deformed by the image of Satan, his slaves and vassals to their own filthy lusts, utterly unsuitable for the enjoyment of God in glory. Such a salvation as that was never purchased by the blood of Christ, and those that seek it abuse the grace of God in Christ and turn it into lasciviousness.[10]

Those who do not set holiness as their goal tend to scoff at those who do, with accusations of legalism and Pharisaism. Watson responds

---

8. Viret, *Du Devoir et du Besoing*, 25.
9. Calvin, *Com.*, 2 Pet 1:9.
10. Marshall, *Gospel Mystery*, 118.

to these: "It is bad to lack holiness—it is worse to hate it. . . . To deride sanctification argues a high degree of atheism, and is a black brand of reprobation."[11] We are to aim at holiness, despite detractors, for God calls us to it.

Some Christians fear committing to growth in holiness, for having battled sin before and failed, they fear more failure. While we can all relate to this, given the weighty preponderance of Scripture, how can we not make holiness our goal? "Let the fruits of chastity, sobriety, moderation, and every good deed proceed from that integrity, that wholeness, which God prizes above all else. That, then, is the goal toward which we must strive if we wish to be approved by our God."[12] Let us set holiness, Christlikeness, as the great goal of our lives and we will find our desire for holiness growing, fueled by the very grace of God, who delights to help his children grow in sanctification.

We Can Grow in Our Desire for Holiness by Remembering Holiness Is Our Certain Future

Few things are as discouraging to pursuing a goal as doubting that it is achievable. On the other hand, when we are confident that we can attain a goal, we are energized to pursue it. Many Christians, believing they will make little progress in holiness, have little desire to try. However, when we remember that holiness is our certain future we more fully desire to pursue it.

Holiness is our certain future, we must remember, because Christ has freed us from slavery to sin by his death. "But now that you have been set free from sin and have become slaves of God, the fruit you get leads to sanctification and its end, eternal life" (Rom 6:22). We are set free not only from sin's penalty and power, but increasingly, the presence of sin is dwindling away. It is like when the stopper is removed from a full tub. All the water is on the way out. It is inevitable, once the stopper is removed, all the water will be gone. Christ's death has removed the stopper and is draining all the sin from us, we will become holy. Calvin comments: "As Christ once died for the purpose of destroying sin, so you have once died, that in the future you may cease from sin."[13] We must remember that,

---

11. Watson, *Body of Divinity*, 247.
12. Calvin, *Sermons on Genesis*, 578–79.
13. Calvin, *Com.*, Rom 6:10.

having died to sin, our growing holiness is certain, and let that encourage our desire for holiness.

Holiness is our certain future, we must remember, because we have been united with Christ in his resurrection. "For if we have been united with him in a death like his, we shall certainly be united with him in a resurrection like his" (Rom 6:5). Christ was raised to new life and we, united to him, are certain to be buoyed upward. It is amazing to watch salvage crews float a long-sunk wreck from the sea bottom. Mired in tons of silt it seems impossible that it should rise. However, they connect airbags to the wreck and inflate them. The force of the flotation powerfully overcomes all the resistance. So too with Christ. Connected to his resurrection life, we cannot help but rise to newness of life, and rising we are. This should encourage us to desire holiness when we understand that we must become holy by the overwhelming force of the risen life of Christ.

Holiness is our certain future, we must remember, because Christ has purchased the perfection of heaven for us. "An inheritance that is imperishable, undefiled, and unfading, kept in heaven for you" (1 Pet 1:4). Heaven waits for every Christian, not merely as a possibility, but as a certainty, and this increases our desire for holiness. When we know we are certainly going somewhere we are motivated to prepare for that new location. Tell a person to learn French when they are living in the United States and they might be somewhat motivated. Tell them they are being transferred to Paris, and they will be terrifically motivated. When we know we are certainly going to heaven, it gives us immense motivation to seek holiness, for growing holiness is the only way to prepare for heaven. Walter Marshall comments on how the certainty of heaven motivates us for holiness now.

> The sure hope of the glory of heaven is made use of ordinarily by God, since the fall of Adam, as an encouragement to the practice of holiness, as the Scripture abundantly shows. Christ, the great pattern of holiness, "for the joy that was set before Him, endured the cross, despising the shame" (Heb 12:2).... The apostles did not faint under affliction, because they knew that it brought for them "a far more exceeding and eternal weight of glory" (2 Cor 4:16–17).[14]

Holiness is our certain future, we must remember, because Christ will certainly complete the good work he has started. "And I am sure of

---

14. Marshall, *Gospel Mystery*, 26–27.

this, that he who began a good work in you will bring it to completion at the day of Jesus Christ" (Phil 1:6). It does not say that he might bring it to completion but rather that he will. Jesus did not go to the cross to purchase the *possibility* of our holiness but the *certainty* of it. Knowing that we will be made holy encourages us to desire holiness.

Let the certainty of our future holiness—our death to sin with Christ, our resurrection to righteous life with Christ, our home in heaven with Christ, our sanctification completed by Christ—encourage our hearts toward holiness now. Since we will certainly be holy, let us desire and strive toward that holiness today.

We Can Grow in Our Desire for Holiness by Understanding How Much God Loves Us

We respond differently in the presence of others in accordance to their degree of love toward us. Around those who reject us, we withdraw. Around those who accept us, we engage with confidence and joy. Understanding the completeness of our justification and adoption assures us of God's loving acceptance and this increases our desire for holiness, wholeness with him.

Our justification means that all of our sins, past, present, and future, have been forgiven. "Blessed is the man against whom the Lord will not count his sin" (Rom 4:8). This means that when we strive for holiness and fail, God does not reject us. It is as if we are performing a trapeze act with a net instead of without one. Without a net the performers are on edge, one slip and they fall to their death. With the net you can feel their ease. They soar higher, and if they do fall, they bounce harmlessly in the net and climb back to the trapeze. In a similar way our justification fuels and frees our desire for holiness. We do not fear condemnation and rejection from God if we fail. Rather, confident in the net of forgiveness that will catch us, we can strive for new heights of holiness.

Justification also means that we are positively imputed the complete righteousness of Christ (Rom 3:22). This means not only that our debt has been paid but our righteousness "credit score" is entirely filled with the perfect righteousness of Christ. Some time ago my wife checked her credit score, we were both surprised at how high it was, since most of our married life until then she had been a stay-at-home mom. Then we discovered that our scores were tied together, my credit was attributed to her. Similarly, our justification is no legal fiction, it is a spiritual reality, our righteousness score is actually united to Christ's so we share the same perfect credit!

This means that when you wake up in the morning and look at the day ahead, you have, in Christ already, perfectly kept the Law. How freeing it is to seek to grow in holiness in an environment where you are already declared righteous. Rather than giving us a license to sin, God means for this justification to give us the freedom to pursue holiness. "How can we who died to sin still live in it? . . . Just as Christ was raised from the dead by the glory of the Father, we too might walk in newness of life" (Rom 6:2–4). The secure state of justification is the perfect encouragement to seek growth in holiness!

Our adoption also frees us to desire holiness in an environment of grace and acceptance. "Because you are sons, God has sent the Spirit of his Son into our hearts, crying, 'Abba! Father!' So you are no longer a slave, but a son, and if a son, then an heir through God" (Gal 4:6–7). God has fully adopted us as his children, with all the rights, privileges, and love due children. Shockingly, we learn that the Father loves us as adopted children even as he loves his Son. "That the world may know that you . . . *loved them even as you loved me*" (John 17:23, emphasis added). How marvelously freeing is it to know that the Father loves us with a love similar to that deep, eternal, abiding love that he has for Jesus!

Knowing that we are forgiven, declared righteous, adopted and loved with an everlasting covenant love from the Father increases our desire to be holy. For the desire to be holy, to be relationally whole with God, cannot be forced upon us, but only induced by God's love. "But the duty of love cannot be extorted and forced by fear, but it must be won, and sweetly allured by an apprehension of God's love and goodness towards us."[15]

It is within this environment of grace—of God's forgiveness, Christ's imputed righteousness, the pouring out of the covenant love of God—where we are perfectly positioned to make holiness our aim. "*I will be a Father unto you* . . . Paul has added it with this view, that a recognition of the great honor to which God has exalted us, might be a motive to stir us up to a more ardent desire for holiness."[16]

---

15. Marshall, *Gospel Mystery*, 20.
16. Calvin, *Com.*, 2 Cor 6:18.

The love of our Father encourages us onward and upward. Imagine two fathers watching their sons playing baseball. The first father is demanding, critical. Each slight mistake invites mean-spirited criticism. His son responds in kind: he is nervous, fearing failure for the condemnation it brings, his performance is tight, insecure, and grows worse. The other father is supportive, shouting encouragements to his son. His son responds in kind: he is at ease, confident, he plays well and with joy.

When we recognize that our Father loves us and accepts us, we are tremendously encouraged toward relational wholeness with him, that is, to aim for holiness. We see the smiling face of our Father and we are eager to run in the paths of his commands, into his arms, for our hearts are set free by his love. "I will run in the way of your commandments when you enlarge my heart!" (Ps 119:32). More fully understanding our justification and adoption increases our desire for holiness.

We Can Grow in Our Desire for Holiness by Knowing That God's Power Makes Holiness Possible

When we mistakenly believe that our holiness is all up to us we may give up on holiness. But when we rightly understand that God is the primary cause of our growth in holiness we are encouraged to pursue holiness. "That you may know that I, the LORD, sanctify you" (Exod 31:13). When we understand that all the power of God is at work making us holy we are very encouraged to join in the battle for holiness.

Suppose a dad asks his four-year-old daughter to move a two-hundred-pound rock. Doubtful of her success, she pushes tentatively but cannot budge such a huge weight. She quits defeated. Imagine instead, this time, that the father is beside the rock and invites his daughter to help him move it. Confident in her father's might she pushes bravely, and with his immense strength, the rock is easily rolled away. This is our reality. God is building us into a "holy priesthood," empowering us to work for holiness as well (1 Pet 2:5). Knowing that God is working to make us holy, we are greatly encouraged to desire growth in holiness.

We Can Grow in Our Desire for Holiness by Hearing Scripture Encourage Holiness and Warn of Sin

The Bible consistently encourages holiness and warns of sin. Everywhere we are told that holiness is God's plan for us. "He chose us in him before the foundation of the world, that we should be holy" (Eph 1:4). Everywhere we are warned away from sin. "For if we go on sinning deliberately after receiving the knowledge of the truth, there no longer remains a sacrifice for sins, but a fearful expectation of judgment" (Heb 10:26–27).

While God's promises of grace stand true, they are true for the repentant. Those who continue in sin either prove they are unbelievers outside the covenant who deserve judgment, or they prove to be wayward children within the covenant who invite fatherly discipline. Either way, we are warned away from sin, for it has no good results for us. "If your eye causes you to sin, tear it out and throw it away" (Matt 18:9). When we see in the Bible the encouragements to holiness and the warnings away from sin, our desire for holiness grows.

We Can Grow in Our Desire for Holiness by Closely Observing Models of Holiness

When we see models of holiness in Scripture and in life our desire for holiness grows. As our Chief example, we should fix our eyes on Christ in Scripture to increase our desire to be like him. "Looking to Jesus, the founder and perfecter of our faith" (Heb 12:2).

The Bible presents many examples of holiness that we might aspire to be like them. "As an example of suffering and patience, brothers, take the prophets who spoke in the name of the Lord" (Jas 5:10). Paul offered himself and other mature Christian as examples to strive after. "Brothers, join in imitating me, and keep your eyes on those who walk according to the example you have in us" (Phil 3:17). Looking on the faith of Abraham, the heart of David, the courage of Daniel, the submission of Mary, the hospitality of Aquila and Priscilla, we are to desire the holiness they display. "Therefore, since we are surrounded by so great a cloud of witnesses, let us also lay aside every weight, and sin which clings so closely, and let us run with endurance the race that is set before us" (Heb 12:1).

We are also to be inspired by godly examples in the life of the church. "Remember your leaders, those who spoke to you the word of God. Consider the outcome of their way of life, and imitate their faith" (Heb

13:7). Christian growth, therefore, happens best in the midst of the church where we have mature believers around us whose lives inspire imitation.

The Reformers well understood the importance of surrounding young Christians with models of holiness. Martin Bucer taught as much by his example as by his words. "His own example was his chief instrument in inspiring all around him to holy lives."[17] Calvin exhorted his congregation to be examples of holiness so others would desire holiness. "Our lives ought so to become shining examples [that others] ... become so inspired as to desire nothing but to serve God."[18] After Calvin's death, his close associate in Geneva, Theodore Beza, marveled at Calvin's helpful example. "We are in no slight degree assisted by his recent and most beautiful examples of both sayings and doings."[19]

When we closely observe models of holiness—Christ, biblical saints, historical or contemporary models of holiness—seeing them increases our desire to be holy like them.

We have seen in this chapter the importance of desiring holiness in order to grow in holiness. We should desire holiness for God desires it for us, holiness is to be like Christ, to be fully human, and because with holiness we avoid the pain of sin and know the blessings of obedience. May our desire for holiness ever increase!

Summary of How to Desire Holiness

1. Realize that God wants us to be holy because he is holy. "You shall be holy because I am holy."

2. Remember that holiness is being like Jesus. The only way to become more like Jesus is to become more holy.

3. Understand that holiness is nothing other than being fully human. The only way to become more fully human is to become more holy.

4. Realize that sin creates tension in our relationship with God, grieving him, while our obedience is a delight to him. The best way to improve our relationship with God is to become more holy.

---

17. Gilbert, "Martin Bucer on Education," 323.
18. Calvin, *Sermons on Micah*, 12.
19. Calvin, *Com.*, Ezekiel, dedication by Theodore Beza.

5. Remember that our sin hurts everyone: us, our family, friends, and it grieves God.
6. Understand that sin invites God's covenant discipline while obedience invites his blessings.
7. Aim for holiness, make it a major goal of your life, for the sake of everyone you love, God included.
8. Remember that you will become perfectly holy in heaven and let that reality encourage your pursuit of holiness today.
9. Mediate on your justification and adoption. Through Christ we are fully righteous today and fully loved as adopted children of God. This provides the safe environment in which to desire holiness.
10. Remember it is God who ultimately makes us holy, for knowing this encourages us to desire holiness.
11. Read Scripture's exhortations to holiness and warnings about sin. Keeping these vividly before us increases our desire for holiness.
12. Closely observe people who are models of holiness: read of Christ and the saints of Scripture, read Christian biographies, and spend time with saints today in your local church. Seeing their holiness helps us to desire holiness as well.

Further Resources

Study Questions

1. Why is desiring holiness important to our growth in holiness?
2. Why does God desire us to be holy? Can you list three reasons?
3. Why should we desire to be holy? List four or five reasons.
4. How can we increase our desire for holiness? List four or five ways.
5. What is your current level of desire to become holy?
6. Which of the motivations for holiness mentioned in this chapter is currently most helpful to you? What could you focus on in the future to most increase your desire for holiness?

For Further Study

Christian biographies. There are thousands, but a few to start:
- Roland Bainton, *Here I Stand: A Life of Martin Luther* (New York: Abingdon-Cokesbury, 1950).
- Corrie Ten Boom, *The Hiding Place* (Peabody, MA: Hendrickson 2015).
- T. H. L. Parker, *John Calvin: A Biography* (Philadelphia: Westminster, 1975).

Martin Luther, *Commentary on Galatians* (tr. Erasmus Middleton; Grand Rapids: Kregel, 1979).

Thomas Watson, *Body of Divinity* (Edinburgh: Banner of Truth, 2015).

3

Rely on God

WHEN WE PURSUE HOLINESS we must stop relying on ourselves and look instead to the Lord. Humanity typically tries to improve itself by itself, but we are incapable of sanctifying ourselves. Even the believer lacks the autonomous ability to grow holy. We must look to God because he is the source of all holiness in the universe and the only one with the power to transform us into the holy. "I, the LORD, sanctify you" (Exod 31:13).

The commands to become holy, however, are real. But they are not given in order that we might seek holiness from ourselves, but rather from the Lord. This is why we are told to turn to the Holy Spirit's power to put to death sin in our lives—"if by the Spirit you put to death"—we cannot do so by our own power (Rom 8:13). Ferguson says it well. "God never throws us back to rely upon ourselves and our own resources. He encourages us rather to grow up as Christians by digging down ever more deeply into the riches of his grace in Jesus Christ."[1]

Theologians throughout history—the Reformers outstanding among them—have understood God's primacy in our sanctification. Pierre Viret writes: "God justifies us through his Holy Spirit in Jesus Christ our Lord, he sanctifies us also."[2] Calvin echoes God's supremacy in our sanctification. "The Lord in this way both begins and completes the good work in us. It is the Lord's doing that the will conceives the love of what is right, is zealously inclined toward it, is aroused and moved to

---

1. Ferguson, *Devoted to God*, 93.
2. Schnetzler et al., *Pierre Viret*, 288.

pursue it."[3] The Puritans also recognized that sanctification was primarily the work of God. "Christian, you could defile yourself—but you could not sanctify yourself. But God has done it."[4]

We must rely upon God for sanctification. Only God can raise the spiritually dead and make them alive in Christ. "But God . . . when we were dead in our trespasses, made us alive together with Christ" (Eph 2:4–5). Only God can forgive and cleanse from sins. "I will cleanse them from all the guilt of their sin against me" (Jer 33:8). Only God can wash away all our filth. "The Lord shall have washed away the filth of the daughters of Zion" (Isa 4:4). Only God builds us into a holy house (1 Pet 2:5). Only God can sanctify us. "Now may the God of peace himself sanctify you completely" (1 Thess 5:23).

In this chapter we will address two broad questions: *Why* should we rely on God to make us holy? and, *how* do we rely on God to make us holy? Our triune God works to sanctify us, the Father decreeing our holiness, the Son accomplishing our holiness, and the Spirit applying holiness to us.

Why Should We Rely on God to Make Us Holy?

The Father Decrees Our Holiness

God the Father in his decree of election chose us to be his holy people. "He chose us in him before the foundation of the world, that we should be holy and blameless before him" (Eph 1:4). Once God has decreed our holiness, it must come to pass.

Before we lift a finger to pursue holiness, God has entirely planned and provided for our holiness in his election. "To those who are elect exiles of the Dispersion . . . according to the foreknowledge of God the Father, in the sanctification of the Spirit, for obedience to Jesus Christ and for sprinkling with his blood" (1 Pet 1:1–2). This is a marvelous picture of the Holy Trinity at work making us holy. God the Father elects us to salvation, God the Son cleanses us with his blood, and God the Spirit sanctifies us applying the blood of Christ. "Our salvation flows from the

---

3. Calvin, *Institutes*, 2.3.9.
4. Watson, *Body of Divinity*, 250.

gratuitous election of God; but that it is to be ascertained by the experience of faith, because he sanctifies us by his Spirit."[5]

It is first, then, the will of God that makes us holy. "And by that will we have been sanctified through the offering of the body of Jesus Christ once for all" (Heb 10:10). Lobstein concludes. "We are chosen by God in order to live a holy and stainless life. . . . Holiness of life cannot therefore be separated from the grace of election."[6]

We should have several responses to the realty that it is God's election that causes our holiness. First, this doctrine should make us humble not proud. We must recognize that all the good in us, all holiness, is from God. "The doctrine of election . . . magnifies the honor of God and reduces us to a status of true humility."[7]

Second, this truth should make us determined, not lax, about holiness. Since it is God's plan for us to be holy we should strive for holiness and make every effort to be what he has willed that we should become. "Therefore, brothers, be all the more diligent to confirm your calling and election, for if you practice these qualities you will never fall" (2 Pet 1:10).

Finally, we should respond to God's election with gratitude not presumption. When we realize that the progress we have known in holiness is from God's election and not primarily our own doing, we are thankful. "But we ought always to give thanks to God for you, brothers beloved by the Lord, because God chose you as the firstfruits to be saved, through sanctification by the Spirit and belief in the truth" (2 Thess 2:13). Truly, God's election gives us an overwhelming reason to rely on God for holiness: he has decreed it.

The Father Decrees to Love Us

God chose us to be his for one simple reason: he loves us. "In love he predestined us" (Eph 1:4). God's love for us is vital to our sanctification. While we will explain this fully in the chapter on apprehending God's love, we will introduce the concept here.

The Father's love for us attracts us to him. Were we not assured of the love of the Almighty, the immense distance between his holiness and our unholiness would leave us terrified. "In this the love of God was

---

5. Calvin, *Com.*, 1 Pet 1:1–2.
6. Lobstein, *Die Ethik Calvins*, 22–23.
7. Niesel, *Theology of Calvin*, 168.

made manifest among us, that God sent his only Son into the world, so that we might live through him" (1 John 4:9). When we see that he loves us, we are irresistibly attracted toward God, we love him and desire to be more holy, walking in his commandments. "For this is the love of God, that we keep his commandments" (1 John 5:3).

The Father Decrees Our Right Fear of Him

The Father's decrees lead us to fear him as well. "Since we have these promises, beloved, let us cleanse ourselves from every defilement of body and spirit, bringing holiness to completion in the fear of God" (2 Cor 7:1). Fear plays a valid part in the Christian's life as well.

Christians are often confused by 1 John 4:18: "There is no fear in love, but perfect love casts out fear." They take this to mean that if we know God's love, and love God, then there will be no fear of God left in our lives. This is erroneous. John is not trying in a single verse to negate a profound biblical teaching that the fear of the Lord is good. "The fear of the LORD is the beginning of wisdom" (Ps 111:10). The apostles, Paul and Peter, affirm the right role of fear. "Therefore, knowing the fear of the Lord, we persuade others" (2 Cor 5:11). "Honor everyone. Love the brotherhood. Fear God" (1 Pet 2:17). Christ affirmed the right fear of the Lord. "But I will warn you whom to fear: fear him who, after he has killed, has authority to cast into hell. Yes, I tell you, fear him" (Luke 12:5).

John is not trying to remove fear as a proper emotional response to God, but trying to qualify it. The rest of 1 John 4:18 makes this clearer. "For fear has to do with punishment, and whoever fears has not been perfected in love." There are two types of fear, a terror of the judgment of God that non-believers should feel, and a reverential fear of the majesty of God that God's children are to feel. The first, as John explains, has to do with the judicial punishment that God deals out as judge of the world. If Christians fear that God will deliver judicial punishment to them, they have not understood the grace of Christ sufficiently. "For you did not receive the spirit of slavery to fall back into fear, but you have received the Spirit of adoption as sons, by whom we cry, 'Abba! Father!'" (Rom 8:15).

So there is still a proper place for the fear of the Lord—a reverential fear, respect, awe—not unlike the feeling a young child has toward their father. To a young child their dad seems so powerful that even though he loves them, his very might and size make him the object of a healthy reverential fear. This right fear is a counter for disrespect. Many of us have seen the casual disrespect some children have for their parents; it is no sign of their love!

We rightly fear God because we are to be aware that our disobedience could bring about God's fatherly discipline. "For the Lord disciplines the one he loves" (Heb 12:6). We see many examples of this in Scripture, few more poignant than David's discipline. "When we see how David was dealt with . . . let us consider walking much more in the fear of God."[8] Yet even here, God disciplines us because he loves us, and disciplines us with love to train us in godliness. For the Christian, fear plays a role in helping us to obey God, but it is a fear of a loving Father, not a tyrannical judge. "Fear must always rest on a firm basis of confidence in God's mercy."[9]

The Father Decrees Our Holiness by Grace

It is not an accident that we must rely on God for our sanctification, he has decreed that we must rely on his grace. "For we are his workmanship, created in Christ Jesus for good works, which God prepared beforehand, that we should walk in them" (Eph 2:10). Surely we must work in our sanctification, as we have made clear. But our work is to take hold of the grace of God, not to "lift ourselves up by our own bootstraps." We are called, by grace, to render the obedience of faith, to fight sin in our lives, in order that we might be sanctified. However, even our obedience, our good work, is ordained by God.

The Father Decrees Our Perseverance Unto Glory

God has decreed that we will persevere in holiness all the way to glory. "For those whom he foreknew he also predestined to be conformed to the image of his Son" (Rom 8:29).

Through God's decree we are certain that we will become what we hope to become—we will be like Jesus. This should not discourage our efforts, but assuring us of final victory, give us all the more reason to strive toward the holiness that God is producing. We may draw a financial analogy. Some people may anticipate a large inheritance. It happens sometimes that this certainty of finances moves a person to greater financial

---

8. Calvin, *Sermons on 2 Samuel*, 542.
9. Wallace, *Christian Life*, 223.

diligence, not less. They budget, plan, set up wills, all to be prepared for the arrival of the fortune, of which they are calmly certain.

This is how God intends the certain inheritance of holiness in heaven to impact us. We are not to worry, but confident of our holiness coming, work diligently today to prepare ourselves for our certain future, our full inheritance. "In him you also . . . were sealed with the promised Holy Spirit, who is the guarantee of our inheritance until we acquire possession of it" (Eph 1:13–14). God's decree seals our perseverance into holiness.

We are right then to rely on God to make us holy. He has decreed our holiness in our election. He has decreed our holiness in love and reverential fear. He has decreed his grace to be the means by which we are sanctified rather than by human effort. He has decreed our perseverance to glory. From start to finish, our holiness is produced by God, we would be foolish then to not rely on him to make us holy. "When a person relying on his own strength wants to acquit himself before God, he cannot lift a finger or have one single good idea as to how it should be done."[10] Let us then look to God and rely on him, his election, his love, his grace, to make us holy!

As the Father has decreed our holiness so has the Son worked to make us holy.

The Son Accomplishes Our Holiness

The Son Sanctifies Us by His Life, Death, and Resurrected Life

Following the decreed will of his Father, Christ gave his life in order to save the elect. Through his sinless life, substitutionary death, and resurrection to new life, Jesus accomplished several key factors in our sanctification.

First, Christ justified us, which involves both the removal of guilt for all our sin—past, present, and future—and the imputation of his own righteousness to us. He purchased our forgiveness through his shed blood on our behalf. "Since, therefore, we have now been justified by his blood, much more shall we be saved by him from the wrath of God" (Rom 5:9). He also secured our imputed righteousness, so that Christ's sinless life is attributed to us, such that we are credited with his compete righteousness (Phil 3:9). Freed from the guilt of sin and declared righteous we are then in a position for God to continue the good work in us.

---

10. Calvin, *Sermons on the Ten Commandments*, 118.

Second, Christ's atonement secures our sanctification by his holy life. "For by a single offering he has perfected for all time those who are being sanctified" (Heb 10:14). Christ's atonement carries with it the power to not only justify his people, but to sanctify us entirely, since we are "perfected for all time." Christ has redeemed us such that our hearts and minds are regenerated and a work of redemption was begun that cannot be stopped.

In one of the Star Trek movies (*The Wrath of Khan*) scientists have created a machine to terraform dead planets, called the Genesis Device. They launch it onto a dead planet and life takes hold. The entire planet is brought to life. Once it is unleashed it cannot be stopped—life is inevitable. The same is true of Christ's atonement, once set loose, life—and in our case, holy life—is inevitable. The power of the cross of Christ is such that we will be holy. "By a single offering he has perfected for all time those who are being sanctified." There can be then a confident, even a restful, approach to our own sanctification, for we can see with confidence that Christ has accomplished our sanctification by a single sacrifice. While we certainly work to be made more like him, we work because he has worked and accomplished this: our perfection in him.

Many Christians have grown so accustomed to thinking of the blood of Christ as only pertaining to justification, that they fail to properly associate it with sanctification as well. "So Jesus also suffered outside the gate in order to sanctify the people through his own blood" (Heb 13:12). Not only does his blood purchase our justification, but it achieves our entire transformation as well. Whatever is required of us in effort as we press on in holiness, we must be clear about this, that the heavy lifting is all done for us by Christ. He has made the way not only possible, but our holiness inevitable. "He has now reconciled in his body of flesh by his death, in order to present you holy and blameless and above reproach before him" (Col 1:22).

The Son Sanctifies Us in His Offices of Prophet, King, and Priest

Christ also actively continues to make us holy as our prophet, king, and priest. As our Prophet, Christ serves as our teacher, leading us into truth through his Holy Spirit and Word. As our King, Christ protects us by defeating our enemies—the world, our sin, and the devil—that we might triumph in holiness. As our Priest, Christ ever lives to intercede for us, asking of the Father those gifts and graces which will contribute to our holiness. Knowing our weaknesses, he knows best how to effectively help us become holy. "For we do not have a high priest who is unable to sympathize with our weaknesses, but one who in every respect has been tempted as we are, yet without sin. Let us then with confidence draw near to the throne of grace, that we may receive mercy and find grace to help in time of need" (Heb 4:15–16). Christ is completely active, both in establishing, and in completing our sanctification.

The Son Sanctifies Us by Uniting with Us

When we look on the cross of Jesus Christ, we may wonder how it comes to be of benefit to us. In a word, Christ unites himself to us. "For if we have been united with him in a death like his, we shall certainly be united with him in a resurrection like his" (Rom 6:5). United to the death and life of Christ, the power of both flow to us from him. Christ actually lives in us and we live in him. "I have been crucified with Christ. It is no longer I who live, but Christ who lives in me" (Gal 2:20a). So powerfully are we united to Christ that we may all say, "Christ lives in me!" This is the power needed to transform us into the very image of Christ.

Jesus spoke of this union in organic terms. "I am the vine; you are the branches. Whoever abides in me and I in him, he it is that bears much fruit, for apart from me you can do nothing" (John 15:5). We are so intimately linked to Christ that his "sap," that is, his vital life, flows through us, enabling us to bear fruit. The good works which we do are done by the abiding life of Christ in us. "Therefore, that joining together of Head and members, that indwelling of Christ in our hearts—in short, that mystical union—are accorded by us the highest degree of importance, so that Christ, having been made ours, makes us sharers with him in the gifts with which he has been endowed."[11]

THE NATURE OF OUR UNION WITH THE SON

We are united to Christ, spiritually not physically, through faith, by the work of the Holy Spirit. Ours is a spiritual union. "He who is joined to the Lord becomes one spirit with him" (1 Cor 6:17). Our union is effected by the Spirit. "If the Spirit of him who raised Jesus from the

---

11. Calvin, *Institutes*, 3.11.10.

dead dwells in you, he who raised Christ Jesus from the dead will also give life to your mortal bodies through his Spirit who dwells in you" (Rom 8:11). We are united through faith. "That Christ may dwell in your hearts through faith" (Eph 3:17). While our union is spiritual we should not think of it as either theoretical or unreal, it is very real and vital to our endeavors in sanctification.

The Benefits That Come to Us Though Union with the Son

All the benefits of Christ flow to us through our union with him, including our sanctification. Because we are "in Christ," the common term used in the New Testament to speak of our union with Christ, we are being made holy. "Because of him you are in Christ Jesus, who became to us wisdom from God, righteousness and sanctification and redemption" (1 Cor 1:30).

More specifically, we have been united to the death of Christ so that sin no longer has mastery over us. "We know that our old self was crucified with him in order that the body of sin might be brought to nothing, so that we would no longer be enslaved to sin" (Rom 6:6). The implications of our union in the death of Christ are stunning. It means that there is an ontological change in us. We are no longer what we were. We were slaves to sin, and enemies of God. Now sin is our enemy and we are slaves to righteousness (Rom 6:17–18). This means that as we fight sin, we do so from a distinctly advantaged position. We are free from sin's dominion and under the dominion of Christ. Union with Christ gives us the winning upper hand against sin. "His death . . . kills the old man in us that he may not flourish and bear fruit."[12]

Having died with Christ, we are dead to sin such that it no longer has dominion over us (Rom 6:14), that is, it cannot force us to obey its passions (Rom 6:12). Having died with Christ, the world, too, has lost its hold upon us so that we may rightly say, "The world has been crucified to me" (Gal 6:14). The world is crucified to us. This is an interesting twist on the concept of crucifixion: it kills the world's hold over us. The world's allures, which captured us before, now more and more repulse us. Our union with Christ frees us from the world's grasp.

Our union with Christ also unites us to the perfectly holy life of Christ. "Therefore, if anyone is in Christ, he is a new creation" (2 Cor 5:17). We live with Christ and he lives in us imparting the vitality and

---

12. Calvin, *Institutes*, 2.16.7.

holiness of his life directly to us (Rom 8:11). Calvin writes of the vivifying power of our union with Christ: "He therefore sits on high, transfusing us with his power, that he may quicken us to spiritual life, sanctify us by his Spirit."[13]

Again, the implications of our union with the life of Christ are stunning. We are alive to God: we can hear him, and love him, and desire to please him. We are alive to righteousness: we love the holy and good, and are magnetically attracted to them. We are alive to obedience: we hear the Word and heed it, and long to run in the path of its commands. We are alive to love: we are filled with the very love of Christ which looks upward to God and outward to our neighbors with genuine affection. We are alive to holiness: we long to be like Jesus.

We are no longer alone in our quest for change, the omnipotent Son of God has taken up residence within us, working to make us holy. United to the holy life of the Son, we cannot become other than holy.

We Are to Rely on the Son to Make Us Holy

Christ, having so completely accomplished our redemption through the atonement, works to make us holy. His sin-killing death, his holiness-producing life, are united to us so that all the benefits of the atonement are at work in us. We would be utterly foolish to think that some other means, some human contrivance, could make us holy. All of our effort in sanctification must be built upon this single foundation: we are united with Christ. If we want to become holy, then, we must look to Christ. "We are not able to find this perfection except in Jesus Christ, through faith in him, through which we are justified and sanctified."[14]

The Holy Spirit Applies Sanctification to Our Lives

The Spirit, who is the *Holy* Spirit, takes the work of the Father and the Son and applies it to us. He regenerates and renews us—giving us a new heart, mind, and will—that we may accept God's free offer of grace and forgiveness (Titus 3:5).

In regenerating us, the Spirit renews our will so that it is no longer opposed to God but able to respond amicably to him. "I also say that [the

---

13. Calvin, *Institutes*, 2.16.16.
14. Schnetzler et al., *Pierre Viret*, 264.

will] is created anew; not meaning that the will now begins to exist, but that it is changed from an evil to a good will."[15]

The Spirit works to renew our minds (Rom 12:2) guiding us "into all the truth" (John 16:13). The truth that he guides us to is the truth about God, ourselves, the world, life and death, and salvation itself. "It hence follows that men are not rightly made wise by the acumen of their own minds, but by the illumination of the Spirit."[16]

The Holy Spirit renews our hearts as well, so that we love what God loves and hate what God hates (2 Cor 3:3). The Spirit's work of regeneration is a wholesale renewal of the person—with renewed mind, will, and heart—all of which now gravitate to the Lord and toward holiness.

The Holy Spirit also creates faith in us, enabling us to lay hold of all the promises of the gospel by belief, not by works (Gal 5:5). Neither the intelligence nor the wisdom of man produces the knowledge of faith, but only the Spirit of God. "And we impart this in words not taught by human wisdom but taught by the Spirit" (1 Cor 2:13). Working faith in us to begin our walk with the Lord, the Spirit continues to supply us with increased faith, through which we gain more of Christ, and more holiness.

The Holy Spirit also unites us to Christ through faith as we hear the gospel.[17] Christ effectively dwells in us by the Spirit, who communicates his life to us. "But if Christ is in you, although the body is dead because of sin, the Spirit is life because of righteousness" (Rom 8:11). Through this Spirit-born union with Christ all the power of Christ to make us holy is no longer outside of us, but at work within us.

The Holy Spirit works continually mortifying and vivifying within us. "The death of the old man and the resurrection of the new . . . happens through the Spirit of Christ who binds us to Him and evokes in us faith and obedience."[18] The Spirit is constantly at war with our flesh, never giving it rest, never showing it any quarter. "For the desires of the flesh are against the Spirit, and the desires of the Spirit are against the flesh, for these are opposed to each other" (Gal 5:17). It is by the Spirit that we do battle with our sin. "If by the Spirit you put to death the deeds of the body, you will live" (Rom 8:13). The Spirit then leads us in the putting off of sin in our march toward holiness. "The same spirit of divine Sonship

---

15. Calvin, *Institutes*, 2.3.6.
16. Calvin, *Com.*, 1 John 2:20.
17. Tamburello, *Union with Christ*, 86.
18. Niesel, *Theology of Calvin*, 128.

... effects in all who are Christ's a continual mortifying and crucifying of their flesh."[19]

The Spirit also vivifies us by communicating the Father's love for us directly into our hearts. "God's love has been poured into our hearts through the Holy Spirit" (Rom 5:5). This love, poured abundantly into our always needy hearts, has a powerful vivifying impact in us. From this love flows our love for God, our desire to be holy, our motivation for obedience, and our relational restoration with the Lord. "For by His Holy Spirit he touches our hearts, which we come to offer him with an open spirit, because he forms our hearts for that purpose. He molds them, and whereas they were once stone, he makes them pliable and soft, so that they are fully prepared to obey him."[20]

The Spirit produces in us all the holy fruits of the Spirit, which conform us to the ideals of the Law and the life of Christ. "The fruit of the Spirit is love, joy, peace, patience, kindness, goodness, faithfulness, gentleness, self-control" (Gal 5:22). The fruit of the Spirit is not our own fruit, but Christ's, who works shaping us into his image. As the mold presses the wax into a new likeness, the Spirit changes us into the very image of Christ who is love, joy, peace, patience, etc.[21]

The Spirit leads us daily in our walk with the Lord so that we will discern what is good and what is not, applying the Word of God to our morally confusing world. "But I say, walk by the Spirit, and you will not gratify the desires of the flesh" (Gal 5:16). Walking by the Spirit is the simple, the organic way, to obey God, for he always leads us in paths that please God and conform to his Word. He always leads away from sin into holiness. Our desire to do good, the good action we carry out, and a humble heart as we obey, are all provided by the work of the Spirit within us. "Certainly, nothing good can be done by us, unless the Spirit of God effects it in us."[22]

The more completely we understand the work of the Holy Spirit in our sanctification, indeed, the more we understand the work of the entire Trinity, the more we come to see that we must learn to rely upon God for our holiness. Since the Father has decreed our holiness, since the Son has accomplished our redemption, and since the Holy Spirit applies the work

---

19. Wright, *Common Places*, 80–81.
20. Calvin, *Sermons on 2 Samuel*, 142.
21. Watson, *Body of Divinity*, 249.
22. Bucer, *In sacra quatuor Evangelia*, fol. 350.D.12–14.

of Christ to us, how could we do other than depend upon the great power of God to make us holy?

Now that we understand how God works in our sanctification we come to ask: How do we actually rely more upon him?

How Do We Rely on God to Make Us Holy?

Stop Relying on Yourself and Human Methods

The first thing we must do in seeking to rely on God is to stop relying on ourselves and human methods of sanctification. Relying on our own strength is futile. "Apart from me you can do nothing" (John 15:5). We can do nothing because the power needed to defeat our flesh does not reside in our flesh. "For I have the desire to do what is right, but not the ability to carry it out" (Rom 7:18).

Attempting to achieve holiness by our own power is the error of legalism which is always doomed to failure. "Those that endeavor to perform sincere obedience to all the commands of Christ, as the condition by which they are to procure for themselves a right and title to salvation . . . shall never be able to perform sincere and true holy obedience by all such endeavors."[23]

Our power is insufficient because no human, even those in the state of grace, has the power on their own to obey the Law in such a way that God would ever count it as righteousness. "Now it is evident that no one is justified before God by the law, for 'The righteous shall live by faith'" (Gal 3:11). It is not human power, but God's grace that works in us to make us holy. "But by the grace of God I am what I am" (1 Cor 15:10). "Let us learn, therefore, that we have nothing that is good, but what the Lord has graciously given us, that we do nothing good but what he works in us."[24]

It is our sinful human nature that very deeply believes we can improve ourselves by ourselves. We must struggle to accept that it is God who works in us. "For it is God who works in you" (Phil 2:13). Certainly we are to seek holiness, but we cannot turn to our power to gain it. We must stop counting on our ability and self-discipline, and look instead to the Lord to strengthen us. "Instead of being able to perfect to the end

---

23. Marshall, *Gospel Mystery*, 76.
24. Calvin, *Com.*, 1 Cor 15:10.

what we have been commanded, we don't even know where to begin. We can't even conceive of one single good idea until God has reformed us, until he has drawn us to himself and given us the heart to do it."[25]

Our hope for holiness lies in the fact that we can depend on God's present grace to sustain our will to obey. "Controlled by grace, [the will] never will perish, but, if grace forsake it, it will straightway fall . . . the direction of the human will toward good, and . . . its continuation in good, depend solely upon God's will, not upon any merit of man."[26]

Nor can we rely on human methods to improve ourselves. Human methods are distractions at best, and more often, absolute harms. Human methods may look good but they do nothing to actually reform us. "These have indeed an appearance of wisdom in promoting self-made religion and asceticism and severity to the body, but they are of no value in stopping the indulgence of the flesh" (Col 2:23).

Human means of sanctification are fruitless, even though they appear to be godly, for they lead away from Christ to the self, and to human religion, which is a religion of self-righteousness. Literally, "Self-made religion" (Col 2:23) means self-imposed piety. Think of the Muslim banging his head on the ground in prayer, the Hindu blood sacrifice, the Christian praying the hours. All appear to be holy actions, none are defined as such by God. Each depends upon personal performance to draw near to God or atone for the self. None promotes real holiness, for these external actions cannot subdue the flesh. Rather, human methods of subduing the body excite the flesh—that is the sin nature—to greater self-sufficiency. The flesh is self-righteous such that beating the body only encourages the flesh to delight in its strength. We cannot fight flesh with flesh. We must seek spiritual means, that is, biblical means, to subdue the flesh.

Benjamin Franklin offers a wonderful example of the futility of trying to improve ourselves by our own power, using human methods. He set out on a course of self-improvement. "It was about this time I conceived the bold and arduous project of arriving at moral perfection. I wished to live without committing any fault at any time."[27] To aid him in this pursuit, he made a little book, listing what he thought were the thirteen cardinal virtues and then daily kept track of his failures.[28] While he

---

25. Calvin, *Sermons on the Ten Commandments*, 274.
26. Calvin, *Institutes*, 2.3.14.
27. Franklin, *Autobiography*, 71.
28. Franklin, *Autobiography*, 73.

experienced slight success in restraining some superficial faults, overall he saw little change, particularly with key areas such as pride and humility. "I cannot boast of much success in acquiring the reality of this virtue, but I had a good deal with regard to the appearance of it."[29] He was able to make progress in the appearance of virtue, just as Paul had warned.

We must come to the end of ourselves, to the end of relying on our power and on human methods to defeat sin. Only then will we to turn to God and rely on his power, and the ordinary means of grace which he supplies. Only then can we hope to strive toward holiness in ways that are truly helpful. "We must always remind ourselves of this word: God must do it. For if it were a question of conforming ourselves to him by our own action, far from doing so, we would discover ourselves to be utterly weak, it would only take a blow to knock us down."[30]

Relying on God for Our Sanctification

How then do we rely on God to make us holy? We struggle, but we struggle by the power of God. "For this I toil, struggling with all his energy that he powerfully works within me" (Col 1:29).

Faith. We must begin by seeking faith. If we believe that God can make us holy, and that we cannot, then the way is opened for us to seek help from God. We must believe that: "It is God who sanctifies us by regenerating our hearts, by renewing us in every part of our being, by mortifying within us the lusts of the flesh."[31]

We must also believe that we are incapable of making ourselves holy. For only when we truly believe that we are too weak to sanctify ourselves will we turn to the Lord. "Heal me, O LORD, and I shall be healed" (Jer 17:14). Calvin comments on our need to know our weakness and thus turn to the Lord. "For every one of us must well know his own infirmity . . . let us learn by the example of the Prophet to hide ourselves under the wings of God, and to pray that he may heal us."[32]

We must depend upon the power of God constantly, even as the world depends on the sun for life. "But as in the world the sun gives and produces the day, so God gives and produces piety. The Sun shines forever

29. Franklin, *Autobiography*, 79.
30. Calvin, *Sermons on 2 Samuel*, 194.
31. Wallace, *Christian Life*, 25.
32. Calvin, *Com.*, Jer 17:14.

and ever, so the children of God must forever be led and impelled by the Holy Spirit."[33] Believing that God can sanctify us, and that we cannot, we rightly turn to him in faith for help.

Repentance. Following on faith we are to come before the Lord in repentance. *The Westminster Shorter Catechism* defines repentance beautifully. "Repentance unto life is a saving grace, whereby a sinner, out of a true sense of his sin, and apprehension of the mercy of God in Christ, doth, with grief and hatred of his sin, turn from it unto God, with full purpose of, and endeavor after, new obedience."[34]

We should note several aspects of repentance here. First, repentance is God's grace: we cannot even repent without his prior movement in our hearts. "Repentance is already a gift of God."[35] Second, it requires faith: belief that we have sinned and that God will show us mercy in Christ. Third, it involves our heart: we must hate our sin. Fourth, it involves our will: we must turn from sin and turn to God. Finally, it involves our effort for obedience: we must turn to God with the desire and the plan to obey. God responds to our repentance with grace to help us.

Means of grace. The ordinary means of grace, unlike human inventions, are provided by God to benefit the one who uses them, in faith, to seek help from the Lord. The Bible, the sacraments, the church, and prayer, are all specifically supplied by God to help us grow in holiness. God uses the Word, particularly its preaching, to impart truth and transformation. The sacraments are used by God to strengthen our faith and therein our union with Christ so that his graces flow more fully into our lives. The church is the body through which God pours out his sanctifying grace. Prayer is the action of faith where we come humbling ourselves before the Lord, and seeking him we "find grace to help in time of need" (Heb 4:16). Together these are God's appointed means to help us lay hold of his grace and advance in holiness.

Obedience of faith. We are to render to God, by his grace, the obedience of faith, which itself helps our holiness advance. "We have received grace and apostleship to bring about the obedience of faith" (Rom 1:5). God greets our obedience of faith with grace and we are helped and encouraged to new heights of holiness.

---

33. Stephens, *Theology of Bucer*, 84.
34. *Westminster Confession of Faith*, 395; Westminster Shorter Catechism, answer 87.
35. Calvin, *Sermons on 2 Samuel*, 567.

Striving yet resting. There is a paradox to the Christian's pursuit of holiness. We are to strive with all the effort we can, but this is to be done with a spirit of rest, confident that God is at work and that the work of Christ is sufficient for us. We strive, but we strive in faith, looking to Christ. In him, even as we strive—we rest—resting from our work to make ourselves holy and turning with all our heart to him. "So then, there remains a Sabbath rest for the people of God, for whoever has entered God's rest has also rested from his works as God did from his. Let us therefore strive to enter that rest, so that no one may fall by the same sort of disobedience" (Heb 4:9–11). Calvin explains that our striving is a restful dependence upon God.

> [Scripture] testifies also that all our progress and perseverance are from God. Besides, it expressly declares that wisdom, love, patience, are the gifts of God and the Spirit. When, therefore, the Apostle requires these things, he by no means asserts that they are in our power, but only shews what we ought to have, and what ought to be done. And as to the godly, when conscious of their own infirmity, they find themselves deficient in their duty, nothing remains for them but to flee to God for aid and help.[36]

This is how we strive for holiness: by fleeing to God for help. We do this through faith, repentance, the ordinary means of grace, and the obedience of faith.

Summary of How We Are to Rely on God

1. To rely on God we must humbly stop relying on ourselves and human methods to make us holy.
2. To rely on God we must have faith that God has the power and the desire to make us holy, and then turning to our triune God in faith, rely on him to actually make us holy.
    a. Since the Father elects us to sanctification by grace, we should be humble and grateful to him. We should also be determined to grow in holiness, confident in his decree, as we rely on his love and his grace, to fulfill his purpose of making us holy.

---

36. Calvin, *Com.*, 2 Pet 1:5.

b. Since Christ unites himself to us, killing our sin and making us alive to righteousness, we should rely on his power at work in us, to make us holy.
   c. Since the Spirit leads us away from sin to holiness we should walk in the Spirit, relying on him to lead us to holiness rather than grieving him by our refusal.
3. To rely on God we should daily humble ourselves before him through repentance, confessing our sins, and seek his grace and power to help us toward new obedience.
4. To rely on God we seek his grace through the ordinary means of grace. Pray to come before him humbly seeking his grace, hear the Word preached and study it to learn of him and find his help, belong to a church and give yourself deeply to her fellowship and work, that God may work through others to help you grow, worthily receive the sacraments, that his grace might abound to you.
5. To rely on God we should aim to render to God the obedience of faith, not of the Law, obeying his Word knowing that we are already justified by grace, and knowing we enjoy the blessings of obedience, even when our obedience is imperfect.
6. To rely on God we strive and rest. We put out all effort to become holy, trusting in God's work, not ours, to make us holy.

Further Resources

Study Questions

1. Why should we rely on God to make us holy?
2. How does the Father's decree of election impact our sanctification? How does his love for us help us grow holy? What is the right role of fear in our relationship with God?
3. How does the Son's union with us help us to become holy?
4. What does the Holy Spirit change about us that advances our holiness? What part does he play in our faith and our union with Christ?
5. Why must we stop relying on ourselves and human methods to make us holy?

6. How does faith help us to rely on God?
7. How does repentance help us to rely on God?
8. What roles do the Bible, the church, prayer, and the sacraments play in helping our holiness?
9. How does our obedience of faith help us to grow in holiness?
10. What human methods have you tried to make you holy? On what do you tend to rely now for holiness? What is one way you could move toward more reliance upon God for holiness?

For Further Study

Henry Beveridge and Jules Bonnet, eds., *John Calvin: Tracts and Letters* (7 vols., Edinburgh: Banner of Truth, 2009).

Richard B. Gaffin Jr., "Calvin's Soteriology: The Structure of the Application of Redemption in Book Three of the *Institutes*," *Ordained Servant* 18 (2009) 68–77.

Dennis E. Tamburello, *Union with Christ: John Calvin and the Mysticism of St. Bernard* (Louisville: Westminster John Knox, 1994).

4

Seek the Twofold Knowledge of God and Self

OUR PROGRESS IN HOLINESS requires that we gain a true knowledge of God and ourselves. "You will know the truth, and the truth will set you free" (John 8:32). Until we see God and ourselves as we truly are—God in his greatness, holiness, and mercy, and us in our smallness, need, and inability—we will not relate to God properly. The true knowledge of God and ourselves leads us to respond to God rightly in relationship: prostrating and exalting before him. In prostration we humble ourselves before him, seeing our smallness before his greatness. In exaltation we worship God, seeing his power and love toward us. The motion of sanctification then is simultaneously twofold: we move downward in prostration and upward in exaltation as we truly see God and ourselves.

The Bible warns us against rejecting this knowledge of God. "For the wrath of God is revealed from heaven against all ungodliness and unrighteousness of men, who by their unrighteousness suppress the truth.... For although they knew God, they did not honor him as God or give thanks to him, but they became futile in their thinking, and their foolish hearts were darkened" (Rom 1:18, 21). Rejecting knowledge of God, humanity became darkened in its understanding, refusing to gratefully exalt God, but rather turning from him in disdain. Sanctification, therefore, requires gaining true knowledge of God which leads us to relate to him well.

Colossians also calls us to have a renewed knowledge of God, as we put on the new self, which is "being renewed in knowledge after the image of its creator" (Col 3:9–10). This renewed knowledge of God conforms us to the image of Christ. Calvin comments: "Newness of life consists in knowledge ... transforming the whole man ... that we are renewed after the image of God."[1]

Romans calls us to be "transformed by the renewal" of our minds, which leads us to understand "the will of God" and to think rightly of ourselves, "with sober judgment" (Rom 12:2–3). As we gain knowledge of God we gain new insights into ourselves as well: "In knowing God each of us also knows himself."[2] We need this new accurate information to replace the lies which we have previously accepted, for his truth transforms our minds and lives powerfully.

This concept of the twofold knowledge of God and self has been taught throughout the history of the church. We read, for example, in Clement of Alexandria (d. 215 AD), "If one knows oneself, one will know God."[3] Basil of Caesarea (d. 379 AD) understood that this knowledge leads us to properly adore God. "If we are penetrated by these truths, we shall know ourselves, we shall know God, we shall adore our Creator."[4] Augustine (d. 430 AD) proclaimed: "I desire to know God and the soul."[5]

The Reformers elaborated upon the twofold knowledge because they were eager to see their congregations grow in sanctification. Martin Bucer wrote: "If we know God and ourselves we will ascribe to God glory in all things, but to ourselves confusion."[6] Pierre Viret wrote of the impact of this knowledge. "The true knowledge of Him ... leads man to honor Him as his God and Creator with the true honor due Him."[7]

Calvin used the knowledge of God and self as a central organizing principle in his *Institutes*. "Nearly all the wisdom we possess, that is to say, true and sound wisdom, consists of two parts: the knowledge of God and of ourselves."[8] He explains the interconnectedness between the knowledge of God and ourselves. "No one can look upon himself without immediately turning his thoughts to the contemplation of God, in whom he "lives and moves." For, quite clearly, the mighty gifts with which we are

---

1. Calvin, *Com.*, Col 3:10.
2. Calvin, *Ioannis Calvini Opera*, 3:37b.
3. Roberts and Donaldson, *The Ante-Nicene Fathers*, 2:271.
4. Schaff, *The Nicene and Post-Nicene Fathers*, Series 2:8:309.
5. Schaff, *The Nicene and Post-Nicene Fathers*, Series 1:7:539.
6. Bucer, *In sacra quatuor Evangelia*, fol. 66v, 25–28.
7. Viret, *Catechism of 1541*, lines 30–31.
8. Calvin, *Institutes*, 1.1.1.

endowed are hardly from ourselves; indeed, our very being is nothing but subsistence in the one God."[9] When we look on ourselves we are forced to see the glory of our Creator.

Calvin also asserted that it is only when we look upon our brokenness and compare it to God's absolute holiness, that we properly understand our need of God.

> Man never achieves a clear knowledge of himself unless he has first looked upon God's face, and then descends from contemplating him to scrutinize himself. For we always seem to ourselves righteous and upright and wise and holy—this pride is innate in all of us—unless by clear proofs we stand convinced of our own unrighteousness, foulness, folly, and impurity.[10]

More recently Dowey has written of our twofold response to the knowledge of God and self. "The reaction is twofold: man stands awestricken in fear, and yet is drawn in love. These two responses are not antithetical, but belong side by side in the pious heart."[11] The Roman Catholic theologian, Hildebrand (d. 1977), demonstrates that knowledge of God and self leads us to humility. "It is only in our encounter with a personal God that we become fully aware of our condition as creatures, and fling from us the last particle of self-glory."[12]

In this chapter we will explain how we came to be in need of this twofold knowledge, how gaining this knowledge helps our sanctification, and then finally, how we may gain this twofold knowledge for progress in holiness.

How Did We Come to Desperately Need the Twofold Knowledge of God and Self?

As we were originally created we fully possessed a right knowledge of God and ourselves. Created in the image of God and walking in complete submission to and fellowship with God, we understood his power and fatherly love. We understood ourselves, as his children, small before his greatness, made by him and loved by him, provided for by his providential care. In the midst of this right knowledge of God and ourselves

---

9. Calvin, *Institutes*, 1.1.1.
10. Calvin, *Institutes*, 1.1.2.
11. Dowey, *The Knowledge of God*, 30.
12. Hildebrand, *Humility*, 24.

we responded to him with humble, thankful hearts which exalted him as our God. Each look up at God and down at ourselves confirmed and strengthened our affective response to God. It drove us to our knees in prostration with arms uplifted in exaltation. So were we in the state of innocence in the garden, our original holiness.

To understand the human condition today—the self-knowledge we need for sanctification—we must contrast what we were as originally created, with our present fallen sinful nature. With humanity's fall into sin, our knowledge of God and of ourselves, and therefore our response to God, was corrupted. Man, who had humbly sat at the feet of God, rose up in pride against him, grasping for knowledge that was beyond him. His mind became defective, he could not reason clearly or even comprehend facts well (Rom 1:21).

This is not to say that human reason and understanding have ceased to function, they still work in part. We may conduct ourselves well enough in the ordinary world, planning and executing those plans. Also, our consciences, with which we can distinguish good and evil, and the "sense of the divine," by which we are aware of God's majesty, still work to some degree.[13] But conscience and the sense of the divine work only well enough to leave humanity without excuse before God's righteous judgment, since they know of God, yet refuse to worship him. "So they are without excuse. For although they knew God, they did not honor him as God or give thanks to him" (Rom 1:20–21).

Our minds cannot, apart from God's grace, acquire a saving knowledge of God, or even a true knowledge of ourselves, since without knowledge of God the latter is not possible. Human reason, conscience, and the sense of the divine, all lead to dead-ends, for "conscience perverts every decision" and "natural reason never will direct men to Christ."[14]

The brokenness of our minds means that we cannot see ourselves rightly. "The human heart has so many crannies where vanity hides, so many holes where falsehood lurks, is so decked out with deceiving hypocrisy, that it often dupes itself."[15] Sin blinds us, and the first thing that it blinds us to is the sin in ourselves. "He has blinded their eyes and hardened their heart" (John 12:40). Because we cannot see our own sin, we have no idea how bad it really is; we live instead with a false notion of

---

13. Calvin, *Institutes*, 1.3.2.
14. Calvin, *Com.*, John 1:5.
15. Calvin, *Institutes*, 3.2.10.

our virtue. We may be able to judge good and evil outside of ourselves to some degree, but not internally. "We always recognize good and evil well enough. But we're totally witless when the case applies to us; so much so that our eyes are dulled, all our senses are lost and, in short, we do not apply it fairly to ourselves."[16]

Our blindness and faulty reasoning are a double curse. Not only can we not see ourselves rightly, but because we cannot see our sin for what it is, we cannot seek the proper cure: help from God. "Through this subtlety Satan attempted to cover up the disease and thus to render it incurable."[17] We falsely believe that we can use self-discipline, education, training, or counseling to improve ourselves, without the help of divine grace. Humanity is then forever left chasing its own tail, trying one remedy after another to improve, but to no avail, while neglecting the one real cure: the mercy of God in Christ.

Our brokenness means that we are corrupted through and through, caught in an ever downward spiral of indulging in sin and moral debasement. A sin principle—sometimes called concupiscence—occupies our hearts, and it lusts for more: more fame, money, and pleasure. "They have become callous and have given themselves up to sensuality, greedy to practice every kind of impurity" (Eph 4:19).

This is not to say, however, that the image of God in humanity is entirely obliterated. The remnants of that glorious image, in our reason, our conscience, our ability to love, to seek justice and truth—at least in part—all point to God's original creation. But this image is a broken ruin, which apart from grace, only speaks a further condemnation over those who deny that the good remaining in them is from the very hand of the God whom they deny. Therefore, all the misguided human efforts to seek after the divine, only lead to idolatry, having "exchanged the glory of the immortal God for images," and not to the true knowledge of God (Rom 1:22–23). "In short, natural reason never will direct men to Christ."[18]

Our Sin Leads Us to Despise God and Exalt Ourselves

In the fall, humanity totally rejected the true God. Humanity exchanged its natural humility for unnatural pride, pride which desires to be exalted

---

16. Calvin, *Sermons on the Ten Commandments*, 525–26.
17. Calvin, *Institutes*, 2.1.5.
18. Calvin, *Com.*, John 1:5.

at the cost of God himself. Our fallen will naturally chooses against God and his Law, so that, constrained only by its own sinfulness, it always wills evil. "The will is certainly by nature always evil."[19] Because the fallen human will opposes God it cannot cooperate with God for its own improvement, apart from special grace. "Therefore simply to will is of man; to will ill, of a corrupt nature; to will well, of grace."[20]

Our hearts and our affections are opposed to God as well. Fallen humanity is not neutral toward God, rather, there is a deep-seated enmity for him. Despising his rightful claim upon us as his creatures, and despising his very presence, we debase God in our own minds.

There occurred then in the fall a great reversal of the natural order of our relationship with God. While we think highly of ourselves, yet in refusing to worship and thank God, we debase him in our thoughts, minimizing his providential contribution to our lives, underestimating his holiness and demand for our holiness, and discounting the debt of worship we owe him. Fallen humanity, reverses the natural order, so that it now considers itself superior to God.

At Creation	After the Fall
God	Man
over	over
Man	God

This is the essential reversal of the fall which must be undone in sanctification.

Rejecting God We Seek Our Own Salvation

Humanity, though flattering itself with any virtue it possesses, is left with a vague awareness of its failings, since the Law of God is still written on our hearts and our conscience still operates partly. Blind to the seriousness of sin and to what might truly help, we flail about seeking self-improvement. Some will try to "improve" themselves by judging their neighbors, so they can judge themselves relatively better. At other times

---

19. Calvin, *Bondage and Liberation*, 183.
20. Calvin, *Institutes*, 2.3.5.

we will try to control our external behaviors giving no thought to the evil within us, satisfied that our actions are slightly improved.[21]

Humanity, recognizing its need and finding little help from its own cures, turns to religion. But our choice for religion is idolatry. Refusing to accept the true God, we create our own gods, making idols of anything we find at hand. "We all possess the seed of idolatry in our nature. Without ever having to go to school, we learn it all too readily on our own."[22]

The Descent into Idolatry

Rejecting the truth about God we create the lies of idolatry as the natural religion of all fallen humanity, past and present. This is why the Bible addresses idolatry so often. "You shall have no other gods before me. You shall not make for yourself a carved image, or any likeness of anything" (Deut 5:7–8). "Therefore, my beloved, flee from idolatry" (1 Cor 10:14).

In the New Testament, the term used most often to describe an idolatrous impulse is desire, or over-desire, *epithumia* (ἐπιθυμία), which occurs about thirty-eight times. For example: "But each person is tempted when he is lured and enticed by his own *desire*" (Jas 1:14).

The downward spiral of idolatry in the human heart is important to understand for our progress in sanctification. For idolatry, along with pride and unbelief, is often the sin more deeply imbedded in our soul, behind an obvious sin. For example, we may be sinfully angry at someone, but the sin behind that sin may be our idolatrous desire for control, which that person threatens.

Romans 1 explains the etymology of idolatry. Hating God we refused to worship him or live in submission to him. "For although they knew God, they did not honor him as God or give thanks to him" (Rom 1:21a). Recognizing our need for help in this life, however, we invent idols: "Exchanged the glory of the immortal God for images" (Rom 1:23). The idols are not just objects, of course, but an entire system of lies around which one's life is to be organized. "Because they exchanged the truth about God for a lie" (Rom 1:25). Through these lying rules, humanity tries to achieve a sense of righteousness, an effort at self-improvement by self-help.

---

21. Calvin, *Com.*, 1 John 5:12.
22. Calvin, *Sermons on Micah*, 37–38.

Humanity invents its own religious approaches to the universe in order to try to obtain righteousness apart from God's mercy in Christ.[23] Trying to live by the lying rules of our various idolatries, however, we are enslaved to them, worshipping and serving them (Rom 1:25). When others oppose our idolatry we naturally hate them, as the Galatians hated Paul (Gal 4:16). We go through life enslaved to the idols, forsaking the love of God that could be ours in Christ. "Those who pay regard to vain idols forsake their hope of steadfast love" (Jonah 2:8).

The Sad State of Fallen Humanity

Blinded to our true condition, our self-help approaches only make us worse. We fight with others to vindicate ourselves and we fight within ourselves trying to validate ourselves. We invent idols by which to declare ourselves righteous but only become all the more unrighteous before our holy God. Rather than advance toward godliness we are thrown backward by efforts at self-help.

The one thing we will not do is turn to God for help. Thinking we are good, we do not seek the right cure, and thinking that God is evil, we neglect the only possible source of our cure. Here we find humanity apart from Christ: helpless to advance toward godliness.

Why must we so precisely understand our bleak human condition? In order to find the right cure for humanity we must have the proper diagnosis of our condition. Historically, there have been three broad diagnoses concerning the human condition: 1) Humanity is generally good and doing well on its own, 2) Humanity suffers from some dysfunction and needs some help, such as education, 3) Humanity is dead in its sin and needs God to save it. Only biblical Christianity offers this final correct diagnosis.

When we rightly understand the nature of our depravity we can see how helpless we are and how much we need God to deliver us. Anselm described it well. "So inexcusable is man, who has voluntarily brought upon himself a debt which he cannot pay, and by his own fault disabled himself, so that he can neither escape his previous obligation not to sin, nor pay the debt which he has incurred by sin."[24]

---

23. Calvin, *Institutes*, 2.8.5.
24. Anselm, *Cur Deus Homo*, 76.

From this stark, but biblically accurate look, we are lead to a few conclusions which will aid our progress in sanctification. First, humanity, deeply sinful, cannot cure itself. This means that we need God to heal us, continuously. Second, humanity is blind to its own condition. This means we need external objective truth to break through our blindness. Third, humanity is without excuse for its sin, and is responsible for rejecting the truth about God and itself. This means that the help we need is not owed to us, it is of grace.

Understanding our helpless state we can now explore how God's grace, in revealing to us the twofold knowledge of God and ourselves, begins to reverse the curse, restoring us to the right relationship with God, where we respond to him with prostration and exaltation.

How Does Growth in the Twofold Knowledge Contribute to Our Sanctification?

The Twofold Knowledge Restores Us to Sanity

Being in a state of sin is a kind of insanity. Humanity is in reality a dependent, weak creature; God truly is good and all powerful. It is sane and natural to believe this and live humbly before God. But in the great reversal of the fall, our pride insanely tells us that we should be honored, even above God. While humility and faith are the natural created order, pride and unbelief are unnatural insanity.

Sadly, we are born into the insanity of prideful unbelief. The process of sanctification, following our conversion, requires the transformation of our minds so that we increasingly see God and ourselves rightly. Sanctification then is a return to sanity, to humility before God. "Pride is the gate, the birth, and the curse of hell. Therefore, it is reasonable to say that nothing can be our redemption except the restoration of the lost humility, the original and only true relationship of the creature to its God."[25]

Thus the twofold knowledge of God and self is essential to our sanctification. As knowledge of God increases, so must, by comparison to him, knowledge of ourselves so that we see more and more clearly how weak and needy we are. "Whoever is utterly cast down and overwhelmed by the awareness of his calamity, poverty, nakedness, and disgrace has

---

25. Murray, *Humility*, 2.

thus advanced farthest in knowledge of himself."[26] It is when these two knowledges come together in us at the same time that we see reality as it is, and then are able to respond to God rightly. Seeing our weakness and need, we look for the right kind of help. Seeing the power and mercy of God, we seek help from him.

Having summarized the impact of this twofold knowledge we will now elaborate upon it.

The Twofold Knowledge Allows Us to See God Rightly

As we grow in knowledge of God we return to the sanity of seeing God as he is. We see his glory. "Great is the LORD, and greatly to be praised, and his greatness is unsearchable" (Ps 145:3). We see his holiness. "Holy, holy, holy is the LORD of hosts" (Isa 6:3). We see that in his holiness he will judge all sin. "Shall not the Judge of all the earth do what is just?" (Gen 18:25). We see the world in a new light. In contrast to the splendid light of God's holiness, all the world, including us, seems now shrouded in darkness. "Woe is me! For I am lost; for I am a man of unclean lips" (Isa 6:5).

Blessedly, we also come to understand God's love more clearly. Were we to only know his glorious holiness, it might send us fleeing in panic. When we also see his mercy, however, we are attracted to him and encouraged to seek his help. "But this I call to mind, and therefore I have hope: The steadfast love of the LORD never ceases; his mercies never come to an end" (Lam 3:21–22). When we see both the holiness and the love of God, we come to understand how worthy he is of worship!

The Twofold Knowledge Allows Us to See Ourselves Rightly

As we gain knowledge of ourselves before the face of God we come to see the reality of the depth of our sin, abandoning our self-flattery. King David finally came to this knowledge of himself regarding his sins of adultery and murder. "Behold, I was brought forth in iniquity, and in sin did my mother conceive me. . . . Purge me with hyssop, and I shall be clean; wash me, and I shall be whiter than snow" (Ps 51:5–7). The fog of self-deception is lifted, and we see that we are the chief of sinners, an understanding that eventually helps lead us to repentance.

---

26. Calvin, *Institutes*, 2.2.10.

Our knowledge of ourselves is enhanced as we look at the cross of Christ. In light of the horror of the cross—the perfect and innocent Christ suffering on account of our sin—we see our sin in all its depravity, painted clearly for us in the blood of Christ. Seeing in the cross God's holy justice as well as his steadfast love, we come to see ourselves as we truly are before him: broken by our sin, yet cherished in his love.

The cross also makes clear God's requirement for our perfect holiness. "You shall be holy, for I the LORD your God am holy" (Lev 19:2). This high standard for humanity, a part of the knowledge of ourselves, no longer allows us to judge ourselves righteous based upon comparisons to others. We come to know our need for personal holiness more deeply.

As we grow in knowledge of ourselves we see that God is not only worthy of worship, but that humanity owes God this honor. Since he has created us, sustained us, and blessed us, we see as never before, the immense debt of worship and gratitude that we owe to God. "You shall worship the Lord your God and him only shall you serve" (Matt 4:10). We see as well the obligation of obedience that we owe God, as part of our honor to him. "So you shall keep my commandments and do them: I am the LORD" (Lev 22:31–32). Seeing our debt of obedience and worship for what it truly is, we feel our lack of both more keenly.

> True knowledge of our status as creatures, however, implies a confrontation of the creature with its Creator: it is not possible except in reference to a personal God. For awareness of our creaturely status is more than a mere awareness of our debility and limitation. It amounts to experiencing not only our relative imperfection and the restrictions to which we are subject, but the infinite distance between us and absolute Being; it requires a full understanding of the fact that we have received "all that we have and are"—except sin—from God.[27]

True knowledge of ourselves also informs us of our cognitive limitations. We see that our reason is still tainted by sin and cannot derive truth on its own. Realizing this we humbly begin to seek the truth from the Word and from the Spirit. "But the Helper, the Holy Spirit, whom the Father will send in my name, he will teach you all things" (John 14:26). Calvin enjoins us: "All our life we are to have God as our Guide, and his

---

27. Hildebrand, *Humility*, 24–25.

Word as the unquestionable standard of right and wrong.... We are nothing but poor brute beasts, unless God gives us reason and intelligence."[28]

The right twofold knowledge of God and ourselves leads us to these new insights but it does not leave us there. From our new insights we enter a new relationship with God.

The Twofold Knowledge Leads Us to Humbly Seek the Help of God

This growing knowledge of ourselves and of God leads us to one inescapable conclusion vital to our progress in sanctification: we must turn to God for help to grow in holiness. "Heal me, O LORD, and I shall be healed" (Jer 17:14). Rather than despising God and running from him, we now turn to God, dependently seeking his help. We come to the single sane realization: there is only one who can help us, the Lord who sanctifies his people (1 Thess 5:23).

We see the truth, that we are utterly and absolutely dependent creatures who must moment by moment depend upon the power and the grace of our God to sustain us and to transform us into his image. "Humility, the place of entire dependence on God, is the first duty of the creature, and the root of every good quality."[29] In humble dependence we turn to God, from whom we have received everything, for help to make us holy. "The legitimate order of nature ... means the order of utter dependence on the mercy of God. Dependence on the mercy of God is order; independence is disorder."[30]

The true knowledge of God and ourselves frees us from the blindness of unbelief, so seeing reality, we turn in deep faith and repentance to God to receive his grace and mercy which then lifts us up in new holiness of life.

The Twofold Knowledge Leads Us from Pride to Humble Prostration

The more we learn of God and ourselves, as the people of God, the more we are led to humility. "For the knowledge of God does truly humble

---

28. Calvin, *Sermons on 2 Samuel*, 51.
29. Murray, *Humility*, 2.
30. Torrance, *Calvin's Doctrine of Man*, 47.

us."[31] Edwards concurs: "Humility does primarily and chiefly consist in a sense of our meanness [lowness] as compared with God, or a sense of the infinite distance there is between God and ourselves."[32]

Humility leads us to relate to God properly, prostrating ourselves, approaching God on bended knee. In the Indiana Jones movie, *The Last Crusade*, Jones is trying to enter the booby-trapped temple which contains the Holy Grail. He has a clue, "only the penitent man will pass." Others have gone before him and died. He realizes at just the right moment that the penitent man goes forward on his knees, so he drops to his knees just as a giant blade slices chest-high over him. It is an apt analogy for our prostration. Only the penitent person may safely enter the presence of God. "Grant, Almighty God, as no other way of access to thee is open for us except through unfeigned humility, that we may often learn to abase ourselves with feelings of true repentance."[33] We no longer vaunt ourselves in our own hearts, but daily cast ourselves prostrate before God. "Humble yourselves before the Lord" (Jas 4:10).

This new humility is the restoration of the true order, where God is exalted and we are cast down before him, the natural way to live. "When the creature realizes that this is true goodness . . . he sees that humility is simply acknowledging the truth of his position as the creature, and yielding to God His rightful place."[34] It is humility that marks the believer's progress in holiness. "The progress of our sanctification shows in the measure of our truly humbling ourselves before God."[35]

Our growing humility encourages us to come more readily to God for help. "For no one is rightly prepared to call on God, except he is cast down in himself and laid prostrate."[36] We give up self-help and come to the divine surgeon, submitting to his scalpel. "Here, then, is what God's truth requires us to seek in examining ourselves: it requires the kind of knowledge that will strip us of all confidence in our own ability, deprive us of all occasion for boasting, and lead us to submission."[37]

---

31. Calvin, *Com.*, Ezek 1:28.
32. Edwards, *Charity and its Fruits*, 131.
33. Calvin, *Com.*, Dan 9:7.
34. Murray, *Humility*, 4.
35. Kraan, "Le Péché et la Repentance," 44.
36. Calvin, *Com.*, Jer 11:14.
37. Calvin, *Institutes*, 2.1.2.

The humility which emerges from the right knowledge of God and self is crucial for it is this very humility which invites the grace of God. While God opposes all the proud, he lifts up—offers mercy and gives grace—to the humble. The very grace that we need to grow in holiness. "Toward the scorners he is scornful, but to the humble he gives favor" (Prov 3:34).

The Twofold Knowledge Leads Us to Thankfully Exalt God

The twofold knowledge also leads us to thankful exaltation. We recognize that all the good in our lives is from him: he has created, prospered, and sustained us. Humbled with the knowledge of our sin and of his goodness we no longer boast of ourselves but in him. "My soul makes its boast in the LORD; let the humble hear and be glad" (Ps 34:2). Boasting in the Lord, we pour out praise for his goodness and mercy to us. "Give thanks to the LORD, for he is good, for his steadfast love endures forever" (Ps 136:1).

Thanksgiving is our chief duty and our chief delight in the light of our growing twofold knowledge. "God's whole purpose in creating us . . . is that we might be moved to continually render praise back to Him."[38] It is this heart of thanks to God—for his merciful blessing and his paternal love—that moves us to exalt God. "Thankfulness . . . is the moving force behind worship."[39] Knowing now the great glory of God, we delight to magnify his name in our worship. "Nothing more frequently meets us than this teaching—that we have been redeemed by God that we may celebrate his glory."[40]

Knowing that we are entirely dependent upon God we turn to him for all things, a turning which does, itself, exalt him as Provider. "Ask, and it will be given to you. . . . How much more will your Father who is in heaven give good things to those who ask him!" (Matt 7:7, 11). This calling upon God is an exaltation of his power and generosity. "Once we have placed our full trust in him, we call upon him for every need."[41]

Knowing more the love of God, we respond with love for God, the central aspect of relational holiness. We come into the presence of God not as slaves who fear the whip of their master, but as children who,

---

38. Wallace, *Christian Life*, 284.
39. Gerrish, "Calvin's Eucharistic Piety," 59.
40. Calvin, *Com.*, Ezek 11:18.
41. Calvin, *Songs of the Nativity*, 38–39.

expecting a warm greeting, run to honor their Father with their love. "For you did not receive the spirit of slavery to fall back into fear, but you have received the Spirit of adoption as sons, by whom we cry, 'Abba! Father!'" (Rom 8:15).

So far we have seen the impact of gaining more knowledge of God and ourselves. This knowledge restores us to humility so that we prostrate ourselves before God in repentance, seeking his grace to transform us, while we exalt God with our thanks, supplication, and our love. Our progress in holiness, therefore, is greatly enhanced by growth in true knowledge of God and ourselves. It remains now for us to explore practically how we may gain this knowledge.

How Do We Gain Greater Knowledge of God and Ourselves?

Growing in the twofold knowledge of God and self transforms our relationship with God as we humbly prostrate ourselves before him and thankfully rise up to exalt him. This simultaneous downward and upward motion leads us to a joyful and bold life. "Our jubilant assent to our own insignificance . . . implies a heavenward aspiration that carries with it a breath of greatness and holy audacity."[42] It may seem odd to think that we are cast down and lifted up at the same time, however this is the essential motion of sanctification, the logic of grace, which we must understand, defying worldly reason.

> Repentance throws men downwards, and faith raises them upwards again. At the first glance these two ideas do not seem easily reconciled. . . . When the sinner comes into the presence of God, he must necessarily fall completely down. . . . Then . . . when God invites them to himself . . . they raise themselves up and overtop the clouds, yea, even heaven itself.[43]

While the concept of the twofold knowledge may seem new to many readers, the way in which we gain it will certainly not.

---

42. Hildebrand, *Humility*, 54.
43. Calvin, *Com.*, Dan 9:18.

The Word of God

We look first to the Bible to gain this twofold knowledge, for the Scriptures "are able to make you wise for salvation through faith in Christ Jesus" (2 Tim 3:15).

We learn best from the Word through its preaching. The Word preached confronts us with views of Scripture outside of ourselves which challenge our limited understanding. "This word is the good news that was preached to you" (1 Pet 1:25). Ignorance is replaced with knowledge, lies with truth.[44] We should not come passively to the sermon but come asking: "What does it teach me of God and of myself?"

We also seek the twofold knowledge in our own devotional study of the Bible. As we prayerfully read the Bible we ask: "What does this teach us about God and ourselves? How does it ask me to respond to God?" "For it is no empty word for you, but your very life" (Deut 32:47). We should daily devote ourselves to the study, memorization, and meditation of the Word. The more the Word shapes our thoughts, the more joy and freedom we know in responding to God rightly in prostration and exaltation.

In all our learning from the Word we should seek knowledge of God regarding his holiness, power, justice, love, mercy, and grace. The more we learn, for example, of his sovereign power the more readily we entrust ourselves to him. "I will trust, and will not be afraid; for the LORD GOD is my strength and my song" (Isa 12:2). Our low view of God must gradually give way to the reality of the God revealed in his Word, so we are changed into his very image.

We should seek to understand ourselves from Scripture: "Where does sin yet linger in my saved soul? How is Christ alive in me?" "So you also must consider yourselves dead to sin and alive to God in Christ Jesus" (Rom 6:11). No psychological textbook will offer such penetrating truth about the human heart, for only the Bible can discern "the thoughts and intentions of the heart" (Heb 4:12).

We should seek knowledge of God's love for us, an understanding which transforms us. "God's love has been poured into our hearts through the Holy Spirit who has been given to us" (Rom 5:5). We should seek knowledge of what God wants from us in obedience. "What does the LORD require of you but to do justice, and to love kindness, and to walk humbly with your God?" (Mic 6:8) As we gain more knowledge

---

44. Schnetzler et al., *Pierre Viret*, 189.

of God and ourselves from his Word, we honor God in our humble relationship with him.

Creation

We should spend time in God's creation enjoying it, but also learning of God's majesty. "The heavens declare the glory of God, and the sky above proclaims his handiwork" (Ps 19:1). In the beauty of creation we can discern his "eternal power and divine nature" (Rom 1:20). We see God's mercy in that he makes the sun to shine on the good and the wicked (Matt 5:45). We learn of his love for all humanity, by the very bounty of creation. "You cause the grass to grow for the livestock and plants for man to cultivate" (Ps 104:14).

While creation teaches us more of God, it teaches us of ourselves, too. From creation we learn of our own finitude. We require the atmosphere to protect us from the harshness of space and the sun's rays. We learn of human dignity as well. God lovingly provided this abundant world *for us*, and *set us* in charge over it. Human depravity and human dignity are both detectable from the book of creation.

Ourselves

We can seek the twofold knowledge within ourselves. Since God has created us in his image, we can understand him by seeing the remnants of his image within us. "Quite clearly, the mighty gifts with which we are endowed are hardly from ourselves."[45] In our longing for purpose, we see reflected God's eternal purpose. Our desire to be loved reflects the eternally fellowshipping Trinity. Our desire for justice reflects the perfect justice of God. We may take the entire list of the communicable attributes of God, and finding them imperfectly cast in ourselves, look upward and see their perfection in God.

Of course we can learn of ourselves as we look inward. We see within ourselves the glorious handiwork of God, our inherent dignity and intrinsic worth. "I praise you, for I am fearfully and wonderfully made" (Ps 139:14). We also learn of our sin, weakness, and need as we descend into ourselves and examine our motives. "Search me, O God, and know my heart!" (Ps 139:23).

---

45. Calvin, *Institutes*, 1.1.1.

Calvin calls this inward look the "descent into the self" where we carefully scrutinize our hearts, thoughts, actions, and motives. Since we must know our sins in order to repent of them, in order to experience God's grace to cleanse, forgive, and heal us, understanding our sin becomes vital to our progress in holiness. "If we confess our sins, he is faithful and just to forgive us our sins and to cleanse us from all unrighteousness" (1 John 1:9). This self-examination for sin should become a daily practice of our devotional life. "Grant, Almighty God, that we may learn more and more fully to probe ourselves, and to discover the faults of which we are guilty."[46]

As we seek to understand our sin, we must not overlook the various idolatries that capture our hearts—the sin beneath the sin—which keeps us from living in the grace of God. Some have suggested that there may be four primary schools of idols: competence, control, approval, and comfort. I have found these categories to be very helpful. Interestingly, they correspond nicely to the four work-styles in the DISC-type indicator. Here the Dominant tends toward the competency idol, Influencing toward approval, Steady toward comfort, and Conscientious toward control. However, anything, anyone, any concept even, may become an idol to us, so we should search our hearts carefully.

It is helpful to regularly analyze our hearts for various idolatries. When we react with more anger, sorrow, or anxiety than any situation biblically warrants, we should ask if there is some idolatry driving us, and discovering it, repent, turning to the Lord for help. For example, years ago, I was planning, with a friend, to complete a one-hundred-mile bicycle ride, which ended at the top of Beech Mountain in North Carolina. We trained for months riding many fifty-to-seventy-mile-long rides.

The week of the ride, however, I came down with bronchitis and could not attempt the ride. The day of the ride I was depressed and surly. Naturally it was disappointing to have a goal and be unable to achieve it, but something else was at work. Suspecting my competency idol, I started to examine my heart. I realized that during the months of training I had imagined myself standing on top of Beech Mountain, arms raised in triumph. I also had imagined telling my friends how I completed this difficult ride, and then imagined how I would bask in their admiration.

Interestingly, as I examined myself closely I realized that I had developed in my mind clear images of those two scenes and had played

---

46. Calvin, *Com.*, Dan 9:21.

them over hundreds of times. I suspect that when we have idols, although we do not usually have external images, we generally create pictures in our hearts of the things that we want. In this case, uncovering the idol, confessing it to God and others, brought growth in this area of my life.

This knowledge of ourselves, and of God, that we gain from looking at ourselves is indispensable to our growth in grace!

Others/The Church

We may gain the twofold knowledge from others. When we hear of God's strength in their stories of deliverance, we come to trust God more as our Father. Our children may excitedly praise God for some small kindness, teaching us of God's love. Over the years I have listened to my wife share insights about God that have filled my heart with new admiration for him. Others in the church may also intentionally teach us about God from his Word.

We can learn of ourselves from others. In community we learn of our failings as we fight with our envy, anger, and jealousy. In community we also learn from others about our sins that are not apparent to us. "If your brother sins against you, go and tell him his fault, between you and him alone" (Matt 18:15).

I have been in accountability groups most of my adult life. In one of those, we were confessing our battle with idolatries. I mentioned to the group my competency idol, then one member asked: "Well what about your control idol?" I was dumbfounded, I had never seen it, never even suspected it. But when I asked for examples the entire group easily rehearsed specific instances. It became clear to me, for the first time, that I had an issue with control.

As we search for true knowledge about ourselves it is vital that we ask others to help us see ourselves as we really are, not as we flatter ourselves to be. "I say to everyone among you not to think of himself more highly than he ought to think, but to think with sober judgment" (Rom 12:3).

Others can also inform us about our growth in grace. We may not see how God is working over the years, but others may more easily see God's progress in us. It is helpful here to ask for feedback to gain accurate information and the encouragement that rightly comes with such growth. "Therefore encourage one another and build one another up" (1 Thess 5:11). The body of Christ is meant to be a great ally in our battle for holiness.

We have seen how the knowledge of God and of ourselves is important for our growth in holiness. The twofold knowledge, gained from the Word, creation, ourselves, and the church, helps us understand reality. Seeing God and ourselves with increasing clarity we come to him as we should, as we must, humbly prostrating ourselves before him and thankfully exalting him as our Savior and Father. We become more and more the transformed people Jesus intends for us to be. "Do not be conformed to this world, but be transformed by the renewal of your mind" (Rom 12:2).

Further Resources

Study Questions

1. Of what does the twofold knowledge consist?
2. Why do we need this knowledge?
3. From what sources may we gain the twofold knowledge of God and ourselves?
4. What do we seek to know about God? What do we seek to know about ourselves?
5. In what ways does this twofold knowledge help us become more holy?
6. Why is the response of prostration before God helpful for our relationship with God?
7. Why is the response of exaltation of God helpful in our relationship with God?
8. What sin patterns and idolatries have you identified in yourself? What steps could you take to discover and root out even more sin patterns in your life?
9. How are you doing in the pursuit of prostration before God? What practical steps could you take, with regard to the twofold knowledge, to grow in humility?
10. How are you doing in exalting God? What practical steps, with regard to the twofold knowledge, could you take to grow in your exaltation of him?

For Further Study

Edward A. Dowey Jr., *The Knowledge of God in Calvin's Theology* (New York: Columbia University Press, 1965).

Elyse Fitzpatrick, *Idols of the Heart: Learning to Long for God Alone* (Rev. ed., Phillipsburg, NJ: P&R, 2016).

Timothy S. Lane and Paul David Tripp, *How People Change* (Greensboro, NC: New Growth, 2006).

Thomas F. Torrance, *Calvin's Doctrine of Man* (Westport, CT: Greenwood, 1997).

5

Engage God's Word

GOD HAS DESIGNED AND given the Bible as a primary instrument to bring his people to holiness. "All Scripture is breathed out by God and profitable for teaching, for reproof, for correction, and for training in righteousness, that the man of God may be complete, equipped for every good work" (2 Tim 3:16–17). God created humanity by the Word of his power and it is his intention to recreate us, restoring us to his very image, by the power of his Word once again.

While we may think that we know how to improve ourselves, when we neglect God's Word we are our own blind guides. "If the blind lead the blind, both will fall into a pit" (Matt 15:14). It is only when we listen to and walk in conformity to the Word of God that we can know that we are headed in the right direction, toward holiness. "Lead me in the path of your commandments, for I delight in it" (Ps 119:35). Within the Word we find God's perfect will revealed for us such that, empowered by the Spirit, we may walk by faith in new holiness of life, pleasing to the Father. "God himself has desired to give them a Law and standard, by which he has shown them, how they should regulate all their affections, and all their words, and all their works, in order to conform them to his will."[1]

Because it is the very Word of God, the Bible, when quickened by the Holy Spirit, has phenomenal power to bring about our transformation. "The word of God is living and active" (Heb 4:12). The Bible works as a template of what humanity is supposed to be. When pressed into us by the Holy Spirit it has the power to bring about our transformation, to

---

1. Viret, *Instruction Chrétienne*, 121.

mold us more into the very image of Christ. "The Word has a transforming virtue in it; it irradiates the mind, and consecrates the heart."[2]

While we may be unaware of this, we all need to have the Bible preached to us so that we can most effectively grow in holiness. Jesus preached, setting the example for all who would minister in his name (Luke 20:1). Those who minister the gospel are commanded to do so by preaching it. "And he commanded us to preach to the people" (Acts 10:42). Through the Word preached God brings us to salvation (1Cor 1:21). It is through the preaching of the Word that we also make progress in the faith (1Cor 15:1–2). People have a need to hear the Word of God, but they cannot hear it effectively unless someone preaches it! "And how are they to hear without someone preaching?" (Rom 10:14).

God has designed the Bible to be most effective in our lives when it is well preached to us, and we attend to it with humble hearts, ready to obey its direction. This is why the *Westminster Shorter Catechism*, answer 89, declares: "The Spirit of God makes the reading, *but especially the preaching*, of the Word, an effectual means of convincing and converting sinners, and of building them up in holiness and comfort, through faith, unto salvation" (emphasis added). To best advance in holiness we must sit under good biblical preaching.

The kind of biblical preaching we need for our advance in holiness only comes from within the local church. It is to the church that the Word, and the ministry of preaching the Word has been given. "So that through the church the manifold wisdom of God might now be made known" (Eph 3:10). This is not to say that other forms of communicating the Word are invalid. Rather, that the one form ordained by God to best transform us is this: his Word, preached by our pastor, in our church.

This preaching comes to us in the church from men, duly ordained by God, but who are simply people like us. Since they are like us, we must learn to not despise this vital ministry because of the failings of preachers, but rather give our utmost diligence to the preaching of God's Word that comes from them. "Let us learn to magnify that reverence which we owe unto the word of God, when it is preached to us, and highly to esteem that inestimable treasure albeit it be in earthen vessels."[3] It is through the ministry of the Word preached in the local church by ordained ministers that God intends to transform us into the image of Christ. "For

---

2. Watson, *Body of Divinity*, 249.
3. Calvin, *Sermons on Election and Reprobation*, 299.

why has God appointed the ministers of his gospel, except to invite us to become partakers of his salvation, and thus sweetly to restore and refresh our souls?"[4]

Whatever has been our view of preaching, we must come to understand that it is central to God's plan for sanctifying us, and understanding this, attend to the Word preached. We must get over the prideful idea that we can feed ourselves sufficiently by our own private study, as important a role as this plays in our lives, and come to submit to the Word preached.

> Pride, or fastidiousness, or emulation, induces many to persuade themselves that they can profit sufficiently by reading and meditating in private, and thus to despise public meetings, and deem preaching superfluous. . . . In order that the pure simplicity of the faith may flourish among us, let us not decline to use this exercise of piety, which God by his institution of it has shown to be necessary, and which he so highly recommends.[5]

The Bible preached to us is the pure spiritual milk for which we are supposed to long. "Like newborn infants, long for the pure spiritual milk, that by it you may grow up into salvation" (1 Pet 2:2). This means that we do not merely attend sermons, or tolerate them, but passionately desire them like a baby craves its next bottle. This does not imply immaturity, however, for this attitude of longing for the pure unadulterated Word of God, is to be the longing of the mature and godly.

Having now introduced the concept of engaging God's Word we will look at 1) how the Word, preached—and studied—helps to sanctify us, and 2) how we can best engage God's Word so as to grow in holiness.

God Works through the Word by the Holy Spirit to Make Us Holy

Hearing a sermon does not automatically help anyone. As powerful as the Bible is, it becomes effective in our lives to transform us only when the Holy Spirit gives us understanding and inclines our heart to believe and respond to the Word. "When the Spirit of truth comes, he will guide you into all the truth" (John 16:13). The two work together in harmony, the Spirit more inwardly, as he illuminates our mind and forms our heart,

---

4. Calvin, *Com.*, Jer 5:14.
5. Calvin, *Institutes*, 4.1.5.

and the Word more externally to point us toward the renewal we need.[6] We need the two together in order to grow in our holiness.

When the Word comes to us preached, even by the weakest of men, and is attended by the power of the Holy Spirit, it has divine power to transform us into the likeness of Christ. "Our gospel came to you not only in word, but also in power and in the Holy Spirit and with full conviction" (1 Thess 1:5). When this occurs it is really as though God were speaking to us personally through the sermon. This is why pastors so often hear: "God was talking to me today in the sermon." We should look to the preaching of the Word, quickened by the Holy Spirit, to hear God speak to us, to have God himself meet with us and change us.

How Does God's Word Help Us Grow in Holiness?

God Works through the Word to Heal Our Hearts

In the hands of the Spirit, the Bible is a kind of medicine that works deep within us to bring about healing. "He sent out his word and healed them" (Ps 107:20). As medicine the Word works deep within our constitution to heal and change us. "Everything that the doctor can do to the human body in face of various disease . . . the Word of God can do for our souls in face of all our evil vices."[7]

The Word works powerfully within us, washing away that sin which might otherwise cling to us. "Having cleansed her by the washing of water with the word" (Eph 5:26). Christ, holy as he is, means to make us a suitable match for himself, so he uses the Word to remove from us every spot, to erase every moral blemish, so that we are entirely holy. "In effecting the reformation of our lives the Word of God works deep within our hearts."[8]

The unclean, the unholy, cannot make itself holy. Dirty laundry can try all day to make itself clean, it cannot. What it needs is the cleansing power of water and soap and agitation, those can make the unclean clean. Sinful humanity lacks the ability to cleanse itself. We must come into contact with the cleansing power of the Word of God, which, when agitated by the Holy Spirit, washes us and makes the unclean, clean.

---

6. Calvin, *Institutes*, 2.5.5.
7. Wallace, *Christian Life*, 210.
8. Calvin, *Institutes*, 211.

Preaching the Word Helps to Produce Faith in Us

Our growth in faith, central to our sanctification, is closely tied to hearing the Word of God. "So faith comes from hearing, and hearing through the word of Christ" (Rom 10:17). Faith only rises from the Word of God, not any insights or wisdom we may have.[9] Faith arises from the Word preached to us as the Spirit works in our hearts. The Word presents God to us that we may look upon him and believe in him—without any images or idols—but with the eyes of faith.

While all the Word may help faith grow, faith rises particularly from the promises of God. Faith, by definition, includes the assurance of God's benevolence towards us, revealed to us largely by his promises. "By faith Abraham, when he was tested, offered up Isaac, and he who had received the promises was in the act of offering up his only son" (Heb 11:17). The promises help give us faith that God will care for us, so that trusting him, we are inclined to follow him.

This growth of faith is important because the more faith we have in Christ, the more firmly we are united to him and hence the more his sanctifying life flows into us. This is in part why the Bible associates the themes of faith and life. "The righteous shall live by faith" (Rom 1:17). God uses the Word, in particular the Word preached, to give us faith, through which we obtain all the promised blessings of Christ, including our sanctification. Because we need more faith, we are encouraged to remain in the Word to grow in faith. "Let the word of Christ dwell in you richly" (Col 3:16).

The Word Gives Us the Truth,
the Twofold Knowledge of God and Ourselves

We live in a world of half-truths and whole lies. Particularly when it comes to spiritual truth, the world propagates such disinformation about God that it lives in darkness. Having been influenced by these lies we need to have the truth cleanse our minds and hearts. The truth of the Word is powerfully sanctifying. "Sanctify them in the truth; your word is truth" (John 17:17). The Spirit takes the truth of the Word and presses it into our hearts, so that we no longer conform to the lies of the world, but to the truth of God.

---

9. Viret, *L'Interim Fait par Dialogues*, 247.

The Word teaches us the truth about God. While creation does reveal some truth about God to us, it is insufficient to engender faith and lead us to salvation. For the complete knowledge of God we must have his Word. "The sum of your word is truth" (Ps 119:160).

The Word teaches us the truth about ourselves. We only gain a perfectly clear view of ourselves, in both our depravity and dignity, when we gaze upon ourselves as reflected in the Bible. This clear truth of ourselves, as we are and as we are meant to be is transforming. "But the one who looks into the perfect law, the law of liberty, and perseveres, being no hearer who forgets but a doer who acts, he will be blessed in his doing" (Jas 1:25).

The Word then is the single most effective source in all the world from which we may gain the truth about God and ourselves, the twofold knowledge which becomes powerfully transforming as the Spirit works within us.

In teaching us the truth, applied to our hearts in great depth by the Holy Spirit, Scripture leads us to respond to God in the humility of prostration. When Moses returned from the presence of the Lord, having experienced God's holiness, and then came to see the sin of his people as they worshiped idols—the twofold knowledge of God and humanity—he responded by prostrating himself before God. "Then I lay prostrate before the LORD as before, forty days and forty nights" (Deut 9:18). The Bible teaches us to be humble before the Lord, as nothing else in the world will. "For Scripture leaves us no reason to be exalted in God's sight. Rather, its whole end is to restrain our pride, to humble us, cast us down, and utterly crush us."[10]

The Word also leads us to exalt God, by revealing to us the magnificent glory and mercy of God. When God had mercifully delivered his people from Egypt they stopped to praise God. "The LORD is my strength and my song, and he has become my salvation; this is my God, and I will praise him, my father's God, and I will exalt him" (Exod 15:2). As we come to see in the Word the glory of God and his goodness to us, despite our weakness and sin, we the redeemed, naturally ascend to him, hearts lifted in praise. "O LORD, you are my God; I will exalt you; I will praise your name, for you have done wonderful things" (Isa 25:1).

It is through the Word that God presents us with the most compelling truths about ourselves and himself, truths that are transformative.

---

10. Calvin, *Institutes*, 3.18.4.

The Word Confronts Us with Our Sin and Calls Us to Repentance

The Word preached to us should pointedly convict us of our sin. This is the pedagogical function of the Law, where we see the holy demands of God and having ourselves weighed against it, find that we have failed, so that we are led to Christ for mercy. The Word is powerful to discern the thoughts and intentions of our hearts and thus convict us of sin (Heb 4:12). We must, therefore, listen to faithful preaching that will teach not only of God's love but convict us of sin. "Hence, when true prophets exhort sinners to hope and predict God's freeness to pardon, they likewise discourse about penitence; they do not indulge sinners, but rouse them, nay, wound them sharply with a sense of God's anger, so as in some way to stir them up, since God's mercy is set before us for that end, that by it we may seek life."[11]

Jeremiah preached this way, sharply pointing out the sins of God's people, that they might be cut to the heart. "Only acknowledge your guilt, that you rebelled against the LORD your God" (Jer 3:13). When the sermon contains "sharp goads"[12] it prods us to see our sin clearly, though uncomfortable, this is absolutely needed for our growth in holiness. Therefore, it is the duty of pastors to convict us, and for us to respond to this conviction. "When God appoints us to proclaim his word, it is as if he were assigning us to be his tort attorneys to explain his rights. . . . Each individual must be rebuked . . . with threats of God's judgment."[13] Brought to this clear knowledge of ourselves by the Word preached, we have the internal desire to change.

We are, however, not left to wallow in the conviction of sin, but are led by the Word from this conviction to repent. Everywhere in Scripture we hear the command to turn, to return, to repent, and come to the Lord. "Come, let us return to the LORD; for he has torn us, that he may heal us" (Hos 6:1). With the clear picture of our failure, we must hear just as clearly from his Word preached the promise of God's mercy to the repentant, or we would never move to find grace. "Return to the LORD your God, for he is gracious and merciful" (Joel 2:13).

By the Word we are convicted of our sin, and by the Word we are led to Christ to find his grace, and by this grace offered to the humbled, we are transformed more into the likeness of Christ. "For the grace of God

---

11. Calvin, *Com.*, Ezek 13:6.
12. Calvin, *Com.*, Jer 9:21.
13. Calvin, *Sermons on Genesis*, 545.

has appeared, bringing salvation for all people, training us to renounce ungodliness and worldly passions, and to live self-controlled, upright, and godly lives in the present age" (Titus 2:11–12).

The Word Shows Us Christ and Bids Us Come to Him

In calling us to repent the sermon must distinctly show us Christ, so seeing him we are truly inclined to seek the mercy he provides. "Come to me, all who labor and are heavy laden, and I will give you rest" (Matt 11:28). We turn not to a principle or to a law but to Christ. "Repent and be baptized every one of you in the name of Jesus Christ for the forgiveness of your sins" (Acts 2:38). Faithful preaching, then, will always be Christ-centered preaching, for God's people always need the grace extended in Christ to change them. Preaching without Christ may be rousing moral encouragement, but it is not Christian preaching. "For Jews demand signs and Greeks seek wisdom, but we preach Christ crucified . . . the power of God and the wisdom of God" (1 Cor 1:22–24).

Seeing Christ presented from the Word, with both his ability and desire to help us, moves us toward him in dependence. "We shall always find him ready and favorable to help and succor us."[14] Faithful preaching then not only invites us to see our sin, but to seek its solution in the mercy of Christ.

The Word Shows Us How to Walk in the Obedience of Faith

As we come to the Lord, seeing our need and finding his grace to help us, we then ask the logical question: How should we live so as to please you? The Word, having pointed us to Christ, points us toward the obedience of faith. "He leads me in paths of righteousness for his name's sake" (Ps 23:3). We could never on our own discern the right way to live, we must have the Word of God to direct us. "How can a young man keep his way pure? By guarding it according to your word" (Ps 119:9). We come to the Word to submit to Christ, who rules his church through his Word preached, guiding, correcting, and comforting. "Jesus Christ wills to rule his church by the preaching of his Word."[15] This is known as the Third Use of the Law, the normative use, where God's Word marks out for

---

14. Calvin, *Sermons on Election and Reprobation*, 209.
15. Calvin, *Sermons on the Beatitudes*, 63.

us the way that we are to live. "We must still practice moral duties as commanded by Moses, but we must not seek to be justified by our practice. If we use them as a rule of life, not as conditions of justification, they can be no ministration of death, or killing letter to us . . . but a better rule to discover all imperfections, and to guide us."[16]

Having been given the righteousness of Christ by grace we do not obey in order to earn our righteousness. The gospel of grace, rather, frees us from the condemnation of the Law, that we might walk freely in heartfelt obedience to the Law. "That you may keep the commandments of the LORD your God that I command you" (Deut 4:2). When the mercy of Christ has won our love *for* him, then to live in love *with* him we are to walk in his commandments. "Whoever has my commandments and keeps them, he it is who loves me" (John 14:23-24).

The Word leads us to obey itself, for the Word as the Law of God lays out for us the very definition of holiness, or what it means to be like Christ. The Law and love are not opposed to one another. The love of God leads us to want to obey him, the Law of God then shows us how to walk in obedience. Gospel and Law are meant to flow together in the heart and lives of believers to bring them to holiness of life. "Without the power of the Spirit we would lack the love for God that energizes us to keep his law. But without the law of God our love for him would lack direction. Thus we discover that the way of Christ leads us more and more into obedience to God's law."[17]

There is a double benefit from our obedience of faith to our growth in holiness. Not only is our obedience of faith holiness, by definition, but as we obey, God purifies us even more. "Having purified your souls by your obedience to the truth for a sincere brotherly love, love one another earnestly from a pure heart" (1 Pet 1:22). In obeying the Word of truth we first believe it and then we do as it instructs. Hence, to obey 1 Pet 1:22 we must have a sincere brotherly love, which leads to a purified soul. That is, the obedience of faith itself, helps to put to death the old nature and revives the new. "For purity of soul consists in obedience to God."[18]

We cannot escape this simple fact: if we belong to Jesus, we will want to be like him. Christ, of course, perfectly kept the Law. He did so that we would *not have* to keep it perfectly in order to find the Father's love, but

---

16. Marshall, *Gospel Mystery*, 85.
17. Ferguson, *Devoted to God*, 187.
18. Calvin, *Com.*, 1 Pet 1:22.

also that we might *be able* to keep the Law at all. We are to be like Jesus. Did he live a holy life? Did he deny himself and take up his cross? Did he love God with all his heart, soul, strength, and mind? Did he avoid sexual immorality? Did he avoid gossip, slander, lying, bragging, and swearing falsely? Did he love others, care for their needs, primarily showing concern for their salvation? Then how can we do other than follow our Lord in all things!

Now we have seen what an immeasurable aid to our holiness is the Word of God. By the Word preached our faith grows, so that we can apprehend the true knowledge of God and ourselves. The Word preached confronts us with our sin, calls us to repent, showing us the mercy of God in Christ, that we might find grace. Having brought us to the heart of Christ where we are transformed by his grace and love, the Word then shows us how we should walk with him, in the obedience of faith. Having seen this, it remains for us to explore how one can engage God's Word to grow in holiness.

How Can We Engage the Word to Grow in Holiness?

Problems to Overcome in Engaging the Word

Before we move to the positive it may be helpful to address some of the issues that hinder us from more productively engaging God's Word.

There is too little able preaching in the church. In his critical work, *Why Johnny Can't Preach*,[19] T. David Gordon asserts that much evangelical preaching is unacceptably poor. Since this is often the case, it is important to find a church with sound preaching. How may you do so? First, find a church that accepts the Bible as God's completely authoritative Word. Second, find a church where the pastor preaches the Word faithfully, 1) explaining what the text means, 2) how it applies, 3) showing forth Christ, 4) our need to repent, and 5) how believing on Christ, 6) we may walk in obedience. Avoid like the plague those preachers who fail these tests but draw crowds through personal dynamism.

We do not know how to listen well to the preaching of the Word. The problem with preaching, of course, is not just preachers, we must be ready to hear the sermon as well. Come well-rested to the sermon by making plans for this rest on Saturday. Do not be distracted during the sermon

---

19. Gordon, *Why Johnny Can't Preach*.

by cell phones or plans for Sunday afternoon. Do not come to judge the sermon (given you have found a faithful Bible preaching church) but to listen to God speak to you through it. When we come humbly submitting to the Word we will find that almost any sermon—faithfully, if not skillfully preached—will aid us in our pursuit of God in holiness. Come with a heart soft toward God, ready to hear and repent. "Take care, brothers, lest there be in any of you an evil, unbelieving heart, leading you to fall away from the living God" (Heb 3:12).

How our hearts come to the preaching of the Word impacts what we take away nearly as much as what is presented. I have noted that when members of our church are in a crisis—fighting cancer, having recently lost a loved one, having been recently fired—they very frequently comment on the effectiveness of the sermon. To them it appears that I have become more effective in preaching. In reality they are greatly changed as hearers. Let us learn from those in trials to always approach the preaching of the Word needy and humble.

The point is simple: If you are not getting much out of preaching, the problem may be you! Come rested, focused, humbly, ready, listen attentively, and see if the efficacy of the preaching in your church does not markedly improve.

We do not know how to study the Bible devotionally. Few of us have been properly taught how to use the Bible devotionally. Using poor methods of study we may derive minimal benefit from the Word and in turn find little energy and therefore time for study. While we will address below some helpful approaches to Bible study, we want here to acknowledge that one of the great problems we face is simple ignorance. We do not know how to study the Bible for greatest benefit. If this is your case, it is best to admit it, and then set about trying to improve your approach to Bible study, certainly do not give up the personal devotional study due to lack of skill!

Engaging God's Word Profitably for Holiness

Diligently Attend to the Word Preached

Attend to the Word preached at Sunday worship. God has appointed his preached Word as a primary means for our growth in holiness, therefore do not voluntarily miss the Word preached each Sunday at your church. Work, children's sports, and family recreational activities all compete for your time on the Sabbath Day. Do not let them win! "Observe the Sabbath day, to keep it holy, as the LORD your God commanded you" (Deut 5:12). Keep the Sabbath Day holy first by worshipping with your local church. Do not expect to grow in godliness if you will not follow the Lord's basic plan. "How presumptuous are we for wanting God to make himself known, and yet not deigning to cast our eyes on the holy Scripture or come to the assembly where it is expounded?"[20]

Certainly there will be times when we are providentially hindered from joining with God's people for worship, illness in particular, may keep us away. But planning to attend games or work overtime instead of worship is not providential hindering, it is poor prioritization. Wherever the Lord takes you on the Sabbath Day plan to join with his people there for worship.

Parents, do you not want to raise children who will value Christ and his kingdom above everything else? What do you teach them, though, if you absent yourself from his church for one of their games or vacation travel? You teach them that sports and vacations are more important than the worship of God—period. They will learn that lesson well!

Preaching is a live communication method through which God has designed to deliver his Word from one preacher to one congregation gathered live in his presence. While there is certainly nothing wrong with supplementing our regular weekly sermon(s) with additional insights gained from webcasts, videos, or recordings, these should not substitute for the live preaching of God's Word.

While in seminary I thought I would only deliver—with due credit—the sermons of the great preachers, reasoning that I would never write one better. Today, I realize how laughable that was. It misconstrues God's intention for preaching. He means for a pastor to preach to his own church. Luther, Calvin, and Edwards were master preachers. But they do not know the issues facing your community or the hopes and sorrows in your church. God has called one particular pastor to preach God's Word, to one particular church, in one particular place, at one particular time, using all that pastor's particular insights, passions, and preparations. During the sermon the Holy Spirit works through that man, in those people, at that place. There is no substitute for the living confrontation between God and his people through his Word preached.

Attend to the Word preached by faithful pastors. There are several criteria by which to search for a church where the Word is preached by

---

20. Calvin, *Sermons on 2 Samuel*, 375.

faithful pastors. First, we should find a pastor who is duly ordained, and not self-appointed. God uses ordination within the church to determine who is fit to preach, separating them from those who are self-appointed (Exod 28:41). "Ought we to put confidence in men who conduct themselves with rashness, and, though they assume authority in God's name, yet have no certain and lawful calling?"[21]

Second, do not mistake eloquence for faithfulness in preaching. Many a gifted communicator can enthrall an audience. But only those called by God can truly feed God's sheep. "God has not chosen men according to the outward show they may have: but contrariwise, that which is accounted most excellent, he forsakes and despises: And that which is as rejected of men, that does he advance."[22]

Third, above all, avoid false teachers. "But false prophets also arose among the people, just as there will be false teachers among you, who will secretly bring in destructive heresies" (2 Pet 2:1). Do not make the mistake of thinking that you can easily recognize them. False teachers will be the nicest, warmest, most likable people you ever meet. This is why they have been so successful at alluring people to their teaching. There is in our day a plethora of false teachers: beware! The primary way to detect false teachers is biblically: do they teach the Bible as it has always been taught, or do they change things, even slightly, with their own unique spin?

However, do not despise an otherwise faithful pastor because he is imperfect. While there should be an overall holiness of life and rightness of doctrine, do not let small imperfections distract you. Edwards read his sermons monotonously, Calvin delivered his sermons with an asthmatic wheeze, Spurgeon was very overweight, yet those who listened to them profited greatly. Be prepared to overlook—not major failings—but the normal human peccadillos which we all possess. God has only at his disposal imperfect men for preachers. Calvin assures us: "How then shall I find my salvation by their means? For I see yet that they are full of imperfections. But . . . God leaves not off to accomplish his work . . . although they be not altogether such as they ought to be. For God uses . . . them."[23]

To come under the preaching of God's Word, let us find faithful pastors—not famous ones, not necessarily eloquent ones—but faithful pastors, who rightly divide the Word of truth.

21. Calvin, *Com.*, Dan 8:19.
22. Calvin, *Sermons on Election and Reprobation*, 75.
23. Calvin, *Sermons on Election and Reprobation*, 252–53.

Attend only to the Word preached, nothing else. Find a church that preaches the Bible. "He must hold firm to the trustworthy word as taught, so that he may be able to give instruction in sound doctrine and also to rebuke those who contradict it" (Titus 1:9). Avoid churches that base their messages on something other than the Bible, or, which only ostensibly use the Bible, perhaps reading it, but really base the message on something else. Faithful preaching is simply delivering the message of God as God gave it. "Son of man, I have made you a watchman for the house of Israel. Whenever you hear a word from my mouth, you shall give them warning from me" (Ezek 3:17).

Attend to the Word preached where Christ is lifted up. Christ should be the central focus of the sermon. "But we preach Christ crucified" (1 Cor 1:23). Many pastors miss this point. They may preach morality, or self-improvement, but fail to point to Christ. Since we make progress in holiness by faith in Christ and reliance upon him, not self-will, therefore sermons should show us Christ and call us to him. This is not to say that every sermon should be primarily evangelistic, but that every sermon should hold forth Christ, as prophet, priest, or king, that the people of God may find from him the grace and help which they need. "Truly faithful ministers preach Christ . . . this must be the object of their sermons."[24]

Attend to the Word preached with boldness. For sermons to be effective they should be delivered with boldness. "As you know, we had boldness in our God to declare to you the gospel of God in the midst of much conflict" (1 Thess 2:2). The preaching of the Word of God is quite literally a life and death matter. Preachers are bound then to deliver the message with boldness, no matter how much opposition they face in the world, or in the stubborn hearts of believers. "It is then necessary, that at the present day the servants of God should also speak more strongly and vehemently, that they may rouse hypocrites and the obstinate from their torpor."[25]

Attend to the Word Preached
by Making Diligent Application of It to Yourself

To most benefit from the preaching of the Word we actively engage the sermon, expecting to hear from God. Do not sit passively and simply allow the sound of the pastor's voice to wash over you like the sound of

---

24. Holder, "The Office of Pastor," 195.
25. Calvin, *Com.*, Jer 4:21.

waves crashing on the beach. "The Word, then, must not be received in a superficial manner but must be allowed deeply and constantly to influence the mind and heart of the Christian."[26] Come asking: What does this message tell me about God? What do we learn of God's love for us? What does this tell me about my sin and where I need to repent? How is Christ presented to me that I may turn to him? Having turned to Christ, how am I supposed to walk now in obedience? We come ready to hear the sermon, listening actively, engaging it fully, then responding with sincere hearts to the urgings, encouragements, and commands from the Word preached. "Be doers of the word, and not hearers only" (Jas 1:22).

Diligently Attend to the Word in Personal Bible Study

Personal Bible reading and study is the first addition to the faithful preaching of the Word. But how are we to study the Bible for greatest growth in holiness? There are many profitable approaches, we will mention several here.

Study devotionally to engage the living God. The goal of personal Bible study is not to spend a certain amount of time or to read a certain number of verses. The goal is to meet with Jesus. To hear from God and to respond to him. Keep this ever before you in Bible study. Don't quit until you have met with God. Be like Jacob who wrestled with the angel of the Lord until finally he was blessed (Gen 32:26).

Engage in reading a book of the Bible devotionally. To do this choose a book of the Bible, start reading in the first verse, then read a few verses that comprise a complete thought. Then ask of the passage some fairly broad questions to begin. What does this passage teach us about God? About humanity? What do we learn of God's love for us? What does it show us of Christ? Where does it call me to repent of sin? How does it urge me toward Christ for help? What new obedience should I seek by grace?

As you answer these questions, pray, strike up a conversation with God around the verse and where it intersects with your life. Does it show sins from which you should repent? Come to him repenting. Does it show the needs of others? Bring them before your Father in prayer. Does it encourage you to worship? Stop and sing praise to your Father.

Engage in a word study in the Bible. Look up all the passages which contain a word or concept. For example, I completed a study of "humility"

---

26. Wallace, *Christian Life*, 219.

throughout the Bible. You can use a concordance, or if you have an electronic Bible, the search function will serve the same purpose. When we are in each passage or verse, ask of it similar questions, as before: What does it tell us about God? About humanity? How does it point us to Christ? What should I do in response to this passage? As we are reading and addressing those questions, engage God in conversation in prayer.

Engage in Bible memorization, meditation, and prayer. The old Bible study technique of *lectio divina*,[27] or divine reading, is making a welcome comeback. In this approach we usually take a single verse or phrase and walk through four distinct steps, meditating deeply on the Word as God has encouraged us. "I will meditate on your precepts and fix my eyes on your ways" (Ps 119:15).

1. Reading: *lectio*

    Read the verse or passage slowly and carefully. Commit it to memory.

2. Meditation: *meditatio*

    Consider how the passage interacts with your life. What does it say to your relationships, tasks, past, future, fears, and hopes?

3. Prayer: *oratio*

    Take the issues brought up in your interaction with the Word and your life to the Lord in prayer. Allow the Word you have taken in to be a means of offering to the Lord your deepest hopes and concerns.

4. Contemplation: *contemplatio*

    As you continue to consider the passage, rest in the presence of the Lord knowing that he has heard you. Wait quietly before him with the Word in your heart.

In all these ways remember that the goal is not to check off for the day that you had personal devotions, but to meet with the living Lord through his living Word. There are, of course, many other helpful ways to study the Bible.[28]

To grow in holiness we must engage God's Word, through sermons and Bible study. The Children's Catechism of 1545 in Geneva taught children how they might profit from the Bible, and offers us a helpful reminder.

---

27. Adapted from a lecture by Dr. Leighton Ford, to whom I am in debt for introducing me to this approach.

28. Warren, *Rick Warren's Bible Study Methods.*

If we lay hold on it with complete heartfelt conviction as nothing less than certain truth come down from heaven; if we show ourselves docile to it; if we subdue our will and minds to his obedience; if we love it heartily; if having it once engraved on our hearts and its roots fixed there, so that it brings forth fruit in our life; if finally we be formed to its rule—then it will turn to our salvation, as intended.[29]

Further Resources

Study Questions

1. Why must we have the Holy Spirit to profit from the Bible?
2. Why is hearing the Bible preached particularly helpful to our growth in holiness?
3. What does the Bible teach us about God and ourselves, in general terms, that proves helpful in our sanctification?
4. How does hearing the Bible call us to particular repentance help us grow in holiness?
5. Why is it important that a sermon present Christ to us?
6. How does the Word assist us in our obedience of faith?
7. In what ways are we to attend to the Bible preached so as to best help our sanctification? Can you name three or four?
8. What should be our goal in personal Bible study? Name one method of personal Bible study.
9. How well are you attending to the Word preached? What one change could you make that would most help your holiness?
10. How well are you attending to the Word in personal devotions? What one change could you make that would most help your holiness?

---

29. Reid, *Treatises*, 130.

For Further Study

Joel Beeke, *The Family at Church: Listening to Sermons and Attending Prayer Meetings* (Grand Rapids: Reformation Heritage, 2008).

John MacArthur, *How to Study the Bible* (Chicago: Moody, 2009).

T. David Gordon, *Why Johnny Can't Preach: The Media Have Shaped the Messengers* (Phillipsburg, NJ: P&R, 2009).

Douglas Stuart and Gordon Fee, *How to Read the Bible for All Its Worth* (Grand Rapids: Zondervan, 2014).

Rick Warren, *Rick Warren's Bible Study Methods* (Grand Rapids: Zondervan, 2006).

6

Apprehend God's Love

APPREHENDING GOD'S LOVE IS essential to our growth in holiness since holiness is a restoration of the love relationship with God, and then, with our neighbors (Matt 22:37). When we are estranged from God, we flee his presence and defy his will, that is, his Word. But when we know that we are loved by God our hearts soften to him, respond in love to him, and desire to obey him, much as a child more readily obeys the parent from whom he senses unconditional love. Jonathan Edwards recognized this centrality of love to the Christian life. "But it is doubtless true, and evident from [the] Scriptures, that the essence of all true religion lies in holy love."[1]

But what does it mean to apprehend God's love? Certainly apprehension of God's love includes an intellectual *understanding* that God does in fact love us. This understanding must begin with the perspective that we are not naturally lovable to God, or else we miss the extraordinary extravagance of his love. For God loves us precisely while we are unlovable. "God shows his love for us in that while we were still sinners, Christ died for us" (Rom 5:8). It is while we were unlovable, indeed while we deserved only wrath, that God moved in love to help us (Eph 2:4–5). Understanding that God has chosen to love us in Christ, although we are naturally unlovable, is the first part of apprehending God's love.

Along with the understanding that God does love us, an apprehension of God's love also includes the experiential reality of *feeling* God's love. "God's love has been poured into our hearts through the Holy Spirit

1. Edwards, *Religious Affections*, 36.

who has been given to us" (Rom 5:5). Apprehending God's love has a visceral nature such that, sensing God's love, we are more than simply cognizant of it, but God's love "utterly ravishes"[2] us. Apprehending God's love includes both the knowledge and the experience of it. "The Spirit himself bears witness with our spirit that we are children of God" (Rom 8:16).

In this chapter we will explain how apprehending God's love helps us to grow in holiness and how we can better apprehend his love for us.

How Apprehending God's Love Helps Us to Become Holy

Holiness Is a Restoration of Loving Relationship with God Which Leads to Heartfelt Obedience

Since holiness is the restoration of our broken—unholy—relationship with God, then God's love for us becomes a vital force in our holiness. Having justified us in Christ, God reconciles us to himself, so that his love for us as his redeemed children flows freely. "We now see how God becomes a Father to us, and regards us as his children, even when he abolishes our sins, and also when he freely admits us to the enjoyment of his love."[3] As God pours his love into our hearts through the Holy Spirit we are changed by that love. Knowing his love for us, we desire to have peace with him, and so love him in return. "We love because he first loves us" (1 John 4:19). Knowing that God loves us, we love him, and want to obey him from this love. "If you love me you will keep my commandments" (John 14:15).

God's love wonderfully serves to restore our relationship not only with him, but subsequently to ourselves. We need his love, in daily doses, in order to feel right about ourselves, to feel at peace within ourselves. Without God's love we vainly seek approval from others, or from various idolatrous systems. With God's love filling that empty place, we are peaceful, assured of our worth in a world that constantly questions it. Catherine of Genoa, the daughter of a wealthy politician, who was converted in 1474 at the age of 27, spent her life serving the terminally ill in St. Lazarus hospital. She knew something of the restoring power of God's love for her personally.

---

2. Calvin, *Institutes*, 3.2.41.
3. Calvin, *Com.*, Hos 14:4.

> I became so consumed with [God's] love that as I stood contemplating this work within me, I felt that even if I were cast into hell, hell itself would have appeared to me all love and consolation . . . with no comfort except in God who was doing this all along through love and great mercy, I came to a place of great contentment.[4]

God's love also changes our relationship with our neighbors. Without the fullness of God's love we approach our neighbor demanding that our desires be met. "What causes quarrels and what causes fights among you? Is it not this that your passions are at war within you?" (Jas 4:1). Loved by God and loving God, we can love others as well. "Whoever loves God must also love his brother" (1 John 4:21).

We find in Scripture a deep connection between being loved by God, loving God, and our obedience. "By this we know that we love the children of God, when we love God and obey his commandments" (1 John 5:2). Often today there is a false dichotomy drawn between love and obedience which says: "Since God loves us he does not care if we obey him, as long as we love him." This directly refutes the teaching of our Lord. "If anyone loves me, he will keep my word, and my Father will love him, and we will come to him and make our home with him. Whoever does not love me does not keep my words" (John 14:23–24).

The love-obedience dynamic cycles upward. Loved, we obey God, as we obey God, we perceive all the more his love for us, as he rewards our obedience with fresh effusions of his love. "If you keep my commandments, you will abide in my love" (John 15:10). Not that we earn his love through obedience, but in the economy of the covenant, there are covenant blessings for obedience (Deut 30:16). God's love then is central to our sanctification, drawing us to love God and from love to obey his commands. The more we apprehend God's love for us in Christ then, the more progress we make in holiness.

God's love lavished upon us has transformed my life as well. After being a believer for twenty-five years I recognized the lack of apprehending God's love in my own life, seen often as duty without delight. For three years, however, I studied God's love in the Bible. I prayed that God would allow me to know his love emotionally, not just intellectually. I needed to feel it, to be filled with his love, as revealed by his Word, as supplied by his Spirit, through the gift of his Son. My request was answered. I wrote in my devotional journal on October 26, 1998.

---

4. Foster and Smith, *Devotional Classics*, 212.

> Psalm 90:14 "Satisfy us in the morning with your steadfast love, that we may rejoice and be glad all our days."
>
> Herein lies the whole relief for our restless searching for fullness, meaning, joy, happiness, love, and significance. We would vainly run from person to person, goal to goal, event to event to find satisfaction but all the while it waits for us in the arms of Christ! The idea of being satisfied (*sabah*) is so deep. To be satisfied is to be filled to the point of being sated, needing no more, the sense of overflow. . . . Do not let us take a step out of bed until your love has filled the boundless appetite we have for affection, for love, for attention, for kindness, for significance.
>
> If you do this then we are able to do two things: to sing for joy, and to be joy-filled. The shout for joy, rejoicing, (*ranan*) is the pinnacle experience of the joyful and satisfied soul. Like the song of a bird when it feels all is right, like the satisfied humming of a wife who feels secure in her husband's love.
>
> To [be glad] (*samach*) is to have the very nature of our heart become one of gladness and levity. . . . But this joy is beyond the world. It is not obtainable by human means, it is only to be found as a result of a heart immersed in the love of the one true God. . . . May your love satisfy me early and that I may sing for joy and be glad! Amen my Lord, my lover, my God!

God's love, experienced fresh daily, had a sanctifying impact in my life. Obedience came more easily, my neighbor was less burdensome to love. True indeed is the Word of the Lord: "If you love me you will keep my commandments."

Now that we have taken an initial look at the connection between apprehending God's love and our holiness, we will explore this in greater detail.

God's Love for Us Replaces Our Dread of Him with Attraction Toward Him

Since we are born estranged from God due to original sin, we naturally dread God, though we are seldom aware of this. Sensing, even unconsciously, God's wrath toward our sin (Rom 2:15), we want to avoid him, and so refuse him worship (Rom 1:21). Apart from Christ, as "objects of his wrath" (Rom 9:22), people naturally move away from God.

This movement away from God may look very religious, as in the case of the ancient Pharisees or modern Islam. It may appear as outright belligerence as with the angry atheist. It may appear as apathy, as with modern "nones." Whatever form it takes, humanity, much like Jonah on his way to Tarshish, tends to flee from the presence of the Lord.

Left to ourselves we would only cower away from God's presence, like a dog who has only known a cruel master slinks away from everyone. But as that dog may be wooed by a kindly new master who holds out a treat and speaks gently, God means to entice us toward him with his love. The Lord woos us, bending low and speaking gently to us in Christ, showing us that he wants to be reconciled. "I will betroth you to me forever. I will betroth you to me in righteousness and in justice, in steadfast love and in mercy" (Hos 2:19). As God speaks of his love and mercy we are drawn to him. "Except his goodness and mercy meet us, when we come to him, dread would immediately absorb all our thoughts; but when God comes forth as if clothed and adorned with mercy, we may then entertain hope of salvation."[5] As the dog with the kindly new master cautiously eases toward his outstretched hand, seeing God's outstretched mercy we move toward him.

After God had lovingly disciplined David for his sin with Bathsheba, God reconciled David to himself, in part by giving their second son, Solomon, a symbolic name, Jedidiah, which means "beloved of the Lord" (2 Sam 12:24–25). God's offer of mercy was meant to win back the heart of David. Calvin explains in a sermon on this passage: "Because God has loved us, next he draws us to himself, and then, when we have felt and known a Father being so kind towards us, from our side also we may be joined to him, and give ourselves to his service."[6]

We are transformed by God's love for us, revealed most powerfully in Christ. "God shows his love for us in that while we were still sinners, Christ died for us" (Rom 5:8). It is not primarily the fear of punishment that brings us back to our Master, but the hope of a loving reception. My wife is fond of observing whenever she sees a dog owner yelling threats at the hapless creature that refuses to return: "Why don't they offer it a treat and call it with love, it would come then!" A truth not lost on our Master, who as our heavenly Father calls us with love and offers us, through Christ, forgiveness, restoration, and love. "God's intent is to draw us unto salvation when he speaks unto us; but here he speaks gently and familiarly, he utters his heart unto us, he shows us which is the way of life."[7]

---

5. Calvin, *Com.*, Lam 3:32.
6. Calvin, *Sermons on 2 Samuel*, 603.
7. Torrance, *Calvin's Doctrine of Man*, 76.

God's Love, Having Wooed Our Hearts, Moves Us to Love God in Return

Knowing that we are loved changes us. Years ago I knew a young business woman who could be rather sullen in her greetings. Usually when I greeted her, she would mumble a hello in response. One morning, however, she smiled and almost sang, "Good morning!" I stopped in my tracks and asked what had happened. After an initial blush, this single woman said: "A guy likes me!" Knowing that we are loved has transforming power.

Scripture is clear, it is only once we know that God loves us that we love him in return. "We love because he first loved us" (1 John 4:19). It is God's love for us that moves us to love him in return. As Bernard wrote: "The cause of loving God is God."[8]

When God, as "the true fountain of all love"[9] in the universe, offers us love, he can easily fill us with love. "God is love, and whoever abides in love abides in God, and God abides in him" (1 John 4:16). Filled with God's love, our love naturally seeks others to love and finds God first.

> But how can the mind be aroused to taste the divine goodness without at the same time being wholly kindled to love God in return? For truly, that abundant sweetness which God has stored up for those who fear him cannot be known without at the same time powerfully moving us. And once anyone has been moved by it, it utterly ravishes him and draws him to itself.[10]

The more filled we are by God's love for us—in his Word, in his creation, in his providence, and in his church—the more we naturally pour out love to him in return.

God's Love Leads Us to Desire Holiness

God's love for us leads us to love him, which then leads us to want to be holy like him, and so keep his commands. "For this is the love of God, that we keep his commandments" (1 John 5:3). Jesus drew this same conclusion. "If you love me, you will keep my commandments" (John 14:15). Each fresh experience of God's fatherly love moves us to want to be holy, much as a child, admiring his earthly father, desires to be like him. "The

---

8. Bernard, *Love of God*, 35.
9. Calvin, *Com.*, Rom 5:5.
10. Calvin, *Institutes*, 3.2.41.

only medicine we need for healing these vices, [is] for us to be able to lift our eyes to heaven and say, 'God is our father, he will provide all that we need.'"[11] Love powerfully increases our desire to be like Jesus.

Conversely, without love as our central motivation, other motives for seeking holiness easily lead to legalism, idolatry, and anger. One night, late, a women we knew showed up at our front door, very upset with her husband. While working on a project in his business that was not going well, this normally friendly man had grown angry, such that his wife had had enough. Though truly a believer he was approaching the Christian life as a series of rules to be followed by his own power. When I explained that God's love is to be our motivation instead, he said: "I have never known the love of God in such a way that I found it fulfilling. I always get my fullness from getting people's respect and performing well." He was helped by finding God's love.

Jonah expressed the same frustration of those who idolatrously strive for their own righteousness. "Those who pay regard to vain idols forsake their hope of steadfast love" (Jonah 2:8). Clinging to the idol of self-righteousness, trying to be good enough to win the approval of God, inevitably leads one to forsake the one thing they most need: the love of God. The word which Jonah uses here for love, *chesed*, is the *covenant love* of God. Like my angry friend, Jonah had forsaken the love of God in a vain effort to make his life work by his own power, which had led him to darkness and despair.

There is no substitute for apprehending God's love as the effective motive for holiness. When we know he loves us, we desire holiness from a heart already filled with love, that is, a heart that is already being made holy. When we strive for holiness while desperately hoping to earn love, the human spirit misfires in idolatry which leads to despair. It is only in apprehending God's love that we desire true holiness and are equipped to rightly pursue holiness, with hearts already filled with his love.

God's Love Leads Us to Seek His Help in Becoming Holy

When we recognize the depth of God's love for us we naturally seek his help. It is only natural that we seek help from those who love us, rather than those who despise us. Since God loves us enough to give his Son for us, this convinces us to look to him. "He who did not spare his own Son

---

11. Calvin, *Sermons on the Ten Commandments*, 196.

but gave him up for us all, how will he not also with him graciously give us all things?" (Rom 8:32).

It is because Christ knows us, because he can sympathize with our weaknesses, having condescended to become one of us, that we know we can approach him for mercy and "grace to help in time of need" (Heb 4:15–16). It is not fear but assurance of his love that leads us to seek help from God. "This then is the true logic of religion, that is, when we are persuaded that God is reconcilable and easily pacified, because he is by nature inclined to mercy."[12] Knowing that God loves us and wants to help us, we seek and find his grace to change us into his likeness.

God's Love Leads Us to Repentance

God's love for us also leads us to repentance. "God's kindness is meant to lead you to repentance" (Rom 2:4). We would never repent were we expecting either cold silence or hot wrath from God. Rather, knowing that we are loved and favored in Christ, we readily turn from our sin to God because we have an "apprehension of the mercy of God in Christ."[13] "When God commands us to return to the right way, our hearts would . . . on the contrary turn away, had we no hope that he would be reconciled to us."[14]

God is like a father with a rebellious child who is drawn back, not with threats of punishment, but with promises of reconciliation upon their repentance. "There is yet room for reconciliation, if you wish; provided you show yourself willing to [repent] . . . I will in return prove myself to be a father."[15] Believing that God loves us we more readily return to him in repentance.

God's Love Encourages Our Obedience

Knowing that God loves us does not lead us to careless living, but rather makes us more eager to obey him. Thomas à Kempis writes: "The noble love of Jesus spurs to great deeds and excites longing for that which is

---

12. Calvin, *Com.*, Mic 7:19.
13. *Westminster Confession of Faith*, 395; Westminster Shorter Catechism, answer 87.
14. Calvin, *Com.*, Mal 3:7–8.
15. Calvin, *Com.*, Jer 6:8.

Apprehend God's Love

more perfect."[16] As a child who feels loved by her father more readily complies with his wishes, the Christian perceiving the love of God wants to obey. "Once we have tasted his mutual love which he reserves for us, then we will be motivated to love him as our Father. For if this love is in us then there will be no doubt that we will obey him and that his law will rule in our thoughts."[17] When we find ourselves lacking zeal for obedience, the cure is not self-will but divine love. "When we are slow to obey God it is helpful to remember His gracious favors."[18]

God's love for us also encourages our obedience for we know that his love means that he will accept and reward our imperfect obedience. "Such children ought we to be, firmly trusting that our services will be approved by our most merciful Father, however small, rude, and imperfect these may be."[19] Otherwise we would hesitate to even try, fearing that our efforts, imperfect and partial, would be rejected by him. But experiencing his graciousness towards us we recognize that even our imperfect efforts are not judged on their own merit but by the grace of Christ. "Whatever you do, work heartily, as for the Lord and not for men, knowing that from the Lord you will receive the inheritance as your reward" (Col 3:23-24).

God's reward for our obedience is all out of proportion to our good works—an eternal inheritance—precisely because it is a reward, not of our merit, but the merit of Christ. Luther extolled the unearned favor with which the Father looks upon us in Christ.

> The Father offers unto me, by His promise, His grace, and His fatherly favor. This remains then, that I should receive this grace. And this is done when I again with this groaning do cry, and with a childlike heart, do assent unto this name, Father.... For by his birth the son is worthy to be an heir. There is no work or merit that brings him the inheritance, but his birth only.[20]

We labor under God's benevolent smile confident in Christ that our labor in the Lord is not in vain but is noticed, accepted, appreciated, and rewarded by our Father, such that even the smallest act brings bountiful reward. "Whoever gives one of these little ones even a cup of cold water

16. Thomas á Kempis, *The Imitation of Christ*, 3:5.
17. Calvin, *Sermons on the Ten Commandments*, 76.
18. Calvin, *Sermons on the Ten Commandments*, 117.
19. Calvin, *Institutes*, 3.19.5.
20. Luther, *Commentary on Galatians*, 250-52.

because he is a disciple, truly, I say to you, he will by no means lose his reward" (Matt 10:42).

We must know he loves us and accepts our works before we would ever obey him willingly and joyfully. "Until men recognize that they owe everything to God, that they are nourished by his fatherly care, that he is the Author of their every good, that they should seek nothing beyond him—they will never yield him willing service."[21] In the kingdom of God, apprehending God's love leads us to gladly obey him.

God's Love Allows Us to Love Others

When we experience the love of God flowing into our hearts we find ourselves filled by him, contented, and ready to love others. "Beloved, if God so loved us, we also ought to love one another" (1 John 4:11). Without the love of God filling us we wander the world passionately vying with others to find fulfilment (Jas 4:1). Those passions are quieted by God's love for us, as a child is soothed by his mother's love. "He will quiet you by his love" (Zeph 3:17). Sated on the love of God we are enabled to genuinely love our neighbors, rather than fight with them. "Easily, therefore, do they grow in love who know that they themselves are more loved."[22]

The more love we apprehend from God the more eagerly we love others. "As soon as, through faith the heart recognizes and holds this truth [that God loves us], so soon the heart is overflowing with love and thereby completely made ready to do good to all men."[23] The love of God then enables us to grow holy by loving our neighbors as ourselves.

We have seen in this first part how the love of God in Christ draws us irresistibly toward him and toward holiness, as a star draws toward itself everything in its orbit. Now it remains for us to understand how we may more effectively apprehend the love of God for us that we might grow in holiness.

How We Are to Apprehend God's Love for Us

Since apprehending God's love is so vital to our growth in Christlikeness God has provided many ways for us to know his love.

---

21. Calvin, *Institutes*, 1.2.1.
22. Bernard, *Love of God*, 12.
23. Bucer, *Christian Love*, 44–45.

Apprehending God's Love in Creation

Creation reveals, in its bounty, beauty, and "immense profusion of wealth," not only God's "eternal power and divine nature" (Rom 1:20), but also his love and "paternal solicitude" for humanity.[24] The psalmist captures God's affection in his abundant provision for us. "You cause the grass to grow for the livestock and plants for man to cultivate, that he may bring forth food from the earth and wine to gladden the heart of man, oil to make his face shine and bread to strengthen man's heart" (Ps 104:14–15).

When we realize what God has done for all humanity in creating a world so extravagantly beautiful and harmonious, we recognize his love. "For if it be asked, why the world has been created, why we have been placed in it to possess the dominion of the earth, why we are preserved in life to enjoy innumerable blessing . . . no other reason can be adduced, except the gratuitous love of God."[25]

This thought struck me one fall day as I stopped to contemplate a Japanese Maple in our backyard. The red of the turning leaves was deep and vivid, almost as if blood coursed through the leafy veins. I stood in wonder at the lavish extravagance of a God who would bother to paint that tree on that day with that particular red. Beauty in our world is an extravagance beyond utility which evidences the care of our Creator who desires that his creation might be "more than sufficient to draw us to his love."[26]

To feel God's love, we should literally stop and smell the roses, watch the birds, wonder at the mountains, walk along the ocean, always knowing that he means in them to send a message to us: "I have done this because I love you, enjoy!" Then, knowing through creation that he loves us, we trust ourselves into his love. "Seeing the good things which come from me, may you learn to entrust yourselves to me . . . since I have given you such good testimony of the love I bear you."[27]

We may see God's love as well in the creation of humanity. For humanity alone was made in the very image of God. "So God created man in his own image" (Gen 1:27). To create us like himself is to shower us with favor. We can perceive his love even as we look into the mirror, for

---

24. Calvin, *Com.*, Gen 1:26.
25. Calvin, *Com.*, 1 John 4:9.
26. Calvin, *Institutes*, 1.5.6.
27. Calvin, *Sermons on Genesis*, 112.

we see in our natures the reflection of his kindness. "God, in creating man, gave a demonstration of his infinite grace and more than fatherly love towards him."[28] To rightly understand God's love we simply look upon his good creation.

Apprehending God's Love in His Attitude Toward Humanity

God has a general love for all humanity. "For he makes his sun rise on the evil and on the good, and sends rain on the just and on the unjust" (Matt 5:45). This love of God for all, even the reprobate, can be asserted because, says Carson, while God's wrath is circumstantial, depending on justice deserved by those upon whom his wrath must fall, his love is essential, intrinsic to his very nature, as he looks upon his creation, even those parts of it which are fallen in rebellion. "Where there is no sin, there is no wrath, but there will always be love in God."[29]

This general disposition of love toward all humanity can be seen in God's accommodation to us. He accommodates himself to us by communicating with words we can understand and often speaking through the voices of fellow humans (Heb 1:1–2). He bends low to us and speaks gently to us through prophets and through Christ, so that we will not be frightened and flee from him.

God allows all humanity to pray to him, although our words may be no more than the babble of a child to his father.[30] We find in Scripture a God who, kind to all, is especially indulgent to his children's prayers. "He not only allows his people to cast their troubles on his breast, but hastens to answer his children quickly when they call."[31]

When we consider the kindness of God to all humanity, and in particular to his people, we begin to recognize that he is "sweetly alluring men to himself."[32] Seeing his kindness to humanity even in his attitude towards us we should clearly perceive that he loves us!

---

28. Calvin, *Com.*, Ps 8:7.
29. Carson, "God's Love and God's Wrath," 388.
30. Calvin, *Sermons on 2 Samuel*, 363.
31. Balserak, "The God of Love and Weakness," 194.
32. Calvin, *Com.*, Ps 119:149.

Apprehending God's Love Both in Good and in Difficult Providences

It is easy to understand that God loves us when he provides well for us in his kind providences. "You gave me life and showed me kindness, and in your providence watched over my spirit" (Job 10:12). Scripture urges us to not take for granted these many kind providences from God but rather to be aware of them and to be thankful. "Let them thank the LORD for his steadfast love, for his wondrous works to the children of man!" (Ps 107:15).

God blesses us daily with kind providences: food and drink, clothing, shelter, health, work, and family all come from his love. When we rightly perceive his loving intention behind each blessing, we rest more securely in his love and find greater peace, joy, and thankfulness.

To rightly apprehend God's love, however, we must also clearly perceive his love for us in the most difficult of providences as well, the trials and crosses we must bear. "For the Lord disciplines the one he loves, and chastises every son whom he receives" (Heb 12:6). While not all of our suffering is directly discipline for our own sin, yet all suffering should be endured as discipline and rightly understood as love. "It is certain that the punishments with which God visits his own children are evidences of his paternal love, as in this way he promotes their salvation."[33]

However, when we undergo difficult providences our natural tendency is to doubt God's goodness. When the diagnosis comes back positive for cancer, when a child turns away from the Lord, or when the boss issues a pink slip, we naturally doubt God's love, assuming that the news is only bad news, or perhaps, random news, rather than loving providence.

To rightly apprehend God's love, we must come to see his loving hand behind each blow we are dealt in this life. "For the moment all discipline seems painful rather than pleasant, but later it yields the peaceful fruit of righteousness to those who have been trained by it" (Heb 12:11). It does not matter the source of the trial—our own sin, the sin of others, disease, financial crisis, weather, technological failures, accidents—his loving providence is behind each one, God is treating us as sons.

There are two aspects of God's nature as our Father which we must consider together in order to find hope in trials: his power and his love. "When these two things are joined together, his great fatherly love for us, alongside of his unlimited power, there is nothing which can hinder

---

33. Calvin, *Com.*, Jer 10:24.

our faith from defying all the enemies which may rise up against us."[34] Confident of both his love and power to lead us through the trial, we can embrace any cross he lays before us as loving direction from our Father.

Perhaps an example will help. When I first begin working on my PhD my writing in the Doctoral Proposal Writing Seminar was much praised. Needless to say, this fed my competency idol to a red hot fury! However, after I submitted my first chapter my experience changed catastrophically. Its direction was utterly rejected by the director of the program. I was thunderstruck as my idols came crashing down around me. I briefly considered quitting.

However, realizing that trials are to be endured as the loving discipline of God, I stopped and asked: "If this difficult providence is from the Lord's love, then what good might he intend?" Two answers came to mind: a new growing academic humility—the obvious need—and, if God wanted the particular project to continue, a new supervisor in another program who would approve of the research direction. Within months, providentially, I had been recommended to a new supervisor who approved the project. I also experienced a newly humbled academic attitude such that, when the new supervisor gave any advice, my default was simply to submit and follow his lead. What initially looked like a disaster, while painful, ended up working to train me in righteousness and was a blessing.

Although we may not always comprehend in this life the beneficial result of the Lord's discipline, when we submit to his difficult providences, we are trained by them and can perceive in them, not the randomness of an uncaring universe, but the love of our Father. This not only brings us comfort and assurance but a positive sense of direction and purpose, leading us to the peaceful fruit of righteousness, that is, our further growth in holiness.

Apprehending God's Love in Redemption

When we consider with what unmerited favor we have been elected, called, regenerated, converted, justified, adopted, sanctified, and bound for glory, we are humbled and made glad by the depth of the love of God for us. To fully apprehend the depth of God's love in our redemption, however, we must first understand that he loved us while we were utterly

---

34. Calvin, *Com.*, Ps 46:7.

unlovable to a holy God: while still dead in our sins (Eph 2:4–5). Such knowledge humbles us regarding ourselves, even while we exalt all the more in the lavish love of our God.

Nowhere does God's love for us in his redemption become clearer than in the gift of his own Son to redeem us. "In this is love, not that we have loved God but that he loved us and sent his Son to be the propitiation for our sins" (1 John 4:10). God's love is most clearly shown and known, in the singular gift of his beloved Son to redeem us even while we were yet sinners. "Christ, then, is so illustrious and singular a proof of divine love towards us, that whenever we look upon him, he fully confirms to us the truth that God is love."[35]

More amazingly, not only are we accepted and forgiven but we are transformed into the children of God. "See what kind of love the Father has given to us, that we should be called children of God; and so we are" (1 John 3:1). When we see that in Christ, we are loved by the Father with the same love that he loves the Son ("You . . . loved them even as you loved me" [John 17:23]), the love of God becomes tangible and life-giving to us.

Do we ever doubt that God loves us? Look to the cross of the Son! Do we wallow in doubt, discouragement, and languish for fear that God has removed his hand of blessing? Look to the cross of his Son. "Now, if you want to see the heart of the heavenly Father entirely open, you may see that in his son Jesus Christ."[36] When we see Christ clearly we are enabled to see God's love for us in him, and that love transforms us, draws us humbly before him to bask in the warm glow of his love. This basking in his love *is* our growing relational holiness which leads us toward obedience as we eagerly yield to the revealed will of the one who has loved us so well. To know God's love we must ever keep Christ and his cross before us.

Apprehending God's Love in the Word

While the Word expresses God's love for us directly, we see his love in the Bible in other ways as well: in its Law, its accommodation, its tone, and its passionate love.

---

35. Calvin, *Com.*, 1 John 4:9.
36. Schnetzler et al., *Pierre Viret*, 193.

While many see the Law of God as severe, for the believer, it should be seen with its loving intention, to lead us in paths of blessing. "But the one who looks into the perfect law, the law of liberty, and perseveres . . . he will be blessed in his doing" (Jas 1:25). Rightly understood, the Law can become a delight, not merely a rule. "His delight is in the law of the LORD" (Ps 1:2). Our loving Father has provided his Law to guide us to him and to life.

God's accommodations to our weaknesses in the manner of the Bible also express his love. The Bible was written by men who are just like us so that we can hear their voices without being undone (Exod 20:19). The Bible uses images which mean something to us: the Passover lamb, the King of heaven, the high priest, the Father, the Son. These accommodations are signs that God loves us enough to stoop low to us.

The tone of Scripture is one of love and concern for humanity, and preeminently, for God's people. "For God so loved the world" (John 3:16). The tone of God's voice in the Bible, when he is not warning, is marked by a paternal affection designed to draw us to him, not frighten us away. "Come to me, all who labor and are heavy laden, and I will give you rest" (Matt 11:28).

We apprehend God's love for us also in the passionate intensity by which our Father bids us to see his love in the Bible. "I will betroth you to me forever. I will betroth you to me in righteousness and in justice, in steadfast love and in mercy. I will betroth you to me in faithfulness" (Hos 2:19–20). The image is movingly passionate. God says to us, in effect: "I love you even more than a husband does his faithless wife, for unlike most earthly husbands, I invite you back, yet again, to be mine. I forgive, and woo, and pursue, and promise you my faithfulness even in the face of your infidelity."

The depth of God's love for us revealed by his Word, struck me years ago as I was reading and praying through Hosea. Here is part of my journal entry.

> March 16, 1999: A touch of love.
>
> Yesterday while reading and meditating on Hosea 6:6 ("For I desire steadfast love and not sacrifice.") I sensed a touch of love from God that brought me to tears and transformed my understanding of our Holy God. This was an encounter with the living God through his living Word that has changed me. What did I experience?

First, was the new awareness of the reality of the superabundant unending overflow of *steadfast* love that fills every molecule of space as an active overflowing force from the Father. No dark corner, no remote sphere sits outside of his love.

Second, I think I saw what I did not expect to see, the readiness of God to receive our love in response to his own. I know this cannot, does not, imply need (Acts 17:25). But the sense that he would gladly receive, waited for, even longed for our love, was new to me. "Love a woman ... even as the LORD loves the children of Israel, though they turn to other gods and love cakes of raisins" (Hos 3:1).

Third, I saw anew the depth of my sin of omission by not loving the Lord with all my heart, soul, mind, and strength. If he is ready for my love and I do not offer it, then I have neglected the most important duty of all: to give him what he most desires, my love.

Here is the compelling picture we receive from God's Word regarding his love for us. The God, who is love, fills the universe with his love, creates the world for us, and us upon it, in his love, redeems us in his love, although we have rebelled against his love, chooses and calls us in his love, desires for us to know his love, that knowing it, we may be moved to love him and find there our highest joy and be satisfied with his love (Isa 55:2–3). Here in God's Word we find the clearest revelation of his love that moves us toward him and therefore forward in holiness.

Apprehending God's Love through the Church

God shows us his love through the body of Christ, the church. In church he provides for us a community, a family, filled with brothers and sisters, fathers and mothers. "Do not rebuke an older man but encourage him as you would a father, younger men as brothers, older women as mothers, younger women as sisters, in all purity" (1 Tim 5:1–2). Here we are to experience his love through one another. "Beloved, if God so loved us, we also ought to love one another" (1 John 4:11).

Within the church God supplies us officers to teach, guide, and correct us, from the love of God. "I exhort the elders among you ... shepherd the flock of God that is among you" (1 Pet 5:1–2). The pastor/teacher is a particular gift of God's love. They proclaim God's love to us while conducting themselves, on God's behalf, as fathers and mothers to us. "But we were gentle among you, like a nursing mother taking care of her own children. . . . For you know how, like a father with his children, we exhorted each one of you and encouraged you" (1 Thess 2:7–12).

The sacraments, too, visibly demonstrate to us the Father's love. Baptism reminds us that God loves us so profoundly that he loves our children for a thousand generations. "Repent and be baptized every one of you. . . . For the promise is for you and for your children" (Acts 2:38–39). The Lord's Supper is a palpable reminder that God loves us so much that he gave his only Son for us to unite himself to us. "This is my body, which is given for you" (Luke 22:19).

Surprisingly, even church discipline is meant to communicate God's love to us and lead us back to his arms. Hence, Paul reminds the Corinthian church to welcome back in love the sinning brother who has repented. "So I beg you to reaffirm your love for him" (2 Cor 2:8). Since discipline is meant to reflect God's compassion in order to lead the wayward to repentance we are admonished to exercise correction carefully, removing the log from our eye first (Luke 6:42), approaching the offender privately to win him over (Matt 18:15), and always disciplining with gentleness (2 Tim 2:25). This affectionate correction assures us of God's love.

The church extends God's love in its compassion as well. Our church ministered tirelessly to a young widow with four children. Particularly touching was a deacon who, with three children of his own, would for years take the widow's children out to dinner on their birthdays. God has placed us in the midst of his beloved people where we concretely experience his great love for us.

Apprehending God's Love for Us in Repentance and Forgiveness

Experiencing God's forgiveness through repentance leads us to a deeper knowledge of God's love. In Luke 7, Jesus confronts Simon the Pharisee over his indignation that Jesus allowed a "sinful" woman to wash his feet. Jesus contrasts the woman to Simon, pointing out that she—having repented of sin more freely than Simon—was forgiven more by Christ and therefore loved Christ more than Simon. "But he who is forgiven little, loves little" (Luke 7:47).

In the parable of the Pharisee and the tax collector Jesus shows that the self-righteous, who wrongly believe they have no need to repent, fail to find forgiveness, while the humble penitent are forgiven.

"I tell you, this man went down to his house justified, rather than the other" (Luke 18:14).

When we take Luke 7 and 18 together, we may then outline the relationship between repentance, forgiveness, and knowing we are loved by God and loving God thus:

1. God graciously offers forgiveness to the repentant.
2. Repenting, we experience God's forgiveness as love.
3. Forgiven and loved by God, we love him in return.

Therefore, to better apprehend God's love, we must regularly repent to experience yet more deeply God's forgiveness. This is why the first of Martin Luther's *95 Theses* called us to repentance. "When our Lord and Master Jesus Christ said, 'Repent,' he willed the entire life of believers to be one of repentance."[37] Calvin too taught the importance of daily repentance. "Every time he gives us the opportunity to repent, let us learn that he wants us to think of our sins, and . . . to bow our head in utter humility."[38] The invitation to repent, given throughout Scripture, is an invitation, not to grovel, but to experience God's forgiveness and thus his love, whose mercies are *new* every morning.

Apprehending God's Love through the Blessings of Obedience

Because God promises to show his covenant love to those who walk obediently within his covenant of grace, we may better know his love through our obedience. "Because you listen to these rules and keep and do them, the LORD your God will keep with you the covenant and the steadfast love that he swore to your fathers. He will love you, bless you, and multiply you" (Deut 7:12–13). As God's children walk in obedience they experience his love as blessings. This does not mean that our obedience merits his blessings, because our obedience is always imperfect, so is blessed only by the grace offered us through Christ, out of God's mercy and love.

God's covenant blessing on our covenant obedience is a pure expression of his love. This dynamic can be seen in covenant blessings within families. Usually something such as this is implied when we give our

---

37. Luther, "Power and Efficacy of Indulgences," 31:25.
38. Calvin, *Sermons on 2 Samuel*, 573.

children a car: "As long as you obey the covenant laws of our family—not speeding, not drinking and driving—I will bless you, letting you use the car. But if you break the covenant law, then I will give you, instead of covenant blessings, covenant discipline. I will take away the car. In both cases I will love you. But your obedience allows you to experience my love as blessing, while your disobedience means my love will feel like discipline. Why not obey and know my love as blessing rather than discipline?"

It is in this context of having a sure covenant relationship with God by his own graceful choice, that he commands us to obey his covenant law and promises us covenant blessings to show us his love. "As the Father has loved me, so have I loved you. Abide in my love. If you keep my commandments, you will abide in my love, just as I have kept my Father's commandments and abide in his love. These things I have spoken to you, that my joy may be in you, and that your joy may be full" (John 15:9–11).

Note the similarities between Deut 7 and John 15: First, there is a pre-existent covenant relationship that does not depend on our actions but on God's graceful choosing. John: "As the father has loved me so I have loved you." Deuteronomy 7:6: "The LORD your God has chosen you out of all the peoples on the face of the earth to be his people, his treasured possession."

Second, based on the covenant relationship, the Lord requires our obedience in order to experience his loving blessing. There is an "if-then" nature to loving relationships in the covenant of grace. John: "If you keep my commandments, you will abide in my love." Deuteronomy: "Because you listen to these rules and keep and do them, the LORD your God will keep with you the covenant and the steadfast love that he swore to your fathers."

Third, the major benefit of obedience is not our salvation but the consistent experience of blessings as love from God. John: "These things I have spoken to you, that my joy may be in you, and that your joy may be full." Deuteronomy: "He will love you, bless you, and multiply you."

The gracious covenant of love God extended to us by faith in Christ still requires our obedience, not to enter the covenant, nor ultimately to remain in the covenant, but rather, to fully experience the temporal blessings of the covenant as love from God. "If anyone loves me, he will keep my word, and my Father will love him" (John 14:23).

We have seen, then, the many ways by which we may come to know God's love more deeply and how his love transforms us into the image of Christ.

Practical Suggestions for Apprehending God's Love

Since apprehending God's love for us aids our growth in Christlikeness we rightly make it our goal to grow in our knowledge of his love. Paul prayed that the Ephesians might more and more: "Know the love of Christ that surpasses knowledge, that you may be filled with all the fullness of God" (Eph 3:17–19). How can we grow in our knowledge of God's love?

1. Set it as your goal to grow in the knowledge of God's love for you in Christ. Start each day with the desire to "know the love of Christ that surpasses knowledge."

2. Stop and wonder at the love of God in creation. Do not take it for granted, see the beauty all around you and accept it for what it is: a sign of God's love for you.

3. Marvel at God's love poured out on all humanity. When you see his mercy falling daily, upon the just and the unjust, allow it to fill your heart with a new awareness of God's love.

4. Appreciate more deeply God's *kind providences* in your life. Do not take for granted your family, friends, work (if you have it), health (to whatever degree you have it), food, clothing, shelter. Give thanks for all the good gifts you receive daily.

5. Understand *difficult providences* as God's love. God has not forgotten us when he walks us through trials. On the contrary, he is just then "treating us as sons." Submit to him in difficult providences, kissing the cross rather than kicking against the goad, he means them as love.

6. Recount daily the great mercy of God in redeeming you through Christ. Let us wonder anew each day, as we did when we were first saved, that Jesus "loved me and gave himself for me" (Gal 2:20).

7. Experience God's love in his Word daily. In his Word, God communicates his love for us, let us read to that end. Consider embarking on a particular study of his love for you, as mentioned above.

8. Give yourself wholly to a local, Bible-believing church and find God's love there. Appreciate and receive as a token of God's love for you his Word preached to you. Savor the fellowship of brothers and sisters, as a touch of the hand of Christ. When the sacraments are offered, wonder at the love of a God who would bind himself to you in such a covenant of grace. Should you be corrected by another

church member, or formally disciplined by the elders, receive it as loving correction from your Father.

9. Repent daily for your sins and receive fresh grace and forgiveness from God's love. "He who is forgiven little, loves little" (Luke 7:47).

10. Walk in obedience and notice the blessings God pours out in love. See those blessings for what they truly are, tokens of his love.

Christ lived with the constant awareness of his Father's love for him. "As the Father has loved me" (John 15:9). For us to become like Jesus we must grow in our knowledge of the Father's love for us. Let us press on, growing in our apprehension of God's love for us.

Further Resources

Study Questions

1. What is the apprehension of God's love?
2. Why is God's love for us so essential for our growth in holiness given that holiness is first a relationship with God?
3. In what ways does God's love help us grow in holiness?
4. How well do you apprehend God's love for you?
5. Which of the various ways listed to grow in an awareness of God's love for you might most help you at this time?

For Further Study

Bernard of Clairvaux, *On the Love of God* (tr. Terence L. Connolly; New York: Spiritual, 1937).
D. A. Carson, "God's Love and God's Wrath," *Bibliotheca Sacra*, 156, no. 624 (1999) 387–98.
Jonathan Edwards, *Charity and its Fruits* (Edinburgh: Banner of Truth, 2013).
———, *The Religious Affections* (Mineola, NY: Dover, 2013).
C. Matthew McMahon, *John Calvin's View of God's Love and the Doctrine of Reprobation* (Crossville, TN: Puritan, 2015).

7

Struggle for Faith

FOR MANY CHRISTIANS, FAITH is a vague concept, and its importance to sanctification is often missed. In this chapter we will explain what faith is, how growth in faith helps us grow in holiness, and how we must struggle for faith as an essential part of the daily Christian life.

What Is Faith?

Faith Is Knowledge of God's Mercy in Christ

We often think of faith as something ephemeral, less real, than knowledge—such as hope, or wishing—but faith is simply another branch of knowledge and no less certain than any other knowledge. Simply put, faith is a way of knowing things that we cannot know through our senses. "Now faith is the assurance of things hoped for, the conviction of things not seen" (Heb 11:1). Indeed, we may be even more certain of those things which we know by faith.

The clearest example of faith as knowledge is when we move from unbelief to faith in Christ. When I was twelve years old I had a fifteen-year-old sister who was killed in an automobile accident. I vividly recall standing in the funeral home and seeing my previously vivacious, beautiful, and popular sister now in her coffin. The Holy Spirit prompted two questions in me: Where am I going and why am I here? I started a spiritual quest exploring various answers offered by world religions until a kindly Episcopalian priest insisted that I should, out of fairness, read the Bible. I did, and there was confronted by the majesty, wisdom, and beauty of Christ in the Gospels.

But I was conflicted over one matter: Jesus clearly claimed to be God. As a logical young man I surmised that God and man were two distinct beings, to be a man is to not be God, to be God is to not be a man. I struggled mightily, but could not accept Christ's divinity. One late night, when I was sixteen, I lay awake crying out to God: "God if you are Jesus you will have to make me believe it, I cannot accept it as true." The next morning my older brother woke me up with the report that the surf was up, since we then lived on the beachfront. I got down to the beach, surfboard under arm, when I asked myself about the night before. I had been praying about wanting to know if Jesus were really God. Then I had a thought I had never had before: "Jesus is God!" I knew it to be true, but did not then know how I knew it to be true. I shouted out praises to God as I surfed: "Jesus is God! Jesus is God!" This I had come to know, and know certainly, by faith, not by sight.

The knowledge of faith is absolutely essential to the Christian life, since much of what we need to know—God, eternal life, forgiveness, love—are all beyond knowing by our senses. Faith is knowledge, in particular, of God and his goodness to us in Christ. Calvin says that faith is a "firm and certain knowledge of God's benevolence toward us, founded upon the truth of the freely given promise in Christ, both revealed to our minds and sealed upon our hearts through the Holy Spirit."[1] Thus faith consists of the knowledge of Christ and the blessings that are ours in him, so that we find in faith the essential ingredient for the Christian life.[2] "For in [the gospel] the righteousness of God is revealed from faith for faith, as it is written, 'The righteous shall live by faith'" (Rom 1:17).

Faith Includes Trust

Faith, while it is a kind of knowledge, is more than merely factual knowledge, for faith includes trust. The bare knowledge of the facts of Christ, without trust in him, is not faith. One may ascent to the historical Christ, even to his divinity, and the redemption possible in Christ, but not have faith. Even the demons believe—with that sort of faith—and tremble (Jas 2:19). Faith not only knows the truth of Christ and the life he offers us,

---

1. Calvin, *Institutes*, 3.2.7.
2. Calvin, *Com.*, John 3:16.

but faith lays hold of that truth by trusting in him. "Faith is trust. It is a trusting and confident knowledge."³ To have faith in Christ we must trust in him, not in ourselves, to save us. "Faith is not just an opinion or a persuasion but rather a personal confidence in the mercy of God. Faith involves not just the mind but also the heart."⁴

Faith Includes Certainty

Biblical faith also includes certainty. This can be the cause of great confusion in the Christian life, for we seldom perceive certainty in ourselves regarding the things of God. This is not because faith itself lacks certainty but rather because we lack faith. While faith is certain, we are a mixture of faith and unbelief. "I believe; help my unbelief!" (Mark 9:24). But the nature of faith itself is certainty.

Hebrews 11:1 says: "Now faith is the assurance of things hoped for, the conviction of things not seen." Here it defines faith as assurance and conviction. The term translated conviction, *elegchos* (ἔλεγχος), means "proof" or "evidence." Faith is itself the proof, the evidence, of the things we do not see, namely that Christ is, and that he redeems us. Faith is, as it were, a tangible bit of the unseen reality to which it corresponds. We can only have faith because it corresponds to the reality of the thing in which we believe, it is, if you will, a small piece of that unseen reality.

Could I travel to the future and return with a newspaper article showing that one of your descendants was to become president of the United States, that article would be evidence of an unseen reality. In a similar way, faith is itself evidence of an unseen reality. The newspaper would not be wishful thinking, or hope, it would be simple reality. Faith is certain evidence that God exists and redeems, for the faith itself comes from him, as the newspaper does from the future.

Faith Gives Assurance

Faith is naturally certain and so gives us assurance. Faith, "contains personal, *subjective* assurance, so that the believer may know that God intends grace toward him."⁵ Faith is our assurance that God loves us and

---

3. Godfrey, "Faith Alone," 272.
4. Lane, "Assurance," 43.
5. Beeke, "Assurance and Faith," 50.

will entirely redeem us. "To every man, therefore, his faith is a sufficient attestation of the eternal predestination of God."[6] The certainty of faith is not something that we create, willing ourselves to believe, just as I could not will myself to believe as a young non-Christian that Jesus was God. Nor can others give us certainty; it is not a human creation. Faith is given to us by God through his Holy Spirit (1 Cor 12:9).

The assurance of faith, inherent in it, is assisted from several quarters.[7] It begins with God's election of us. Since he chose us he will certainly bring our salvation to fulfillment (Rom 8:30). The Holy Spirit also makes our faith assured as he gives testimony to us that we are indeed the children of God (Rom 8:16). When we see that God is really at work in us, putting to death sin and bringing to life new works of righteousness, these good works serve as a minor help to our spiritual assurance in Christ. "And by this we know that we have come to know him, if we keep his commandments" (1 John 2:3).

But the central assurance and certainty of faith is Christ himself. "And there is salvation in no one else, for there is no other name under heaven given among men by which we must be saved" (Acts 4:12). It is not the strength of our faith that saves us but the object of our faith—Jesus Christ. The least amount of real faith, faith that is knowledge, trust, and certainty, all in Christ, is a saving faith.

How Does More Faith Help Us Grow in Holiness?

Growth in faith means growth in holiness because more faith gives us more of Christ, who makes us holy. It is by faith that we are united to Christ and share in the life, death, and resurrection of Christ, such that the power of his life is at work in us. "The life I now live in the flesh I live *by faith* in the Son of God, who loved me and gave himself for me" (Gal 2:20b, emphasis added).

Since faith instrumentally unites us to Christ, the more faith we have the more of Christ we have, as it were. Not that there is more *to* Christ, but that we know more *of* him through increased faith. Faith has been well-likened to a pipeline through which water flows. The smaller the diameter of the pipe the less water flow, the larger the diameter the greater the flow. More faith means a more vital flow of the life of Christ

---

6. Calvin, *Com.*, John 6:40.
7. Lane, "Assurance," 34–36.

into our lives. Hence, we must always be growing in faith. "We ought always to give thanks to God for you, brothers, as is right, because your faith is growing abundantly" (2 Thess 1:3).

Christ is in us by faith, and we live, and progress as Christians, through faith. "That according to the riches of his glory he may grant you to be strengthened with power through his Spirit in your inner being, so that Christ may dwell in your hearts *through faith*" (Eph 6:16–17, emphasis added). United to Christ by faith, from him come all the benefits of our salvation—union, justification, sanctification, and glorification—it all depends on this organic union by faith with Christ. "True faith is also the fountain of sanctification, love, and repentance."[8]

When we grow in faith we grow in knowledge of and trust in Christ by which he transforms us into his image. "We are again taught in this place how strong and efficacious is the knowledge of Christ; for it transforms us into his image."[9] Faith uniting us to Christ, he works to sanctify us, for as Christ says, believers are: "sanctified by faith in me" (Acts 26:18). As we are justified by faith, so too are we sanctified by faith, a double grace.[10] It is not human power properly that makes us holy, though our effort is clearly required. It is divine power, working though faith, that transforms us, so that we conform more and more to the likeness of Christ.

Because faith unites us to Christ, growing faith is essential to our growth in holiness. One might even say that growth in sanctification *is* growth in faith. All of our progress in holiness is directly linked to our growth in faith.[11] "Since this Christian and godly life flows entirely from a true and living faith in Christ the Lord, it can be clearly seen that if Christians are to be kept, guarded and encouraged . . . it must above all be insured that they are healthy in the faith."[12]

Martin Bucer was so convinced of the connection between faith and sanctification that he would say: "All deficiency of life comes from deficiency of faith."[13] This means that the good pastor or Christian counselor should always recognize that when a Christian is struggling,

---

8. Godfrey, "Faith Alone," 274.
9. Calvin, *Com.*, 1 John 3:7.
10. Calvin, *Institutes*, 3.11.1.
11. Selderhuis, "Faith Between God and the Devil," 197.
12. Bucer, *True Care of Souls*, 179.
13. Bucer, *True Care of Souls*, 165–66.

the thing they most need is not self-esteem, confidence, or even good problem-solving, but simply more faith.[14]

Growth in faith means more of Christ, which means more growth in Christlikeness. "You are to believe assuredly that there is no way to be saved without receiving all the saving benefits of Christ: His Spirit as well as His merits, sanctification as well as remission of sins, by faith."[15] But why is this difficult? Why do we struggle so for more faith?

Why Is the Entirety of the Christian Life a Struggle for More Faith?

Faith Struggles Against Unbelief

Faith is confidence in Christ, but the Christian's heart is not filled with only faith so that it is always tranquil. Rather, there rages in the heart of the believer a constant struggle between faith and unbelief. This is so because while faith possesses by its nature confidence, humanity by its fallen nature possess doubt. For the Christian, the struggle is not primarily an external one, fighting for morality, but first an internal one, "the struggle between faith and doubt, certainty and fear, belief and unbelief."[16] Calvin emphasized the battle that is the struggle for faith. "We rightly aim for an increase in faith, but the increase itself is a struggle."[17] This struggle is not an occasional one for the believer, but one that we engage regularly: "Our faith cannot and should not exist without battle."[18]

We see throughout Scripture that the chief conflict of the life of the believer is this struggle for faith. When God promised Abraham that his children would be as numerous as the stars in Gen 15, Abraham had to fight against the doubt in his heart, so he would not "weaken in faith," aware as he was that he and his wife were beyond childbearing years, so that he might rather believe God and grow "strong in his faith" (Rom 4:19–21).

Israel's chief problem during the years of wilderness wandering was not that God would not help and protect them, but rather that they would

---

14. Bucer, *True Care of Souls*, 103–4.
15. Marshall, *Gospel Mystery*, 168.
16. Schreiner, "Calvin's Concern with Certainty," 119.
17. Calvin, *Com.*, John 2:11.
18. Calvin, *Ioannis Calvini Opera*, 53:29.

not *believe* that he would, so they doubted and their unbelief kept them out of the promised land. "So we see that they were unable to enter because of unbelief" (Heb 3:19).

Throughout the Gospels, Jesus consistently rebuked his disciples for unbelief. While Jesus slept and the disciples feared the storm in the middle of the lake he rebuked them: "Why are you afraid, O you of little faith?" (Matt 8:26). When Peter began to sink, Jesus rebuked him: "O you of little faith, why did you doubt?" (Matt 14:31). When the disciples wondered why they could not cast out a certain demon, he rebuked them: "Because of your little faith" (Matt 17:20). When the disciples huddled in fear after the crucifixion, Jesus: "rebuked them for their unbelief" (Mark 16:14). When Thomas demanded that he see Jesus' wounds before he would believe, Jesus rebuked him: "Do not disbelieve, but believe" (John 20:27). The chief struggle for the Christian is between faith and doubt!

The Struggle for Faith Is a War between Two World Views

The nature of this struggle is essentially a struggle between two competing worldviews. Faith offers a view of this world in which our loving God is in control, always watching over, providing for, and protecting his people, even during trials, and will deliver them ultimately to heaven. Unbelief offers the opposite worldview: that God has forgotten his people, they are on their own, chance rules the day, not the kind providence of God, so that hope in God is ill-placed and one had best take matters into their own hands, rather than trust God. Unbelief encourages us to *see* the pressing reality of the difficulties, focusing on what is *seen*, doubting what God has said. Faith bids us to *hear* the Word of God's promise, to look beyond what is seen and take God at his Word. Faith bids us believe what we cannot see, doubt to believe only what we can see. Faith bids us believe that God is good; doubt bids us to doubt his goodness.

The devil, the world, and the flesh lead to doubt. The devil is skilled at rubbing our faces in the difficulties of this life, while tempting us to doubt God's promise. "See the hardship, how can a good God allow you to suffer so? Abandon hope in him and take matters into your own hands!" Selderhuis summarizes this strategy calling it a "theology from below," that is, the devil's theology starts and ends only with what we experience in this broken world. "Satan takes advantage of such a theology [from below] and the feelings generated by it. . . . We do not feel anything of

God's benefits, and so, we think, he has probably forgotten us."[19] The devil is always tempting us to listen to his doubts rather than God's Word of faith. "In the heart of the believer there are two voices, the voice of God and the voice of God's adversary. God's voice comes through the promise and generates hope but that other voice points to circumstances in that way to make a person despair of God."[20]

The world system works in cooperation with the devil, urging the Christian to live by sight and not by faith. The world tells us that we should succeed in the things of the world—money, fame, power, sexuality—and then count on the world to reward our success, rather than counting on the Lord to provide for us. The world tells us not to trust God to provide for us, instead we must self-promote and self-care precisely because, from the world's view, one cannot leave something as important as ourselves in the care of God. Hence friendship with the world, living in accordance with its externally-oriented, success-here-and-now mantra is opposed to walking by faith. "Do you not know that friendship with the world is enmity with God? Therefore whoever wishes to be a friend of the world makes himself an enemy of God" (Jas 4:4).

The devil and the world are assisted by our own sin nature which gravitates always to walk by sight and not by faith. "Believers are in perpetual conflict with their own unbelief."[21] The old nature musters doubt in God's goodness and unbelief in his Word. "The struggle with the flesh means a constant inward struggle, not only against wrong desires but also against false ideas and unbelief, for unbelief is also an activity of the flesh (our old nature), whose judgment about God and our situation is always opposed to faith."[22] It is the unbelief arising from the flesh, masquerading as our helper, which serves as our greatest opponent in the struggle for more faith. "Take care, brothers, lest there be in any of you an evil, *unbelieving heart*, leading you to fall away from the living God (Heb 3:12, emphasis added). So we struggle against unbelief in our own sin nature. "When the flesh tells us that God is opposed to us, and that there is no more hope of pardon, faith at length sets up its shield, and repels this onset of temptation, and entertains hope of pardon.[23]

---

19. Selderhuis, "Faith Between God and the Devil," 200.
20. Selderhuis, "Faith Between God and the Devil," 201.
21. Calvin, *Institutes*, 3.2.17.
22. Wallace, *Christian Life*, 256.
23. Calvin, *Com.*, Jonah 2:4.

The Struggle for Faith Is the Normal Christian Life

While this struggle sounds terrible and we may want to avoid it, this daily struggle for faith *is* the normal Christian life. The devil will tell us that our very struggle for faith is a sign of our failure, but this is not true, for the struggle itself is evidence of the Christian's faith. We should not be discouraged by this necessary part of the Christian life, but rather encouraged, for through Christ we will have the ultimate victory of faith! God deliberately leads us to places where we must struggle for more faith so that we will grow closer to him and grow in faith. As Jacob wrestled with the angel of the Lord, so too, God delights to have us bring our wrestling for faith to him, for he loves us.

Consider, for example, that we may today have a certain level of faith, say, a six on a one-to-ten scale. The level-six faith is enough to meet our normal challenges. Then a new challenge arises, for example, the doctor tells us that we have a serious cancer—which demands, say, level-nine faith. Now the level-six faith is inadequate and we experience a "faith gap." Immediately the struggle for faith ensues. The devil tells us that God has forgotten us, the world tells us to put all of our faith in medicine since God has allowed us to have cancer and cannot be trusted, our flesh bids us to resent God for doing this and to look for our own means of escape. But faith responds: "Trust God, he is good, he loves you, he is in charge, live or die, he means for you to walk though cancer with him now, 'the righteous will live by faith.'" And so goes the struggle until we emerge triumphant again by the grace of God, closer relationally to God, and with greater faith.

This is the normal Christian life and it is necessary, for faith grows, as does a muscle, when it is exercised by new challenges. As we struggle for faith, we find triumph by faith in Christ, a growing faith, more of Christ, and more of his holiness in us. While we must struggle for faith all this life, our final victory in Christ, that which overcomes the world, is our faith! "And this is the victory that has overcome the world—our faith" (1 John 5:4).

If we must struggle for faith to grow in faith and holiness, we then need to understand precisely how we may grow in faith.

How Can We Grow in Faith?

Faith Grows from the Word and Spirit

Faith is a gift of God; we cannot create it (Eph 2:8–9). This gift is not partly God's work and partly ours, but all of God. "Faith is a work of God."[24] Although faith is a gift from God, it is a gift that we can and should seek from God, from his Holy Spirt, and his Word. "Faith comes from hearing, and hearing through the word of Christ" (Rom 10:17). The Holy Spirit quickens and energizes the Word such that faith grows in our hearts. "For the Spirit is not only the initiator of faith, but increases it by degrees, until by it he leads us to the Kingdom of Heaven."[25]

There is simply no other source for growth in faith like God's Word whose voice speaks contrary to the world, the flesh, and the devil, always leading us to the truth about God's goodness to us. "From childhood you have been acquainted with the sacred writings, which are able to make you wise for salvation through faith in Christ Jesus" (2 Tim 3:15). Faith arises, not from the words of men, but only from the Word of God. "For the faith of true believers is not founded on their particular opinions, nor on the opinions of men, but on the pure and explicit Word of God."[26]

Faith grows from the Word, all of the Word, but in particular faith is aided by the promises of God in the Word. "For it is certain that faith cannot stand, unless it be founded on the promises of God."[27] What is God's promise to us in the Word? Generally speaking, that he will love us, save us, and deliver us to the kingdom of heaven, through faith in Christ. "We know that for those who love God all things work together for good, for those who are called according to his purpose" (Rom 8:28). While we believe all of the Word of God, his promises uniquely give us faith in his goodness to us. "For, if you have faith in the histories etc., but do not trust the promises, it is not possible that you have faith."[28] It is not simply information about God which helps us, rather when we learn that he loves us and will care for us, our faith in him is greatly increased.

Faith arises from the Word and its promises to us, but even more particularly, faith rises as we look to Christ in the Word. "Faith comes

---

24. Calvin, *Com.*, John 6:38.
25. Calvin, *Institutes*, 3.2.33.
26. Viret, *L'Interim Fait par Dialogues*, 247.
27. Calvin, *Com.*, Gen 12:2.
28. Timmerman, "Martin Bucer as Interpreter," 58–59.

from hearing, and hearing through the *word of Christ*" (Rom 10:17, emphasis added). Jesus Christ is himself the ultimate promise of Scripture in whom we find God's great "Yes." "For all the promises of God find their Yes in him" (2 Cor 1:20). The Word reveals Jesus as the great yes: "Yes, I will forgive. Yes, I will make you my people. Yes, I will cleanse, renew, and make you holy. Yes, you will triumph through the trials of this life and reach heaven." Therefore, when we go to the Word for increased faith the first sight we need is of Christ. "First, then, we ought to believe that Christ cannot be properly known in any other way than from *the Scriptures*; and if it be so, it follows that we ought to read *the Scriptures* with the express design of finding Christ in them."[29]

We seek growth in faith from the Scriptures by "finding Christ in them." While all the Word of God is good for faith and life, every jot and tittle, it is especially Christ and the promises fulfilled in him that grow our faith in the goodness of God. We should seek Christ when we struggle, and we should offer him to all who struggle between faith and unbelief as well. "It is therefore the duty of a godly teacher, in order to confirm disciples in the faith, to extol as much as possible the grace of Christ, so that being satisfied with that, we may seek nothing else."[30]

Faith Grows in the Exercise of Prayer

Prayer is another biblical aid to faith. Indeed, prayer and faith have a special relationship, for prayer is the principle exercise of faith. To pray is to believe that God exists and that he rewards those who seek him (Heb 11:6). When we pray we are expressing certainty in the unseen, in the power and goodness of God; and negatively, we are expressing our belief in the limited power of ourselves and the world, all actions of faith. Faith teaches us what we need and where we may find our help—in God alone—then faith seeks God through prayer.[31] "Prayer is the inevitable outcome of the presence of faith in the human heart, for wherever faith exists it cannot be sluggish. It is bound to break out spontaneously and immediately into prayer."[32]

---

29. Calvin, *Com.*, John 5:39.
30. Calvin, *Com.*, 1 John 5:13.
31. Calvin, *Institutes*, 3.20.1.
32. Wallace, *Christian Life*, 271.

Prayer is humble in essence, since it seeks help, yet when we pray scripturally, it is right for these prayers to be confident, even bold. "Let us then with confidence draw near to the throne of grace" (Heb 4:16). Wallace says this well. "When it is founded upon the Word of God in the way that has been described, prayer becomes characterized by true boldness."[33]

Prayer is indeed essential to all the disciplines of grace—self-denial, cross bearing, repentance—all of the life of the Christian is intimately tied to prayer, the heart of faith coming before the throne of God in submission and supplication and there finding grace to help in time of need. "The primary exercise which the children of God have is to pray; because here indeed is the true proof of our faith."[34]

Faith Grows in Knowledge, Trust, and Certainty

As we grow in faith through the Word, Sprit, and prayer, our faith grows in knowledge, trust, and certainty. We grow in knowledge as we grow in faith (Heb 11:6). We come to understand God, his ways, his promises, his character, and his work, seeing more and more clearly God for who he truly is. We grow in trust as well. Seeing his mercy, power, and love, we see that we are right to trust him with all things, ourselves first of all. We grow in confidence and assurance as well. "Faith grows in stability and clarity as it increasingly apprehends the exaltation of Christ."[35] As faith grows rising to meet each new challenge, we become more certain of the faithfulness of God to his Word of promise. So grows "the firmness of your faith in Christ" (Col 2:5). Things may look bad, faith reminds us—but they have looked bad before—and he proved himself true.

Our faith grows through the Word, the Spirit, and prayer and as it increases we gain more of Christ and become more holy through him. "So that Christ may dwell in your hearts through faith" (Eph 3:17). This is the ordinary process of the growth of faith. But how especially are we to struggle for faith during those times of trial?

---

33. Wallace, *Christian Life*, 279.
34. Calvin, *Ioannis Calvini Opera*, 53:125.
35. Wallace, *Christian Life*, 328.

How Do We Struggle for Faith?

Expect Life to Be a Struggle for Faith

We must recognize that, while we may have periods of peace, the struggle for faith is the normal life of the Christian. The Christian life is not lived aboard a cruise ship but rather a battle ship. If you are on a battle ship, but think you are on a cruise, you will be unpleasantly shocked when shells start to explode around you. We should be prepared for battle. "Beloved, do not be surprised at the fiery trial when it comes upon you to test you, as though something strange were happening to you" (1 Pet 4:12). This is the battle that will test and grow your faith. "Count it all joy, my brothers, when you meet trials of various kinds, for you know that the testing of your faith produces steadfastness" (Jas 1:2–3). When we expect to do battle against unbelief we are better armed to fight back with faith in God through his Word, Spirit, and prayer.

Struggle for Faith with the Word

We must delve into the Word of God as we struggle for faith. Especially we need to hear the preaching of the Word. "And how are they to believe in him of whom they have never heard? And how are they to hear without someone *preaching*?" (Rom 10:14, emphasis added). "And this is a remarkable passage with regard to the efficacy of preaching; for he testifies, that by it faith is produced."[36] One of the great tragedies of modern evangelicalism is that, precisely when a believer struggles most for faith, they often absent themselves from the preaching of the Word. It would be like an ill person avoiding the hospital, the very treatment they need to cure them. When you are engaged in the struggle for faith attend to the preaching of the Word with utter diligence.

Attend to personal study of the Word. The Lord speaks to us today, not through audible voices, but through his voice in the Word. "The word that evokes faith must be some one particular word in which God personally addresses us by name and speaks precisely to our situation."[37] It is wise to find particular passages of Scripture which address your struggle. Does the devil tempt you to doubt God's material provision? Fight back with Matt 6:31–33, which assures us that, "all these things will be added

---

36. Calvin, *Com.*, Rom 10:17.
37. Wallace, *Christian Life*, 213.

to you." Does the world tempt you to doubt God's sovereign power to direct all things for your good? Fight back with Rom 8:28, which reminds us that "all things work together for good." Does your own flesh tempt you to doubt God's love? Fight back with Lam 3:22–23, which proclaims: "The steadfast love of the LORD never ceases." For every attack of doubt, the Word of God holds an answer that will increase our faith.

Struggle for Faith by Walking in the Spirit

Seek to walk in the Spirit. While the Holy Spirit is always with us, during times when we struggle for faith against unbelief we need to listen to the Spirit who teaches us the truth about God against all the lies which bombard us. "When the Spirit of truth comes, he will guide you into all the truth" (John 16:13). We need his still small voice to apply the Word to our situation and lead us from error to find repose in the truth of God's Word.

Since it is uniquely the Holy Spirit's office to increase our faith, it only makes sense that as we struggle for faith we listen to him and follow his teaching. Remember that the nature of the battle for faith is between two worldviews, the view of the flesh is diametrically opposed to the view of the Spirit, so we need to listen to the Spirit far more than to our flesh. "But I say, walk by the Spirit, and you will not gratify the desires of the flesh. For the desires of the flesh are against the Spirit, and the desires of the Spirit are against the flesh, for these are opposed to each other" (Gal 5:16–17). Our flesh will lead us to despair, but the Spirit to hope and faith.

Struggle for Faith in Prayer

Be quick and constant in prayer. While the command to pray without ceasing always applies (1 Thess 5:17), during periods of great struggle for faith this is doubly true. Prayer as the unique exercise of faith is needed precisely to strengthen our faith. Having regular times of prayer during the day is a time-honored and wise practice. "It is good that . . . we observe particular and fixed hours for our secret devotions. Making such rules can save our prayer-life from dying out."[38]

The Reformers struggled mightily between faith and doubt, given the intense opposition of Roman Catholicism of the day. The devil could easily play on their hearts, so they rose as men of resolute prayer. Luther

---

38. Wallace, *Christian Life*, 294.

was devoted to prayer. "I have so much to do that I shall spend the first three hours in prayer."[39] Calvin prayed as though his life depended upon it, indeed, his longest chapter in the *Institutes* is the one on prayer. "Calvin began each day with prayer. He prayed a lot because he expected so much from it."[40] When we battle for faith we must do so with the great tool of faith: prayer. Taken together these disciplines of grace will help our faith grow and triumph as we struggle against unbelief.

Summary of How to Struggle for Faith

1. Recognize that a normal part of the Christian life is the struggle between faith and unbelief. When crises reveal "faith gaps" in your own heart, engage the struggle fully, using all the means of grace. Know that the devil will want to rub your face in your hard circumstances and be ready to counter with the truth of the Word.

2. Dive into the Word of God, listen regularly to biblical preaching, read and study the Word, memorize key verses which directly oppose the particular lies that you are hearing, seek the biblical encouragement of others.

3. Walk in the Spirit who is the Spirit of truth and who uniquely gives us faith. Listen to his voice which will always affirm the Word of God and the unseen promises of God over against the World.

4. Pray without ceasing. Since prayer is the unique exercise of faith, during times when you struggle for faith, exercise faith by praying all the more.

Further Resources

Study Questions

1. What is faith?
2. How does growth in faith help us grow in holiness?
3. What is the struggle for faith?

---

39. *Official Report*, 221.
40. Selderhuis, *Pilgrim's Life*, 161.

4. Why is the struggle for more faith a necessary part of the Christian life?

5. How can we best struggle for more faith?

6. What has been a recent struggle for faith in your life? What perspective do you gain from this chapter on your own recent struggle for faith?

For Further Study

Joel R. Beeke, "Does Assurance Belong to the Essence of Faith? Calvin and the Calvinists," *The Master's Seminary Journal* 5 (1994) 43–71.

A. N. S. Lane, "Calvin's Doctrine of Assurance," *Vox Evangelica* 11 (1979) 32–54.

Walter Marshall, *The Gospel Mystery of Sanctification* (Grand Rapids: Reformation Heritage, 1999).

Herman J. Selderhuis, "Faith Between God and the Devil: Calvin's Doctrine of Faith as Reflected in His Commentary on the Psalms," in *John Calvin and the Interpretation of Scripture*, edited by Charles Raynal, 188–205 (Grand Rapids: CRC, 2006).

8

Repent Regularly

As a young believer I struggled with pornography for years, as mentioned previously. In shame I had repeatedly vowed: "I am finished with it!" Only to return to it again. Unless you have experienced it, it is difficult to communicate the shame and hopeless defeat that occupies a Christian who feels trapped in sexual sin. Then, shortly after hearing a convicting sermon on hidden sin, I was asked by a new believer for encouragement in his own sexual purity. We were scheduled to meet the next day, and, not wanting to lie to him about my own hope for purity, I asked God—again—that I might be delivered.

Only this time I thought I heard the still small voice of the Spirit say distinctly, "No." "But wait a minute," I countered in prayer, "you have to help me when I ask." Again it seemed to me that the Spirit's response was something like, "Yes, I help the repentant, but you only want to manage your sin for today, so you can return to it later. That I will not do." I was cornered.

That night I looked back on my years of "repentance" and recognized in my heart an unwillingness to actually desire a future without pornography. Then I confessed to the Lord, "You are right, I do not really want to repent. Will you grant me the desire to actually repent, the desire to want to be free from this sin?" He did, and my life was changed from that moment. Not that I never struggle, but the struggle is regularly one of victory over sin, not defeat by it.

I have counseled many struggling with sin, who have half-heartedly "repented." I typically ask: "Do you really want to be free from your sin? Or do you actually only want to manage it because you cannot imagine your life without it?" Many of them have come to know the freedom of real repentance. I have from this adopted a simple maxim: *It never gets better until you really repent.*

What is repentance? It is well defined by *Westminster Shorter Catechism* answer 87:

> Repentance unto life is a saving grace, whereby a sinner, out of a true sense of his sin, and apprehension of the mercy of God in Christ, doth, with grief and hatred of his sin, turn from it unto God, with full purpose of, and endeavor after, new obedience.[1]

We will explain repentance at length in the following section, but for now let us notice that repentance is at its heart a turning from sin to God, a relational return to God. In fact, in the Old Testament, the primary term used for repentance is simply "turn" or "return," both one Hebrew word, *shub* (שׁוּב). God's people sin by turning away from him—breaking relationship—most often turning toward other gods, which are only idols. "They have turned back to the iniquities of their forefathers, who refused to hear my words. They have gone after other gods to serve them" (Jer 11:10). To be restored in relationship then requires a relational change, a turn away from whatever sin has lured us, back to the Lord. "Return to me, and I will return to you, says the LORD of hosts" (Mal 3:7). Calvin uses the concept of turning in his definition of repentance. "It is the true turning of our life to God."[2]

Now we will expand on the meaning of repentance, then we will explore precisely how repentance helps us grow in holiness, and then finally, explain the way to practice repentance in order to become more like Christ.

What Is Repentance?

Repentance Is a Work of God's Grace

We are sometimes confused by the command to repent: "Repent, for the kingdom of heaven is at hand" (Matt 4:17). Since it is a command, many wrongly assume that we have the ability, in ourselves, to obey the command. However, the commands of God are not given in order to indicate our ability, but rather our duty. In order to fulfill this duty God means for

---

1. *Westminster Confession of Faith*, 395; *Westminster Shorter Catechism*, answer 87.
2. Calvin, *Institutes*, 3.3.5.

us to turn to him, to "the aid of his grace,"³ to enable us to obey. We are commanded to repent, but since repentance is a gift of God, and "men cannot turn except God turns them,"⁴ we are to seek the gift from the Giver, who readily grants it.

Indeed, our very *inability* to repent is meant to humble us so that we will more readily turn to God for help, asking that he grant the very repentance he requires. "Having made trial of our own strength and having been convinced of our weakness . . . [we are] compelled to say to God: give what you command, and command which you will."⁵

Scripture is clear that repentance is a work of God. "God may perhaps grant them repentance leading to a knowledge of the truth" (2 Tim 2:25). Here, "grant" is simply the common word for "give." This is the word used in Acts as well: "Then to the Gentiles also God has granted repentance that leads to life" (Acts 11:18). "To give repentance to Israel" (Acts 5:31). Calvin underscores this point: "It is the peculiar work of God when a sinner repents . . . it cannot be ascribed to human powers, as though men could of themselves turn to the right way."⁶

God grants repentance, and it is particularly the work of the Holy Spirit to bring it about in us. "When [the Spirit] comes, he will convict the world concerning sin and righteousness and judgment" (John 16:8). We cannot produce conviction of sin, brokenness of will, and a heart soft to God, but the Holy Spirit can as he moves within us. "When men really repent, they do so through the special influence of the Spirit."⁷

Although repentance is ultimately produced by God in us, we are responsible to pursue it. "Now he commands all people everywhere to repent" (Acts 17:30). We are to turn to the Lord, striving for repentance, seeking from him the very repentance he requires.⁸ We seek repentance from God knowing that he is eager to bring us to repentance, for there we return to him in relational holiness. "If my people who are called by my name humble themselves, and pray and seek my face and turn from their wicked ways, then I will hear from heaven and will forgive their sin and heal their land" (2 Chr 7:14). In the midst of God granting us repentance

---

3. Calvin, *Com.*, Rom 15:13.
4. Calvin, *Com.*, Jer 31:19.
5. Calvin, *Bondage and Liberation*, 168.
6. Calvin, *Com.*, Jer 31:19.
7. Calvin, *Com.*, Hos 2:7.
8. Calvin, *Institutes*, 3.3.20.

we are to be continually active: humbling ourselves before him, agreeing with the conviction of sin, confessing, and seeking his grace. "With genuine repentance, [we ought to] bow our heads, confess our sin, and implore God's forgiveness."⁹

Repentance Requires Faith

To repent we must have faith that we will find "the mercy of God in Christ." Did we not believe in God's mercy, we would be unwilling to repent, for repentance is an admission of guilt which would only lead to further condemnation, were God merely a judge and not our Redeemer. However, believing in God's mercy, we are willing to lay down in confession before him. "When we refer the origin of repentance to faith . . . we mean to show that a man cannot apply himself seriously to repentance without knowing himself to belong to God [by] God's grace."¹⁰

The faith which leads to repentance always has a keen eye upon God's mercy. "Evangelical repentance . . . is always accompanied by a certain knowledge of the grace and the mercy of God."¹¹ We most effectively call others, and ourselves, to repentance by focusing upon the mercy of God in Christ. "The foundation of repentance is the mercy of God."¹² It is the very kindness of God—his mercy and love—which lead us to repentance. "God's kindness is meant to lead you to repentance" (Rom 2:4).

We have faith in God's mercy, but another part of the faith that produces repentance is faith in God's judgment upon sin, that is, the fear of the Lord. "The fear of the LORD is a fountain of life, that one may turn away from the snares of death" (Prov 14:27). Therefore it is right to connect fear and repentance. "Repentance proceeds from an earnest fear of God."¹³ While God's mercy is our primary motive for repentance, this godly fear supports it, as well. This fear is faith—faith in God's hatred of sin, faith in his eventual destruction of all sin and all unrepentant sinners—and this faith-filled fear leads us away from sin toward God.

However, not all fear of God's judgment leads to repentance. The fear of unbelief only anticipates God's wrath, not his mercy, and therefore

---

9. Calvin, *Sermons on Micah*, 11.
10. Calvin, *Institutes*, 3.3.2.
11. Kraan, "Le Péché et la Repentance," 41.
12. Calvin, *Com.*, Matt 3:2.
13. Calvin, *Institutes*, 3.3.7.

leads one to flee from the presence of the Lord, "tormented by a sense of their own punishment,"[14] rather than to seek his clemency. Here is the worldly sorrow that may be mistaken for repentance, but only leads to death. "Worldly grief produces death" (2 Cor 7:10). This kind of fear-only induced repentance is a repentance of the Law, which seeks in the short-term to avoid the punishment of God, but does not earnestly seek to renew relationship with him. "Through [repentance of the law] the sinner, wounded by the branding of sin and stricken by dread of God's wrath, remains caught in that disturbed state and cannot extricate himself from it."[15]

The right fear of the Lord, however, is ultimately meant to lead us to the mercy of God. "We are to examine our whole life, and . . . being influenced by the fear of God, we are to return to him."[16] The faith which leads to repentance affirms the reality of our sin and its penalty, but above all it believes in the limitless mercy of God. This kind of faith leads us to godly sorrow and to life. "For godly grief produces a repentance that leads to salvation without regret" (2 Cor 7:10).

Repentance Requires the Twofold Knowledge of God and Ourselves

In order to repent we must have knowledge of God and ourselves. Concerning ourselves we must be aware of our sin, for if we are oblivious to our sin, we feel little need to repent. But when we become aware of our sin, as Scripture is held before us by the Spirit, we are inclined toward repentance. "Because the beginning of repentance is a preparation unto faith. I call the displeasing of ourselves the beginning . . . [of seeking] some remedy."[17]

Concerning God we must know his character, that he is holy so judges sin, and yet he is merciful to the repentant. Believing that we are sinful and that God is holy yet merciful, leads us to the inescapable conclusion that we must repent in order to find God's mercy. The knowledge of God and ourselves supplies the "true sense of his sin, and apprehension of the mercy of God in Christ" upon which true repentance is based.

---

14. Calvin, *Com.*, Heb 12:17.
15. Calvin, *Institutes*, 3.3.4.
16. Calvin, *Com.*, Lam 3:40.
17. Calvin, *Com.*, Acts 20:21.

Repentance Requires an Emotional Response from the Heart: Grief and Hatred of Our Sin

True repentance, while it leads to external actions, is not primarily about external actions, but about the movement of the heart. "'Yet even now,' declares the LORD, 'return to me with all your heart'" (Joel 2:12–13). True repentance is the inward turning of the heart away from sin toward God.[18]

Many in church history have misconstrued repentance to be the performance of certain outward rites that in themselves expunge guilt, satiate God's justice, and merit mercy. While we must repent to find grace, we must not think that our repentance in any way merits grace. "Repentance is a response to God's grace and judgment, but never a means of obtaining grace."[19] We may sit down to eat a meal. The sitting puts us in a posture to eat but does not earn the meal. In a similar way our repentance puts us in the posture to receive grace, but never merits it, for repentance is a gift from God (2 Tim 2:25).

The inward heart attitude will be marked by grief and hatred of *our sin*. We will not hate the one who confronts our sin, nor the church which holds us accountable for our sin. Rather, our enmity will be for our sin, and to some measure, ourselves for committing the sin which harms others.[20] Although many in our age wish to outlaw all sense of shame, biblical repentance resounds with a proper sense of shame for the damage caused by our sin. "Wake up from your drunken stupor, as is right, and do not go on sinning. . . . I say this to your shame" (1 Cor 15:34). Calvin concurs: "This then is the fruit of penitence, this is true humility, flowing from genuine shame."[21]

The truly repentant person owns up to their sin and the humiliation that it brings upon them. "The sinner has not been won back until he has been moved and brought to the point of saying: 'I have sinned, I desire grace, I want to reform,' and is really struck down and humiliated because of his sin."[22]

David demonstrated this heartfelt grief and hatred over his sin as he acknowledged that it deserved God's punishment. "Against you, you

---

18. Calvin, *Com.*, Jer 4:14.
19. Wallace, *Christian Life*, 99.
20. Calvin, *Sermons on 2 Samuel*, 555.
21. Calvin, *Com.*, Ezek 20:43.
22. Bucer, *True Care of Souls*, 102.

only, have I sinned and done what is evil in your sight, so that you may be justified in your words and blameless in your judgment" (Ps 51:4). David rightly understood that it was not the external rituals which God desired from his repentance, but a heart sick over its sin and ready to run to God. "For you will not delight in sacrifice, or I would give it; you will not be pleased with a burnt offering. The sacrifices of God are a broken spirit; a broken and contrite heart, O God, you will not despise" (Ps 51:16–17).

While the repentant grieve over their sin, this is not done as self-flagellation, in an effort to punish oneself in order to atone for sins. Gospel repentance seeks mercy from God, not the appeasement of God by self-punishment.[23] Self-flagellation leaves one doubting that repentance could ever be deep enough and leads to "truly miserable consciences,"[24] while gospel repentance assures us that we are restored entirely.

True repentance will however always show itself in outward fruit, so that a lack of such fruit is one indicator that repentance has not occurred. "Bear fruit in keeping with repentance" (Matt 3:8). Repentance begins in the heart but moves outward from it to action. When a person is truly repentant we can expect to see great transformations in their behavior. They gladly yield to church discipline. They frankly accuse themselves for their sin rather than blaming others. They readily offer restitution. They patiently endure whatever lack of trust their sin has earned them, rather than demanding that they be restored immediately. They weep readily over their sin and the damage it has done. "We can simply say that [with true repentance] . . . there will always be this lamenting, weeping, praying, pleading, confessing and repenting."[25]

But outward actions by themselves are neither the cause of, nor necessarily the result of, real repentance. One may easily fake repentance, mouthing the right words, even shedding false tears. There may even be some minor amendment of life, but without the change of heart, no true repentance has taken place. Such superficial repentance contrasts sharply with "gospel repentance" from the heart. "We see 'gospel repentance' in all those who, made sore by the sting of sin but aroused and refreshed by trust in God's mercy, have turned to the Lord."[26] Outward works are merely fruits of repentance, not the root of repentance, and of no value

23. Calvin, *Com.*, 2 Cor 7:11.
24. Calvin, *Institutes*, 3.4.2.
25. Bucer, *True Care of Souls*, 119–20.
26. Calvin, *Institutes*, 3.3.4.

without the root.[27] From the hatred and grief over our sin, to the earnest desire to seek the Lord, we have seen that true repentance is a matter of the heart that eventually manifests itself in outward actions which align with the new heart.

Repentance Is Action, It Is Turning "Turn from [Sin] Unto God"

The essential activity of repentance is turning, turning from sin to God, with our hearts, minds, and often, with our bodies. "Repent"—and its Old Testament equivalent, "return," is one of God's most persistent commands. "Return, O faithless children, declares the LORD" (Jer 3:14). John the Baptist preached it. "Repent, for the kingdom of heaven is at hand" (Matt 3:2). Jesus preached it. "Repent, for the kingdom of heaven is at hand" (Matt 4:17). Peter preached it. "Repent therefore, and turn back, that your sins may be blotted out" (Acts 3:19). When we are sinning there is only one right action—turning.

This turning is not a motion we undertake by ourselves. As we have already mentioned, we are told what to do—repent—but this does not imply our independent ability to repent. Rather, it shows us our responsibility to turn, which leads us always back to God to supply the powerful grace required for repentance. "God may perhaps grant them repentance" (2 Tim 2:25). To turn from sin to God, we begin by asking God for the grace to repent.

The request for God to grant us repentance begins with the confession of sin, for we cannot seek the grace to repent if we do not acknowledge our sin before him. "If we confess our sins, he is faithful and just to forgive us our sins and to cleanse us from all unrighteousness" (1 John 1:9). This confession is to be serious, a deep rending of our hearts before God, who is displeased with our sin. The initial turn from sin to God is strengthened by him as we are given grace and enabled to see the greater offense of our sin and our greater need for forgiveness.

Our confession is first to God but may involve confessing to others, where others are wronged by our sin: "confess your sins to one another" (Jas 5:16). "Therefore, a willing confession among men follows that secret confession which is made to God."[28]

---

27. Calvin, *Com.*, Jer 7:5.
28. Calvin, *Institutes*, 3.4.10.

The confession itself is the start of our turn from sin. When we admit that our action, thought, or word is sinful, we demarcate it as lawbreaking and seek to move away from it by confessing it. The proper confession is simple and direct, "I have sinned," never, "mistakes were made," which seeks to obscure our fault. David confessed well, when he sinned by numbering the people, rather than trusting the Lord. "I have sinned greatly in what I have done" (2 Sam 24:10).

Repentance requires, where possible, our physically turning away from sin. The story is told that when Norman Vincent Peale was a boy he found and began smoking a cigar. Surprised by his father, he hid the cigar behind his back and tried to divert his father by pointing to a billboard for a circus, asking his father to take him. His father replied, "Son, never make a petition while at the same time trying to hide a smoldering disobedience." We are not actually repenting from sin if we are at the same time making plans to continue in sin. "If my people . . . *turn from their wicked ways*, then I will . . . forgive their sin" (2 Chr 7:14, emphasis added).

Repentance is a move downward, as we humble ourselves before God in confession. "Let us fall down before the majesty of our good God, in acknowledging our faults."[29] We must humbly prostrate ourselves, as a defeated canine will lie down with its neck bared to its enemy, as a sign of submission. David prostrated himself humbly, admitting that God would be just to condemn his sin. "Against you, you only, have I sinned and done what is evil in your sight, so that you may be justified in your words and blameless in your judgment" (Ps 51:4). This is the motion which restores the natural order, where we are rightly humbled before God, and God is exalted before us.

Repentance contains an upward motion as well. We anticipate God's mercy in Christ so our hearts move upward in thanks toward God. David moves from the prostration of confession to the upward motion which glories in God's transforming grace. "Deliver me from bloodguiltiness, O God, O God of my salvation, and my tongue will sing aloud of your righteousness" (Ps 51:14–15).

Repentance combines this twofold motion: downward in prostration before God—confessing sin—and upward in exaltation of God—thanking him for mercy. Repentance is never just one without the other. Were we to only prostrate ourselves we would be like those who flagellate themselves hoping to repay God. Were we only to thank God, we would

---

29. Calvin, *Sermons on Election and Reprobation*, 47.

be like the self-congratulating Pharisee of Jesus' parable (Luke 18:11). Only when our turn involves both the downward and upward movements are we truly repenting. "When a man is laid low by the consciousness of sin . . . and afterward looks to the goodness of God . . . he returns from death to life."[30] David shows both motions of grace—prostration and exaltation—when he proclaims, "O LORD, be gracious to me; heal me, for I have sinned against you!" (Ps 41:4).

Repentance calls for action, for turning. It begins with humble confession but it leads to heartfelt rejoicing in the Lord, as our turning to him, by his grace, is met with his wholehearted embrace, and he lifts us up. "To abase ourselves so that we may be lifted up by him."[31]

Repentance Is New Obedience, "Full Purpose Of, and Endeavor After, New Obedience"

Although repentance must begin in the heart, it always leads to external changes. It is never enough in repentance to simply say, "I am sorry." The admission of sin must be accompanied by a change of life as well. The Apostle Paul applauded the fruit of repentance displayed in the Corinthians. "For see what earnestness this godly grief has produced in you, but also what eagerness to clear yourselves, what indignation, what fear, what longing, what zeal, what punishment!" (2 Cor 7:11).

One may easily enough profess repentance without being truly penitent. "Repentance, which is attested by words, is of no value, unless it be proved by the conduct."[32] Many a "caught sinner" has deceived the church by apologizing with no other sign of repentance. "It is not enough reason to loose anyone completely from his sins and admit him to the holy supper, that following the commission of grosser transgressions he has said: 'I am sorry, I won't do it anymore,' . . . if he shows no other signs of true repentance."[33] The true turning from sin changes behavior, as Edwards noted. "All true and saving repentance tends to holy practice."[34]

True repentance includes our desires and plans to walk in obedience to the Lord. "They should repent and turn to God, performing deeds in

---

30. Calvin, *Institutes*, 3.3.3.
31. Calvin, *Institutes*, 4.17.42.
32. Calvin, *Com.*, Matt 3:8.
33. Bucer, *True Care of Souls*, 160–61.
34. Edwards, *Charity and its Fruits*, 237.

keeping with their repentance" (Acts 26:20). We lay firm plans: to stop slandering but rather to bless, to stop stealing but rather to earn a living, to stop lying but rather to speak the truth. A lack of changed behavior is ample proof that the repentance professed was false. "Works are the only testimonies to real repentance."[35]

There is, along with the new behavior, a new attitude present in the repentant person—one of notable humility and softness. Rather than blaming others, or expressing anger for being caught in sin, the repentant person accepts responsibility and the consequences of their actions. "He that once was of a proud heart, and under the dominion of pride in his conduct, if afterward he has his heart changed to a humble heart, will necessarily have a corresponding change in his behavior. He will no longer appear in his demeanor as proud, and scornful, and ambitious as once he was."[36]

The repentant person shows this humility with their willingness to accept discipline from church authority. Whereas the unrepentant bristles at any effort by the church to restrain their sin, the repentant yields gladly. "[The truly repentant] will also with great humility and eagerness of spirit subject himself to the church's discipline . . . and make amends to those whom he has injured through his sin."[37] The repentant heart, changed by grace, will always yield gracious fruit.

Now that we have expounded the definition of repentance we will demonstrate how it contributes to our sanctification.

How Does Repentance Help Us to Grow in Holiness?

Repentance Humbles Us before God Where He Extends Grace Which Transforms Us

Humanity must be humbled before God in repentance. There is a spiritual dynamic inherent in God's plan of redemption: "God opposes the proud but gives grace to the humble" (1 Pet 5:5). In the fall humanity vaunted itself before God, exchanging its natural humility for pride. However, since only God is rightly exalted, he must oppose the proud until they are humbled before him. Only then will he extend them grace.

---

35. Calvin, *Com.*, Dan 4:27.
36. Edwards, *Charity and its Fruits*, 238.
37. Bucer, *True Care of Souls*, 161.

For sanctification to move forward, we must be humbled before God by repenting of our sin. If we do not, God will actively oppose our pride. God has two hands, says Calvin, the one is like a hammer with which to strike down the proud and the other is open to lift up the humble.[38] God will use his Law in part as the hammer to knock down our pride, showing us our sin and our need to repent. "The law was given to accuse you; that accused you might fear; that fearing you might beg forgiveness."[39]

Brought low in repentance we find the grace of God to help us. When in repentance we humble ourselves before God, God delights to help. "Humble yourselves before the Lord, and he will exalt you" (Jas 4:10). Our humble repentance before God, enabled as always by his own grace, invites mercy from his hand. There at the bottom, prostrate and looking up to God, we are finally where God wants us, where we should be, and God delights in helping those who seek his grace. "But you are a God ready to forgive, gracious and merciful" (Neh 9:17).

Calvin will quote Augustine with approval on the necessity of this humility before God. "If you ask me concerning the precepts of the Christian religion, first, second, third, and always I would answer, 'Humility.'"[40] While the proud mountains remain dry, in the low place, in the valley of repentance, God's grace abounds. "Let that man, therefore, become a valley, who is desirous to receive the heavenly rain of God's spiritual grace."[41] Every time we humbly flee to the mercy of God, we find him merciful. "[May we] be touched with real and deep sorrow, and thus learn to flee, not only once in our life, but every moment, to thy mercy."[42]

Receiving God's grace for the lowly we are transformed by this grace. We are transformed as we receive God's grace. We are made more humble and thankful as we experience his mercy upon us in our sinfulness. The entire repentance-forgiveness-restoration cycle also increases our faith as we see God's grace at work. "Humility is the best preparation for faith."[43] Our faith grows, and as it grows our union with Christ is more firmly established such that the holy life of Christ grows in us. "Whoever abides

---

38. Calvin, *Com.*, 1 Pet 5:5.
39. Calvin, *Institutes*, 2.7.9.
40. Calvin, *Institutes*, 2.2.11.
41. Calvin, *Com.*, 2 Cor 12:9.
42. Calvin, *Com.*, Jer 14:20.
43. Calvin, *Com.*, Jer 16:21.

in me and I in him, he it is that bears much fruit, for apart from me you can do nothing" (John 15:5).

The grace of God continues the work of reshaping us by purging our hearts from the sin he has forgiven. "If we confess our sins, he is faithful and just to forgive us our sins and to cleanse us from all unrighteousness" (1 John 1:9). This process moves onward in life with each fresh repentance. "God wipes out in his elect the corruptions of the flesh . . . that they may practice repentance throughout their lives."[44]

The repentant heart is shaped by the grace of God such that we more and more *want to* obey God's Word. "We are indeed sanctified . . . with our hearts formed to obedience to the law."[45] The ultimate fruit of repentance is a heart made whole for God, purified by him, desiring to serve him in holiness. As grace leads us to greater obedience we are blessed by God for our obedience of faith with an even closer relationship with him, which is holiness.

So we see how God uses repentance to increase our holiness: humbled before him in confession of sin, we prostrate ourselves and seek his grace, seeking his grace from the humility of repentance we find it, and are transformed by grace more and more into those who love and serve God from a pure heart.

Indeed, repentance—along with faith and the obedience of faith—comprises the central dynamic of our sanctification. The practices of cross bearing, self-denial, and meditation on the future life all contain elements of repentance. "Therefore, the doctrine of repentance contains a rule of good life; it requires the denial of ourselves, the mortifying of our flesh, and meditating upon the heavenly life."[46] For example, to bear the cross well we must repent of our resentment that God has brought suffering into our lives. The other disciplines of grace also require our repentance. Submitting to the Word of God requires us to repent of our own wisdom. Engaging the church requires us to repent of our independence. Seeking the twofold knowledge of God and self requires us to repent of self-flattery. Repentance is woven throughout the entire sanctification process, so it is important to understand it, and to practice it well. We will now turn to the right practice of repentance.

---

44. Calvin, *Institutes*, 3.3.9.
45. Calvin, *Institutes*, 3.14.9.
46. Calvin, *Com.*, Acts 20:21.

How Do We Practice Repentance to Grow in Holiness?

Recognize that it is always really hard to repent. We should not think that repentance will ever be easy. I was disappointed, naively expecting repentance to become easy, like a tennis swing well practiced, until I read these words from J. I. Packer.

> In speaking of habitual repentance, I do not mean to imply that repentance can ever become automatic and mechanical, as our table manners and our driving habits are. It cannot. Every act of repentance is a separate act and a distinct moral effort, perhaps a major and costly one. Repenting is never a pleasure. Always, in more senses than one, it is a pain, and will continue so as long as life lasts.[47]

Repentance never becomes easy for us because it is always a death of the old nature. We are always giving up the sin we want. We are perpetually like the child who must give up his toy. This usually means a fight with our screaming, spoiled flesh which clings to sin. For example, every time I have a disagreement with my wife and realize I need to repent, my consistent first response is to ask myself: "Is there some way other than repenting? Is there some way that we can make this about her sin instead of mine?"

I never want to repent, and I suspect I am not alone. This is critical to understand about yourself, you will not want to repent—ever—no matter how needed. You must seek the grace of God to make you willing to repent. Do not expect repentance to ever come naturally or easily, it is a spiritual wrestling match every time.

Understand: It never gets better until you really repent! This is a maxim for me and I suggest it become one for you. When we have sinned there is one direction in which we can go to find help: Repent. All other directions are dead-ends that will fail. All the other strategies we try—blaming others, arguing, excusing, anger, withdrawal—will all fail. "There are many who will attempt to lessen their offenses in this way, and say: 'Now look, we are all sinners.' . . . They think that they ought to be absolved. This is nothing but thoroughly wicked impudence."[48] Don't try

---

47. Packer, *Rediscovering Holiness*, 111–12.
48. Calvin, *Sermons on 2 Samuel*, 560.

other strategies. It never gets better until you really repent. *You* never get better until you repent.

Repent frequently not occasionally. There are some who mistakenly think that repentance should only be an occasional practice, reserved for the really serious sins, like David's with Bathsheba. This is not the case. When Martin Luther wrote the *Ninety-Five Theses*, he began by showing how to find God's grace. His very first thesis said: "When our Lord and Master Jesus Christ said, 'Repent,' he willed the entire life of believers to be one of repentance."[49] The entire life of believers! Every day, multiple times a day, we are called to repent. Packer agrees. "Christians are called to a life of habitual repentance, as a discipline integral to healthy holy living."[50]

Since it never gets better until we really repent and we *do* sin daily we must learn to practice daily repentance. While major sins may require the formal kinds of repentance which happen through church discipline, daily sins need daily repentance.[51] Following the model of the Lord's Prayer we should practice repentance daily, praying, "forgive us our debts." We should expect to repent daily, searching for the opportunity to return to the Lord and find refreshment.

Repent hopefully, not fearfully. While repentance is always difficult at first—for it is humbling, even humiliating—it leads to the joy of experiencing the mercy of God in Christ. King David knew that repentance was the only path to joy in the Lord. "Let me hear joy and gladness; let the bones that you have broken rejoice" (Ps 51:8). To help us overcome our reticence to repent, we should keep this in mind: repentance is ultimately the path, not only to holiness, but to joy. "Restore to me the joy of your salvation" (Ps 51:12).

Self-examine every day for sin, using Scripture. The practice of daily self-examination is a healthy one. As a regular part of our daily devotions we should allow the text that we are reading to convict us of sin and lead us to repentance. When we discover one sin, we can use it to detect others, as pulling at one vine often leads to others in the garden.[52] This self-examination, *descensus in se* (descent into the self) in Calvin's terms, must be a brutally honest evaluation that avoids the deception of self-flattery.

---

49. Luther, "Power and Efficacy of Indulgences," 31:25.
50. Packer, *Rediscovering Holiness*, 111.
51. Bucer, *True Care of Souls*, 121.
52. Calvin, *Com.*, Ps 51:6.

> If then, we wish to be healed of our vices, let us ever begin in this way—let us carefully examine our thoughts and our motives, and not please ourselves nor deceive ourselves by empty flatteries, but strive to shake off whatever is reprehensible and vicious. The very beginning of true repentance is to renounce all deceptions.[53]

We generally overlook most of the sins we commit. But Scripture reveals them, since it is useful "for teaching, for reproof, for correction, and for training in righteousness" (2 Tim 3:16). To allow it to correct us we need to read it, discern what it says to us, and then inquire: "How does this passage expose my sin?"

For example, when the passage says, "do not be anxious about anything" (Phil 4:6), we can candidly search our hearts for those things which cause us anxiety. Recognizing the items over which we are anxious—perhaps a health challenge we may face—we can go to the Lord and repent, praying something like this: "Father, rather than trusting you to care for me, I am worried, doubting your goodness or your power to superintend my health. Forgive me for my anxiety Lord, help to trust your love and your power."

This should become our daily practice, allowing the Scripture to lead us to repentance. It can also be helpful to think through the prior day—your thoughts, words, and deeds—examining where you sinned against others. When you discover these, make your repentance to God, and where appropriate, include confession of sin to those you wronged. We must learn to detect and repent of sins, rather than overlook them. "What is first necessary for repentance is, that the sinner should call himself to an account; for as long as we rest secure in our sins, it is impossible for us to repent. It is hence necessary that everyone should examine himself, so as to call himself to an account, and in a manner to summon himself before God's tribunal."[54]

Heed the church as it calls us to repentance. We should carefully heed the preaching of the Word where it calls us to repent. We should, therefore, be members in a church whose preaching regularly calls us to repentance. "This sermon must continually sound in the Church, repent."[55]

---

53. Calvin, *Com.*, Jer 8:4–5.
54. Calvin, *Com.*, Jer 8:6.
55. Calvin, *Com.*, Acts 2:38.

We must hear not only of our sin, but even more so, the sermon must speak of the glorious grace of Christ awaiting the repentant.

The faithful pastor will, however, take aim at the sin in his congregation for God's sake. "This is what we must . . . always hear from Christ's ministers: Repent, for the kingdom of God is near."[56] We, therefore, should go to worship prepared to repent, rather than resisting the conviction of sin which the preached Word brings us. "Every time we come to the sermon, let us keep before our eyes the fact that God is making his case to demand his right."[57]

In addition to the sermon, corporate confession of sin may help our repentance. The Lord's Prayer again is our model, for it says, "Forgive *us our* debts," not "Forgive *me my* debts," for it is intended to lead the church into confession. We should not approach corporate confession of sin as an empty ritual, but allow the words of the confession to touch our hearts and lead us to repent for the sins enumerated in it. This applies as well to the pastoral prayers which may helpfully call us to repentance. Additionally, the sacrament of the Lord's Supper summons us to search our hearts and come to the table, not excusing any sins we find, but repenting of them, for our restoration. "Let a person examine himself, then, and so eat of the bread and drink of the cup" (1 Cor 11:28).

The church also helps us repent through church discipline. It is the duty of church leadership to examine our lives for sin and to call us to repent wherever that is found. "For what have I to do with judging outsiders? Is it not those inside the church whom you are to judge?" (1 Cor 5:12). It is our duty to listen to the judgment of the church and allow it to lead us to repentance, not to defend ourselves or run to another church in anger. "And if he refuses to listen even to the church, let him be to you as a Gentile and a tax collector" (Matt 18:17).

Too often, the response to confrontation is a proud assertion of innocence, as was the case in Calvin's day. "Every day in the course of the examination . . . most people say, 'I am innocent.'"[58] Rather than running from such accountability in the church we should welcome it, for we are blinded by our own sin such that God uses the church to force open our eyes. "Let us seek to have our vices actually pointed out and preferred to

---

56. Bucer, *True Care of Souls*, 210.
57. Calvin, *Sermons on Genesis*, 547.
58. Calvin, *Sermons on Genesis*, 580.

be pricked in the very place where, because of our wicked lusts, we only ask to be flattered."[59]

Accountability for our sin may lead to formal church discipline but it should begin with informal accountability as we call one another to repentance. "If your brother sins against you, go and tell him his fault, between you and him alone" (Matt 18:15). We should confront others in sin, speaking the truth in love. So too, when we are confronted by others about our sin, we should yield to those who admonish us. "Brothers, if anyone is caught in any transgression, you who are spiritual should restore him in a spirit of gentleness" (Gal 6:1).

The healthy church will find members gently and lovingly admonishing one another, and also welcoming such admonishment when it comes. "One should point out and reveal the sin to the sinner in such a way that he is convinced of sin and overwhelmed by it, and thus be brought back through true repentance."[60] Our churches are vital tools in helping us find the grace of repentance.

Repent deeply not superficially. We should practice repentance that is thorough, not superficial. We must feel the "grief and hatred" of it that are necessary for our hearts to move away from sin and toward God. To help us feel this hatred for our sin, we need to turn to the Spirit and the Word, to convince, convict, and lead us to deep repentance.

We must come to God confessing our sins. "Since it is the Lord who forgives, forgets, and wipes out sins, let us confess our sins to him in order to obtain pardon."[61] Christ invites the burdened sinner to come to him for refreshment. "Come to me, all who labor and are heavy laden, and I will give you rest" (Matt 11:28). We should actually go to Jesus in Word, prayer, and Spirit, and ask him to lift the burden of our sin through his forgiveness and cleansing.

When our sins have hurt others, repentance should include confessing to them, apologizing, and making restitution, if needed. Our level of willingness to confess to others and provide restitution is a real measure of the depth of our repentance. The person who is merely sorry will hesitate to be so humiliated, the deeply repentant will not care for their reputation. "We fight to seem honorable at all times, to keep our reputation unblemished and unembarrassed before men. . . . Therefore . . . that

---

59. Calvin, *Sermons on 2 Samuel*, 521.
60. Bucer, *True Care of Souls*, 101–2.
61. Calvin, *Institutes*, 3.4.9.

we will be brought low, which is what God requires ... let us learn to bear our shame before all the world, since we have merited it."[62]

We may also want to confess to accountability partners. "Confess your sins to one another and pray for one another, that you may be healed" (Jas 5:16). This can be very helpful in fighting sin. I have been part of a prayer-triad for over twenty-five years. It is marvelously healing to have our sins, even those that may be deemed private, known to others. This is because one of the devil's basic tricks is to isolate and corner us with our sin, convincing us that, were others to know our sins, they would despise us. However, when others, after admonishing our sin, accept and love us, it is powerfully helpful in breaking the spell of secret sin in our lives. "Therefore, a willing confession among men follows that secret confession which is made to God, as often as either divine glory or our humiliation demands it."[63]

Turning to God means that we turn away from sin toward new obedience. We should lay firm plans to aid our new obedience. For example, the one struggling with gluttony may need to be rid of certain foods in their home. The one struggling with pornography may need to cancel cable and install internet monitors. While these examples may sound trifling, they are real efforts at new obedience, inherent to true repentance. Overall this point is fairly simple: do not think that saying you are sorry is the end of repentance, rather it is just the beginning.

We must repent deeply and thoroughly. For the truly repentant finds grace and new holiness of life with God.

Further Resources

Study Questions

1. How would you distinguish a truly repentant person from one who is merely trying to manage their sin? What characteristics would you look for in each case?
2. Why do you think that repentance must be first a work of God's grace?
3. What faith do we need to repent, what must we believe before we will repent?

---

62. Calvin, *Sermons on 2 Samuel*, 492.
63. Calvin, *Institutes*, 3.4.10.

4. How does knowing God and ourselves better contribute to our repentance?
5. Why is grief and hatred of sin important to our repentance?
6. In repentance, what do we turn from and what do we turn toward?
7. What role does new obedience play in our repentance?
8. How does repentance help us to grow in holiness? What is the essential dynamic that occurs in repentance before God?
9. How difficult is it for you to repent, generally speaking? How frequently do you repent? Where now do you need to repent?
10. What practical steps could you take to add more repentance to your daily life? Is there someone who is, or could be, an accountability partner for you?

For Further Study

Sinclair Ferguson, *The Grace of Repentance* (Wheaton, IL: Crossway, 2010).

J. I. Packer, *Rediscovering Holiness: Know the Fullness of Life with God* (Grand Rapids: Baker, 2009). Particularly chapter 5 on repentance.

R. C. Sproul, *What is Repentance?* (Sanford, FL: Reformation, 2014).

Thomas Watson, *The Doctrine of Repentance* (Carlisle, PA: Banner of Truth, 1988).

9

Deny Yourself

What Is Self-Denial?

JOHN CALVIN WAS EXPELLED from Geneva in 1538, a painful personal failure. In 1541 he was invited back by the same city council which had driven him away. The last thing he wanted to do was to return to the city where his prior three-year tenure had been torn by rancor and ended with deep humiliation. However, Calvin's guiding star was not his own will, but the Lord's.

He wrote to his friend William Farel, who had encouraged him to return to Geneva. "Had I the choice at my own disposal, nothing would be less agreeable to me than to follow your advice. But when I remember that I am not my own, I offer up my heart, presented as a sacrifice to the Lord. . . . Therefore I submit my will and affections, subdued and held fast, to the obedience of God."[1] This was perhaps the single greatest example of self-denial in the storied life of Calvin, one that led to his greatest triumphs for the Lord. Yet, it all began here with a simple act of self-denial.

Self-denial is denying our own will while embracing the will of God, as revealed in the Bible and providence. To advance in holiness one must constantly look for opportunities to deny oneself and embrace God's will. Doing this is the daily practice of faith and repentance which embraces more grace. "We are not our own: let us therefore not set it as our goal to

---

1. Beveridge and Bonnet, *Tracts and Letters*, 4:280–81.

seek what is expedient for us according to the flesh.... We are God's: let his wisdom and will therefore rule all our actions."[2]

Self-denial contains a twofold movement—first, away from one's will, mortifying it, and then toward God's will, in vivification—prostration and exaltation. Self-denial must begin with laying down our own will, before we can take up God's. Self-denial is at the heart of the invitation that Jesus issues. "If anyone would come after me, let him deny himself and take up his cross and follow me" (Matt 16:24).

"Let him deny himself." These four little words introduce a world of struggle, and an entirely new way of living. Turning in repentance from our wants, we embrace by faith what God wants for us, however painful. Calvin thought that self-denial was the first motion of sanctification: "Self-denial may be said to be the commencement of piety."[3] Thomas Watson agreed: "Self-denial is the first principle of Christianity."[4] It is the movement that begins all other movements of mortification, entirely necessary for our advance in grace.

Self-Denial Is Enabled by Our Union with Christ

Self-denial depends upon the grace of God, as in all of our efforts in sanctification.[5] Particularly, the grace of our union with Christ empowers our self-denial by his death and by his life.[6]

Christ' self-denial in his death frees us to deny ourselves. He had to deny himself the glory of heaven to descend to Earth as a man (Phil 2:6–7). Even more, he denied himself life here by embracing death on a cross, and, worst of all, bearing our sin for us. "For our sake he made him to be sin who knew no sin, so that in him we might become the righteousness of God" (2 Cor 5:21). It is through our union with Christ that we are enabled to deny ourselves—dying to ourselves—as Christ did for us. "Self-denial is always to be thought of as the human accompaniment of a very real and powerful process of dying with Christ

---

2. Calvin, *Institutes*, 3.7.1.
3. Calvin, *Com.*, John 3:12.
4. Watson, *The Duty of Self-Denial*, 2.
5. Calvin, *Com.*, Ezek 20:12.
6. Winecoff, "Mortification," 98.

which takes place within the Christian through living communion with the death of Christ."⁷

As we daily struggle to die to our will and embrace God's we must rely upon the reality that Christ has crucified our sin nature (Gal 5:24) and that he lives within us so that we are no longer forced to obey sin (Rom 6:12). Here the whole power of our union with Christ's death comes to bear, killing off our sinful self-will and freeing us to submit to the will of God in self-denial. This is precisely what Paul meant when he wrote: "I have been crucified. It is no longer I who live, but Christ who lives in me" (Gal 2:20). God has, in uniting us to Christ, united us to his death by which our sin nature is dealt the final fatal blow.

Yet at the same time in that union we find vivification, for Christ lives in us. What more potent force of sanctification could exist than this: Christ himself, through his Holy Spirit, takes up residence in our person. Christ dwelling in us liberates our will from the devil and sin so that it is actually more free, not less. Our will is free to obey, free to flee sin, free to deny ourselves.

Self-Denial Is an Inward Mortification Where We Deny Our Sinful Will and Reason

Unlike cross bearing, which generally entails outward struggles, self-denial is an inward fight that requires us to wrestle in our own hearts. We must resist, and by grace, subdue the flesh, denying its attempts to rule over us. Since we are new creatures, the old nature, the flesh, has lost its power to dominate us. "You, however, are not in the flesh but in the Spirit" (Rom 8:9). Since we are now in the Spirit it is only natural that we should deny the flesh and follow the Spirit.

We must wrestle as well with our own reason, denying it by recognizing that it is faulty and limited. Instead we submit ourselves to the Word of God, wherever it runs contrary to our reason. For example, a man may reason that having an affair would be good. To deny himself, he must deny his thinking that the affair would be good, and submit himself to the Word of God which commands, "Thou shall not commit adultery."

When we deny our reason and will as the ultimate arbitrators of what we should do, then we take an important step toward humility and find the grace of God to guide us toward holiness of life. "Whenever,

---

7. Wallace, *Christian Life*, 63–64.

therefore, God does not seem to work as our carnal reason dictates to us, we may learn, by the Prophet's example, how to restrain ourselves, and to subject our reason to God's will, so that it may suffice us that he wills a thing so, *because* his will is the most perfect rule of all justice."[8]

Self-Denial Is an Inward Vivification Where We Embrace God's Will over Our Own

It is not enough to merely reject our fleshly will and reason, we must substitute for them the will of God. This occurs primarily by understanding how his will, revealed in his Word, runs contrary to our own, and then following his will. Because of this we might call self-denial instead: God-affirming.

This is similar to when a parent disciplines a child. Ultimately the child learns self-discipline, that is, to deny themselves and bend their will to their parent's will. For example, a child may want to flick his peas on the floor during dinner for fun. Several spankings later the child determines that his parents' will—to keep the peas off the floor—is preferable to his will. To arrive at this conclusion the child had to struggle against his own will. Ultimately denying himself, the child embraces his parent's will.

So too, we must wrestle with our will, denying it, deciding to follow God's will instead. It is an inward struggle which no one can achieve for us. At some point we must finally relent and respond to God's will in obedience if we are to deny ourselves.

Suppose a person really wants a job and does not get it, much to their sorrow. In response, they can either embrace God's providential will or live in defiance. Embracing God's will as revealed in his providences means the person accepts the "No," thankfully, knowing that God's will is best. Alternately, if they do not deny themselves, they complain loudly, they grudgingly return to their current job, and only half-heartedly do what the Lord has laid before them to do. One path is the way of self-denial, the other of self-indulgence. We may resist or yield to the rein of God, as a horse may to its rider. Self-denial means we yield to Christ's rein, embracing his direction for our lives, over our own.

---

8. Calvin, *Com.*, Ezek 9:9.

Self-Denial Is a Vivification Where We Offer Ourselves to God

There is in self-denial a dying to the self where we offer ourselves to God. In 1991 the Center for Church Planting that I had been asked to launch in Orlando, failed. It had been a dream come true, its failure the death of a dream. This failure was public before my denomination and personal, as I told my wife, who hugged our two small children and wondered at her unemployed husband. During the six months that I spent searching for another call, by grace, I embraced God's will, in a prayer of self-denial. "Lord, I do not need to do anything big, if you want me to sweep the streets, I will, only let me serve you." It was a prayer of surrender to the will of God, rather than demanding my own will.

Wallace describes this offering of ourselves to God as a kind of self-immolation, of being consumed by the will of God.[9] Calvin founded his personal motto on this concept, as mentioned previously, and imprinted it on his signet ring: "My heart I offer as though slain in sacrifice to God."[10] It sounds wonderful, doesn't it, a heart slain in sacrifice? But we must remember that this comes only at great personal cost: the slaying of the self, the loss of dreams, and ultimately, offering ourselves to God.

Self-Denial Is an Inward Vivification Where We Embrace Our Neighbor's Will over Our Own

Self-denial requires not only that we submit to the will of God, difficult enough, but also to the will of our neighbor. "You shall love your neighbor as yourself" (Matt 22:39). This command puts our neighbor's needs on par with our own. God presents us here with ample opportunity to deny ourselves as we are confronted by the needs of family, friends, church, and all those the Lord brings into our path.

For example, a son needs help with homework, while we want to go for a run. A friend needs a ride, while we have work to do. We are presented an endless stream of opportunities to deny ourselves in order to serve our neighbors. Calvin is blunt. "Therefore, whatever man you meet who needs your aid, you have no reason to refuse to help him."[11] Martin

---

9. Wallace, *Christian Life*, 29–30.
10. Calvin, *Ioannis Calvini Opera*, 11:100.
11. Calvin, *Institutes*, 3.7.6.

Bucer wrote an entire booklet to this effect, which was entitled: *Everyone should live not for himself but for others.*[12]

Self-denial encourages us to love others by setting aside our plans and meeting their needs. To do so, we must consider them more important than ourselves. "In humility count others more significant than yourselves" (Phil 2:3). Humbled through self-denial, realizing the God-given value of the other person, we are moved to compassion and then to service. "Let each of you look not only to his own interests, but also to the interests of others" (Phil 2:4).

Denying ourselves frees us to love our neighbor and to serve God, submitting to their wills even as we deny our own. This is precisely the motive that brought Jesus to the cross and redemption to us. This, we are told, is to be our mindset as well. "Have this mind among yourselves, which is yours in Christ Jesus, who, though he was in the form of God, did not count equality with God a thing to be grasped, but emptied himself" (Phil 2:5–7). How though does all this self-denial help us to grow in holiness?

How Does Self-Denial Help Our Growth in Holiness?

Self-Denial Reverses the Cursed Impact of the Fall

In the fall, the natural order of human humility before the exalted God was perverted such that humanity exalted itself in pride and laid God low, at least in its own mind. Self-denial, as a work of God's grace, leads to humility, reversing the curse. The curse of thinking more highly of ourselves than we ought—pride—and of thinking more poorly about our neighbors, and God, than we ought, is reversed. Sanity returns to us.

At the same time, with self-denial, we exalt God. God again rightly reigns supreme in our hearts as we bow before his will. We exalt him as we honor his image in others. The curse is reversed as we are brought low, prostrating ourselves before God, and God is lifted up by our ready obedience.

With self-denial we no longer follow the pattern of sinful humanity, where everyone would be king, but are conformed more to the pattern of Christ—who humbly considered our needs before his own. "But whoever would be great among you must be your servant, and whoever would

---

12. Bucer, *Christian Love*, 21.

be first among you must be slave of all. For even the Son of Man came not to be served but to serve, and to give his life as a ransom for many" (Mark 10:43–45). Christ came in part to transform us from masters into servants, servants of God, and servants of one another. Becoming self-denying servants like Christ, we become more holy.

Self-Denial Is Faith and Repentance at Work in Our Daily Lives

Self-denial is not merely human effort, but the everyday practice of faith. We must believe that God will bless us in Christ for our self-denial, as he has promised, before we will deny ourselves. "If anyone would come after me, let him deny himself and take up his cross and follow me. For whoever would save his life will lose it, but whoever loses his life for my sake will find it" (Matt 16:24–25). Without this faith that Christ will give us life in response to losing our lives in self-denial, we never could deny ourselves. "The denial of ourselves . . . is impossible except by faith in Christ."[13] Self-denial then is the daily practice of faith as we look to Christ to bless our sacrificial service, rather than trusting ourselves to obtain the good life.

Self-denial is also the everyday practice of repentance. To deny ourselves we must repent, turning from the direction our will was leading us and instead go in the direction of the Lord's choosing, revealed in the Bible and in the providence of others' needs. If my wife's need for help conflicts with my desire to watch TV, then I must repent, turning from my selfish desire, and instead look to Christ to renew me, while I fully endeavor after the new obedience of helping her. Self-denial is repentance in the trenches of daily life.

Since holiness is growth in faith and obedience, and self-denial grows our faith in God as it trains us in obedience to submit to his will, self-denial helps our holiness. Since holiness is also progress in repenting of sins and finding grace, and self-denial requires daily repentance, self-denial again helps our holiness. Through self-denial, as the daily application of faith and repentance, we are transformed by the grace of God more and more into the image of Christ, who was a humble servant. As humble servants of God and others, we bow before God, gratefully embracing his will in self-denial. This is holiness, and the only path that leads there is self-denial.

---

13. Wendel, *Origins*, 248.

Self-Denial Puts Us in the Low Place Where God's Grace Helps Us

In self-denial we are humbling ourselves before God where we find his grace to help sanctify us. "God opposes the proud but gives grace to the humble" (1 Pet 5:5). Self-denial leads us downward, where meeting us, Christ transforms us with his grace more and more into his own likeness.

In self-denial we are lying down on the operating table where Christ does his holy surgery upon us. "The lesson of this knowledge [of our poverty before God] is that we learn to humble ourselves, cast ourselves before God, seek His mercy."[14] He operates on us; he removes the corruption within us replacing it with new living tissue. "Having prostrated ourselves in the dust before him, he may raise us up."[15] Such self-denial is then the path downward to grace where Christ helps us upward in holiness.

Self-Denial Helps Us to Love God and Our Neighbor

Self-denial is the everyday expression of love to God as we grow in loving obedience to him. "Whoever has my commandments and keeps them, he it is who loves me" (John 14:21). When our children were small they would show their love for us—or their lack of love—by the readiness of their obedience. So too, we express love to God by our submission to his will in the denial of our own. But our self-denial not only expresses love for God, but increases it, for each act of self-denial is a move toward God relationally, to embrace him. Growing in love for God, we are growing in holiness through self-denial.

In a similar way, as we deny ourselves and favor our neighbor, we express love for them. We also grow in love for them, for those we willingly serve, we grow to love. Self-love is replaced by neighbor-love as self-denial rips "from our inward parts this most deadly pestilence of love of strife and love of self."[16]

Self-denial, as the spiritual practice which daily applies faith and repentance in a hundred small decisions, leads us to holiness as we grow in love for God and our neighbor.

Self-denial leads us to a holy happiness. The world tells us that happiness lies with self-indulgence, not self-denial. But self-indulgence is a

---

14. Battles, *The Piety of John Calvin*, 4.
15. Calvin, *Com.*, Ps 34:18.
16. Calvin, *Institutes*, 3.7.4.

never-satisfied desire that leads us to be "greedy to practice every kind of impurity" (Eph 4:19), while it supplies less and less joy. Self-denial, although initially painful—for mortification is the painful killing of the flesh—leads finally to the joy of contentment with Christ. "It hence at length follows, that man becomes happy by self-denial."[17] This joy is only found on the other side of losing our life for Christ.

I vividly recall one instance of self-denial where I experienced this "happiness" in one of the most unusual circumstances: my father's funeral. Dad died suddenly after a short hospital stay. The next few days became a blur of self-forgetful service. Several days sped by with planning for the service, preparing a message, comforting Mom and others. At the end of these days I realized that I had hardly had a thought of myself. The needs of the moment—of those around me, of the glory of God in the memorial to my dad—had entirely consumed me. It was a joy in the midst of sorrow that I had rarely known before. Self-denial had led, as Christ promised, to life, even in the face of death.

Self-denial is the unavoidable doorway which leads to growth in holiness. This does not, however, lead to a glum and joyless existence. We find in self-denial a deeper joy of submission, service, and wholeness. It is the completely surprising result of living life the way Jesus did, by the power that Jesus gives, and finding the joy that Jesus promises.

As important as self-denial is then to our growth in holiness we should now explain how to practice it.

How Do We Practice Self-Denial to Grow in Holiness?

When Jesus said, "let him deny himself" (Matt 16:24), he meant that our lives would be marked by daily self-denial, as was his. Indeed, it is the life of Christ in us that enables us to deny ourselves, holding more tightly to Jesus, as we loosen our grip on our lives. Here are some particular applications to help our growth in self-denial, essential to our growth in holiness.

---

17. Calvin, *Com.*, Heb 4:10.

Faith: Believe That God Blesses the Life of Self-Denial by Looking to Scripture

Self-denial is impossible without faith, which increases as we look to the Bible. God assures us that he will care for our needs now when we look after the needs of his kingdom before our own. "Seek first the kingdom of God and his righteousness, and all these things will be added to you" (Matt 6:33). God assures us that he will reward us with a "hundred-fold now . . . and in the age to come eternal life" (Mark 10:29–30), when we give up now for his service. Scripture often motivates us with future reward as an encouragement to serve others now, the essence of self-denial. "Sell your possessions, and give to the needy. Provide yourselves with moneybags that do not grow old, with a treasure in the heavens that does not fail, where no thief approaches and no moth destroys" (Luke 12:33).

Living a life of self-denial requires faith. Let the truth of God's Word—studied, memorized, and meditated upon—convince you more and more, decision by decision, that the way of self-denial is the only way to abundant life, now and forever. The world will tell you the opposite, as will your flesh. Feed yourself on the truth of the Word to enable your self-denial.

Repentance: Examine Yourself Daily for Areas Where You Are Indulging Rather Than Denying Self

To practice self-denial we must examine ourselves daily for those areas where we are indulging our will and denying the will of God and others, and repent of these. Are we indulging our desires at home, church, or work, only being served and not serving others? Let us repent and, denying ourselves, look for opportunities to serve others.

We should repent not only for our self-indulgent actions, but for our self-indulgent attitudes, emotions, and thoughts. Aided by the Spirit, the Word, and our conscience, we should seek out self-indulgence in our thoughts and emotions. When we find that our passions rule over us—anger, judging, jealousy, covetousness, fear, worry—we confess these sinful attitudes and thoughts, bringing them to God. In this repentance we deny ourselves and seek to have our hearts reformed so that we feel and think what God wants us to feel and think.

> When I feel passions within myself that are excessive and violent, like boiling water which is foaming over, then I must renounce my rights and forget the injuries which have been done to me. Now in this way, God is wanting to show that I do not belong to myself, but I am his, and that he must gently control all my emotions.[18]

When we notice sinful self-indulgence in action or attitude, we first confess that sin to God, and others as necessary, then seek grace-enabled change. For example, if you notice that you are not giving your child the help with homework that they need, start by confessing that to God and them. Turn to the Lord for forgiveness and the power to put yourself second to your child. Then plan the time you will help them, and strengthened by Christ, do so.

Examining ourselves daily to repent of self-indulgence is self-denial that helps our holiness.

Put Out Spirit-Empowered Effort at Self-Denial

Sanctification requires real effort from us. In this effort we are yielding to the Spirit. "But I say, walk by the Spirit, and you will not gratify the desires of the flesh" (Gal 5:16). When we walk by the Spirit we listen to him rather than our sinful nature as he prompts us toward obedient self-denial.

The flesh would keep us from following the Spirit in self-denial. "I am too tired to extend them my energetic hospitality." "I need this money for myself so I will not tithe to the church." In each case the Spirit working with our new spiritually-oriented nature strives against the flesh. "Yes, you are tired, but so was Christ when he bore your cross, so that you can serve when you are tired." "Yes, you could use the money, but Christ gave up riches so that you could give up that pittance and trust God to supply." Where sin arises, God stirs his Spirit within us to provide a way of escape, which we should endeavor to take.

Since the flesh strives against the Spirit of Christ within us, we must continually strive against the flesh by the Spirit. "Disobedience and rebellion against the Spirit of God pervade the whole nature of man. If we would obey the Spirit, we must labor, and fight, and apply

---

18. Calvin, *Sermons on 2 Samuel*, 636–37.

our utmost energy; and we must begin with self-denial."[19] Self-denial is Spirit-led warfare!

In this warfare we must struggle against our desire to impose our will on those around us. This is not to say that we never express our opinions, but that our opinions are first sifted through the grid of self-denial to ascertain whether we are seeking the good of God and others, or just our preferences.

For example, I used to think as moderator of our church's elder board that my job was to get the session to agree with my good ideas. That leads to warfare and bad decisions. I now understand that my job is to lead us all to seek the Lord's direction. I often repeat to myself this simple truth: "While I know what I want, what God wants will be revealed as we discuss and seek the Lord *together*." This is self-denial applied to leadership, as we surrender control and follow the leadership of the Holy Spirit.

Self-denial requires very real, Spirit-empowered effort, which yields a life of greater peace and joy.

Seek Opportunities for Self-Denial Rather Than Seeking to Avoid Them

We should actually *seek* opportunities for self-denial. We may find these opportunities as we look to the needs of those we encounter daily. We are surrounded by an unending chorus of needs. Generally, we have become deaf to them, as we listen far more carefully to our own desires. Christ bids us to heed the opportunities around us, and letting go of our plans, to serve others as we deny ourselves. "If anyone would be first, he must be last of all and servant of all" (Mark 9:35).

You may want to try this simple experiment in self-denial: Try to meet the first need you notice today. This is not to say, of course, that we are to meet every need we see every day. We must walk by the Spirit, who will tell us when, where, and how to die to ourselves. But since we are so used to indulging, rather than denying ourselves, it may not hurt to try this experiment. I did. The first need I saw the day I wrote this was that my wife's closet light was not working in the morning, due simply to the lack of a string to pull it. Though I was running late for work, and therefore disinclined, I stopped long enough to find a string and fix her light. Nothing really, such a small thing, but I have to say, it felt good to

---

19. Calvin, *Com.*, Gal 5:17.

put her needs before mine, even in such a small way. Let us, walking in the Spirit, seek opportunities to deny, not indulge, ourselves all day long.

Seek Your Neighbor's Good to Deny Yourself

In seeking opportunities to deny ourselves, our neighbors offer us nearly endless possibilities. The command to love our neighbor as our self leads us to care for the needs of the poor, widows, orphans, and sojourners in our midst. "Religion that is pure and undefiled before God, the Father, is this: to visit orphans and widows in their affliction" (Jas 1:27). Self-denial bids us to not merely wait for such opportunities, but to seek them out and to be helpful in systematic ways.

Our enemies provide us another fruitful venue for self-denial. "Love your enemies and pray for those who persecute you" (Matt 5:44). Is there someone who has made themselves your enemy? What might you do to bless them? Start with forgiveness and a refusal to hold a grudge. This is self-denial on the emotional level, for we delight to ruminate about getting even. "You shall not take vengeance or bear a grudge . . . but you shall love your neighbor as yourself" (Lev 19:18).

Of course no neighbor is closer to us than our own families, so self-denial starts at home. "But if anyone does not provide for his relatives, and especially for members of his household, he has denied the faith and is worse than an unbeliever" (1 Tim 5:8). In general, the closer the relationship we have with anyone, the greater the obligation to meet their needs through self-denial. Therefore, opportunity for self-denial presses outward from family to friends to church members to co-workers, etc.

Deny Yourself What the World Says You Must Have, So That You May Give More to Others

Another facet of self-denial is refusing to follow the dictates of the world which tells us to indulge ourselves with luxury. "We should be very careful not to become slaves to the palate, and thus be drawn off from our duty and from obedience and the fear of God, when we ought to live sparingly and be free from all luxuries."[20] As Christians, we are free to enjoy all things, but are to be mastered by none, being moderate in our tastes, so as not to love the world. "Do not love the world or the things

20. Calvin, *Com.*, Dan 1:14.

in the world" (1 John 2:15). Self-denial bids us to let go of worldly ambitions, and hold loosely to wealth, as did Christ. "Christ's Kingdom lies in the Spirit, not in earthly pleasures or pomp. Hence we must forsake the world if we are to share in the Kingdom."[21]

Does the world say we should have a house over a certain square footage to show that we have arrived? Perhaps self-denial will lead us to intentionally buy one smaller. Does the world dictate that those in our social class drive a certain level of luxury car? Self-denial may teach us to enjoy something more modest. Does the world dictate a certain level of financial security? Self-denial may lead us to give away more wealth than the world judges prudent. "Do not lay up for yourselves treasures on earth . . . but lay up for yourselves treasures in heaven" (Matt 6:19–20).

We have a plethora of biblical examples where self-denial meant giving up the easy life which the world offered. Abraham left his home. Moses turned his back on the wealth of a king. All the prophets put their lives and fortunes at risk. Paul left behind a great career. By self-denial we grow far less concerned with acquiring riches for ourselves and far more delighted with enriching others, at our expense. "A need satisfied, or good fortune received will not delight us so much as that His will is seen perfectly fulfilled in us and by us."[22]

This denial of the worldly materialism is aided through giving the whole tithe. "Bring the full tithe into the storehouse, that there may be food in my house" (Mal 3:10). Christian giving only begins with the tithe, it does not end there. Seek to grow in generosity, funding missionaries, students, widows, anyone the Lord brings before you.

As we deny ourselves the luxuries that the world insists are our rights, we have more financial freedom to love our neighbors as ourselves. Self-denial leads us to lives of moderation where, in sowing generously to help others, we reap lives of lasting—everlasting—joy.

Keep the Sabbath Day Holy as a Weekly Habit of Self-Denial

The world tells us that our time is ours, but God has laid particular claim to the Sabbath Day. "Remember the Sabbath day, to keep it holy" (Exod 20:8). The Sabbath is a denial of the self, where we set aside one day in seven to come away from the world to be the Lord's. "The Sabbath was

---

21. Calvin, *Institutes*, 2.15.5.
22. Bernard, *Love of God*, 44–45.

the sign of mortification. God, therefore, sanctifies us."[23] When we deliver to the Lord one day in seven, we learn the true demands of God upon our time: every moment of every day.

In denying our right, as it were, to our very time on the Sabbath we yield our lives to God in an uncompromisingly clear way. We say to him: "This day is yours Lord, how shall I use each minute of it?" This is why the *Westminster Shorter Catechism* instructs us to give "all that day" to God. "The Sabbath is to be sanctified by a holy resting all that day."[24]

The Sabbath was made for man and what a gift it is! God has given this gift as a foretaste of heaven: a day where we rest from all our striving and achieving and are simply quiet before God, basking in the glow of his loving face. What joy to know rest in a restless world. We are to be a Sabbath people, a people at peace in a troubled world. To grow in holiness, practice the self-denial of Sabbath-keeping.

Follow Jesus in Self-Denial

Christ is the standard of self-denial to whom we look and by whom we are encouraged toward self-denial. "The Son of Man came not to be served but to serve, and to give his life as a ransom for many" (Matt 20:28). In ways large and small Jesus constantly denied himself and served others. A person in the crowd demands his time, Jesus yields his schedule to their needs. His mother wants wine for a wedding, wine it is. Someone has a sick child, Jesus drops everything to heal them.

At every critical decision point in his life Jesus took the path of self-denial. Would he retain his glory above or take on humanity? Take on humanity. Would he be honored or despised? Despised. Would he live long on Earth or die young? Die young. Would he die in some painless way or painfully on the cross? The cross.

This ultimate act of self-denial led to the ultimate blessing in the universe—for us and for him. "Therefore God has highly exalted him and bestowed on him the name that is above every name" (Phil 2:9). His example encourages us, for we see that his self-denial led to an even greater joy. "That all are happy who, along with Christ, voluntarily abase

---

23. Calvin, *Com.*, Ezek 20:12.

24. *Westminster Confession of Faith*, 386–87; *Westminster Shorter Catechism*, answer 60.

themselves, he shows by his example; for from the most abject condition he was exalted to the highest elevation."[25]

In all our self-denials we should fix our eyes on Jesus, who through self-denial became our servant and through self-denial became the most joyful. "Looking to Jesus, the founder and perfecter of our faith, who for the joy that was set before him endured the cross, despising the shame, and is seated at the right hand of the throne of God" (Heb 12:2). Self-denial is the road to holiness and the way to the deep joy that lies in fellowship with Christ.

Summary of How We Can Grow in Self-Denial

1. Grow your faith by reading the Bible promises of life and reward, here and in heaven, for those who deny themselves. Memorize some verses that especially grab your heart.

2. Repent daily of your self-indulgences—whether deeds, thoughts, feelings, or words—when you could have denied yourself. Listen to the Holy Spirit as he convicts you of sin and turn to Christ in new obedience as you deny yourself.

3. Put out Spirit-empowered effort to deny yourself. Do not go with the flow of your flesh but follow the Spirit. Stop trying to impose your will on others and follow the will of God as revealed in Scripture and evident in providence.

4. Seek opportunities for self-denial, rather than trying to avoid them. Look to the needs of those around you and the commands of Scripture. Try noticing and meeting the very first need presented to you today, if the Spirit so moves.

5. Focus on the needs of neighbors—your family, friends, co-workers, church members, others—to see if opportunity arises to serve them and deny yourself. Remember: the closer the relationship, the more natural obligation exists to meet those needs. Do you have enemies you need to forgive and bless? Don't forget those neighbors either.

6. Deny yourself those things the world insists you must have. To honor God and to leave you more resources for others, buy smaller, spend less, and give away more. Start with the full tithe, if you are not yet tithing, and grow from there.

25. Calvin, *Com.*, Phil 2:9.

7. Keep the Sabbath Day as holy to the Lord. By living the whole day unto the Lord, we deny ourselves and focus our time on the Lord, a pleasing sacrifice to him.
8. Follow Jesus in self-denial. His self-denial redeemed us, that we might follow him in self-denying service of God and others. More than an example, Christ lives in us to empower us to follow the way he went, the way of self-denial.

Further Resources

Study Questions

1. Define self-denial in your own words.
2. Why might self-denial be called "God-affirming" as well?
3. How is self-denial faith and repentance at work in our daily lives?
4. Why must we deny even our own reason in self-denial?
5. Name two or three ways in which self-denial helps us to grow in holiness.
6. How can self-denial lead us to a "holy happiness?"
7. Of the eight ways to practice self-denial which one seems most helpful to you at this time?
8. What is one realistic step you could take to grow in self-denial as you walk with Christ?

For Further Study

Martin Bucer, *Instruction in Christian Love*, trans. Paul Traugott Fuhrmann (Eugene, OR: Wipf and Stock, 2008).
Jeremiah Burroughs, *Moses' Self-Denial* (Grand Rapids: Soli Deo Gloria, 2010).
Thomas Manton, *A Treatise of Self-Denial* (Pensacola, FL: Chapel Library, 2014).
Thomas Watson, *The Duty of Self-Denial and Ten Other Sermons* (Morgan, PA: Soli Deo Gloria, 1996).

10

Bear the Cross

What Is Cross Bearing?

ONE OF OUR GROWN sons and I were out for dinner on a Friday night at a familiar restaurant in Charlotte, North Carolina. He had gone through struggles with his faith during college and even now was not doing well. That night, aged twenty-five, he was living back in Charlotte and I had invited him to join a short-term mission team going to the Middle East. I was glad that he wanted to go and what the close association of the team might mean for his growth in faith.

That night in the restaurant, one week before our mission team was to leave, I would find out the true state of his soul. "Dad, I am not a Christian. I do not think that I ever really was." While I was happy that he trusted my love enough to tell me, this was devastating news. I suspect that these words are every Christian parent's worst fear.

The next day, Saturday, my wife and I felt just as if someone had died. The same sense of loss, of sorrow, with cold grey clouds of depression, swept over us both. Then on Sunday I was trying to prepare to preach. I could not. I was so lost under the weight of sorrow that I could not muster the faith to proclaim the goodness of my God. In prayer I was convicted that I must, in one sense, let my son go. That I must bow before this difficult providence. "Whoever loves son or daughter more than me is not worthy of me" (Matt 10:37). I prayed: "God please show him mercy and save him. But if you want to cast him into hell I will still praise you. I surrender him into your hands. Lord, for now you want me to be the father of an atheistic son, ok, I will do it. Please help me to faithfully follow you with this son." It was a prayer of release, and I could again take up the Word to preach.

This is cross bearing: the voluntary submission to involuntary suffering brought to us by the providence of God. Jesus was clear that all who follow him must bear the cross. "If anyone would come after me, let him deny himself and take up his cross and follow me" (Matt 16:24). While the crosses come from the providence of God, cross bearing itself is our submissive endurance of them. We say with Jesus before the cross, "Nevertheless, not my will, but yours, be done" (Luke 22:42). Where self-denial may be entirely self-initiated, in cross bearing, God takes the initiative, whether or not we desire to progress in holiness.

Cross bearing must involve real suffering, with emotional pain that requires endurance. Crosses appear in all aspects of our lives: health, finances, relationships, vocation, church-life, family, friends. Trials in any of these are to be seen as suffering from the hand of God. "Beginning with Christ, his first-born, he follows this plan with all his children."[1] Every Christian *must* bear the cross, for there is no son or daughter, without discipline. "For the Lord disciplines the one he loves, and chastises every son whom he receives" (Heb 12:6).

We must understand this about cross bearing, we suffer because God loves us and knows that in our suffering we will turn to him and be transformed by him. I would marvel how, after lovingly disciplining my young children, they would immediately want to be comforted by me. So, too, God sends us trials that we will seek our comfort and help in his arms.

The crosses God gives us are ultimately designed to put to death our old sin nature and lead us step by painful step into conformity with the image of Christ. Cross bearing is so important to our transformation that God may pile them upon us until it seems that he, "treats his children more harshly than he does strangers."[2] Since God is concerned that his children grow in holiness, he will often leave the reprobate to indulge in their ease, while his children suffer. The psalmist notes this with lament: "For I was envious of the arrogant when I saw the prosperity of the wicked" (Ps 73:3). Thus it is true that, "God spares men when he does not spare them," the cross, and for the reprobate, "when God spares them" the cross, "he does not spare."[3]

---

1. Calvin, *Institutes*, 3.8.1.
2. Calvin, *Sermons on Micah*, 61.
3. Calvin, *Com.*, Hos 9:7.

Cross bearing is perhaps the one Christian doctrine which runs most contrary to the American Christian's cultural training and so is extraordinarily difficult for us to understand, accept, and follow. We expect the American success story to happen to us even as Christians. We will be born, do well—then do better—and then die at an old prosperous age.

I was surprised to find this same false expectation in myself while I was in seminary. Through the blessing of God we lived rent-free for fourteen months in a very nice home. When we had to move out, we could only find a small expensive apartment. I was perplexed. If God had once supplied that nice home why not a nicer one now? My wise younger brother pointedly asked: "What did you expect? What in Scripture, with all the trials of the saints, would make you believe that God would deliver to you the American Dream?" Indeed, Paul never said: "I have learned to go from luxury to even more glorious luxury." But rather he wrote: "In any and every circumstance, I have learned the secret of facing plenty and hunger, abundance and need" (Phil 4:12). The biblical pattern includes periods of want and periods of plenty, not an uninterrupted climb up the social-economic ladder. These periods of want may then be financial crosses.

I was very much like the imaginary sufferer Calvin describes. "If God singles us out first for chastisement and in the meantime we observe that others are enjoying their ease we murmur: 'Whoa! What is this? What's going on here? Are we more vile than these people over here or those over there?' That is how we react."[4] Yet Scripture is abundantly clear that suffering and trials will be the normal lot of the Christian. Consider:

> Beloved, do not be surprised at the fiery trial when it comes upon you to test you, as though something strange were happening to you. (1 Pet 4:12)

> We rejoice in our sufferings, knowing that suffering produces endurance, and endurance produces character, and character produces hope, and hope does not put us to shame, because God's love has been poured into our hearts through the Holy Spirit who has been given to us. (Rom 5:3–5)

> Count it all joy, my brothers, when you meet trials of various kinds, for you know that the testing of your faith produces steadfastness. (Jas 1:2–3)

---

4. Calvin, *Sermons on Micah*, 53.

Scripture teaches us that we must bear the cross for our good and ultimate joy, but how are we to understand the various types of crosses we bear?

The Types of Crosses We Bear

Although we may suffer in dozens of different ways, it is helpful to consider four broad categories: crosses God uses to display, discipline, develop, or deploy us.

Display: Suffering in Order to Display God's Glory

One way in which we suffer to display God's glory is when we are persecuted for righteousness. "Blessed are those who are persecuted because of righteousness" (Matt 5:10). God's people always have been, and always will be, persecuted until Christ returns. "All who desire to live a godly life in Christ Jesus will be persecuted" (2 Tim 3:12). Whether this persecution comes in milder forms, such as being excluded and derided, or the more severe forms of being jailed, tortured, and even killed, it is all persecution, a cross to bear, not for any sin in us, but rather because Christ's righteousness is in us and God wishes to show it to others.

God intends that our righteousness will be on display in our suffering such that our tormentors and others will see the power of God. "Yet if anyone suffers as a Christian, let him not be ashamed, but let him glorify God in that name" (1 Pet 4:16). This is our consolation and encouragement to endure. "Now, to suffer persecution for righteousness' sake is a singular comfort. For it ought to occur to us how much honor God bestows upon us in thus furnishing us with the special badge of his soldiery."[5]

We also display God's glory when we suffer righteously through various trials. "You have been grieved by various trials, so that the tested genuineness of your faith . . . may be found to result in praise and glory and honor at the revelation of Jesus Christ" (1 Pet 1:6–7). God will allow such suffering to display his glory through his children as he did to the blind man: "It was not that this man sinned, or his parents, but that the works of God might be displayed in him" (John 9:3).

---

5. Calvin, *Institutes*, 3.8.7.

We had a fifty-seven-year-old woman in our congregation pass into the presence of Christ after a battle with ovarian cancer. Her months of suffering were a testimony to the God who loved and supported her. Her memorial service, packed with 1,600 people because she was well known and loved, was a singular display of the glory of God. One of the more glorious moments of the service came when her husband read her journal from the very day she had discovered that she had a terminal cancer. She wrote to God: "I know you love us and have a plan, be my hope, my comforter, and my great physician." Her husband remarked that he was struck not only by what she said but by what she had not said, there was no bitterness or questioning. God proved himself to be her, and her family's, hope and comfort as they powerfully testified to God's glory before a watching world. Many people at that service expressed a desire to know more about the God who had borne her on eagle's wings. God does allow his children to suffer in part to display his glory.

Discipline: Suffering as Chastisement for Our Sin

While not all suffering in the Christian's life comes as discipline for sin, some of it does. "My son, do not make light of the Lord's discipline" (Heb 12:5). God, as a good and loving father, wants to train his children away from sin, so he sends chastisements our way.

David experienced this discipline for his sin with Bathsheba, as Nathan announced on God's behalf. "The LORD also has put away your sin; you shall not die. Nevertheless, because by this deed you have utterly scorned the LORD, the child who is born to you shall die" (2 Sam 12:13–14). A painful lesson certainly, but one that would help shape David into the man the Lord wanted him to become.

When God sends us suffering as discipline we must understand that this discipline is not a judicial punishment, but a fatherly chastisement. Since Christ has borne the punishment for our sin, we cannot be punished again. "For Christ also suffered once for sins, the righteous for the unrighteous" (1 Pet 3:18). Judicial punishment means to exact a price from God's enemies for their past sins, moved by his wrath. Fatherly chastisement means to correct his children for the future, moved by his love. A father disciplines his young children not in order to exact a pound of flesh from them out of spite, but lovingly applies the rod to train them for the future. It is vital for us to understand this difference as we suffer correction from our heavenly Father.

Development: Suffering to Sanctify Us and Deepen Us

Much of the suffering that comes into our lives is intended by God to develop our hearts and our faith. "Count it all joy, my brothers, when you meet trials of various kinds, for you know that the testing of your faith produces steadfastness" (Jas 1:2–3). Suffering humbles us and makes us more God dependent. The Apostle Paul was trained by his "thorn in the flesh," to depend on the strength of God, not his own. "Therefore I will boast all the more gladly about my weaknesses, so that Christ's power may rest on me" (2 Cor 12:9).

Calvin referred to this type of suffering as medicinal suffering. God as the great physician knows just what cures each person requires and so he writes a prescription for suffering that will heal and develop us, individually. He will use shame for this one, disease for that, relational trials here, financial trials there, always using the "appropriate remedy"[6] designed to be help the individual grow in holiness. This suffering is not to discipline vice but to develop virtue. "We rejoice in our sufferings, knowing that suffering produces endurance, and endurance produces character, and character produces hope" (Rom 5:3–4).

Deployment: Suffering to Move Us Out for Ministry

God brings suffering into our lives at times to deploy us, moving us to new locations, vocations, or relationships, in order to advance his kingdom. God may give us the loss of a job here, a broken relationship there, in order to relocate us, for his kingdom purposes.

We see this in the persecution of the church in Jerusalem which spread them throughout the Roman Empire for the rapid advance of the gospel. "There arose on that day a great persecution against the church in Jerusalem, and they were all scattered throughout the regions of Judea and Samaria, except the apostles" (Acts 8:1). Paul was deployed to Rome in chains, where the gospel went forward. David fled to the Philistines where he was further readied to be king. Joseph was painfully deployed

---

6. Calvin, *Com.*, Ps 119:67.

to Egypt in order to save Israel from the coming famine (Gen 50:20). God uses suffering to deploy his people.

Now that we understand the common types of crosses, it will be helpful to understand the common purpose God has behind all of our crosses.

The Overall Purpose of Cross bearing

While God may use the suffering of the cross for his glory, to correct us, or to advance his kingdom—God has a common purpose toward us in each cross—to help us grow in holiness. "God disciplines us for our good, that we may share in his holiness" (Heb 12:10). The crosses we bear *thrust* holiness upon us. Rarely would we choose disease, persecution, poverty, loneliness, or conflict. But God lovingly chooses them for us to help us become more like Jesus.

Paul explains this dynamic behind his suffering. "For we were so utterly burdened beyond our strength that we despaired of life itself. . . . But that was to make us rely not on ourselves but on God who raises the dead" (2 Cor 1:8–9). Paul learned through trials, in lessons that could never be taught by mere words, that he must despair of his own strength to rely instead upon God. This is the lesson of suffering that leads us to know and love God more deeply.

In the early 90s another leader and I worked with a leadership development program for young Christian leaders. We noticed that the young leaders fell neatly into two broad categories: those who had, and those who had not yet, endured a deep cross. Those who had not yet been broken by a cross tended to minister for their own glory, by their own power. Those who had suffered like Paul, "utterly burdened beyond our strength," tended to work for God's glory and by his power. These young cross-shaped leaders were humbled enough to be teachable and benefited most from the training.

Calvin addresses our need to have the cross break our fleshly confidence: "The fleshly confidence with which we are puffed up, is so obstinate, that it cannot be overthrown in any other way than by our falling into utter despair. . . . Nor are we brought to true submission, until we have been brought down by the *mighty hand of God*."[7] We must bear the cross to become those who in humility depend upon God's power and work for his glory from a heart of love.

---

7. Calvin, *Com.*, 2 Cor 1:9.

But how does bearing the cross actually work to help us become more like Christ?

How Cross Bearing Helps to Make Us Holy

Cross Bearing Humbles Us, Bringing Us to the End of Our Own Resources

We are naturally blind to our sinfulness and to our inability to fight sin alone. When we bear the cross, God brings us to the end of ourselves where we see the seriousness of our sin and our inability to defeat it, so that we will turn from self-dependence to seek help from him. This is the cross's mortifying impact.

When our lives are going well externally there is little motivation to change. God lovingly sends us crosses to wake us from our slumber in sin. If a man sins, say by regularly viewing pornography, he is usually blind to its destructiveness and its hold over him. But allow his wife to discover this and threaten him with divorce, then this crisis, this cross, will force him to see both the destructiveness of his sin and his inability to defeat it on his own. God uses the cross as an aid to our repentance by destroying our confidence in our flesh, so humbled we will turn to him.

Ultimately the crosses we face threaten us with types of death, because this is the way that God best gains our attention. Failure threatens the death of our reputation, financial trials threaten the death of our independence, relational trials threaten us with death by isolation, and, of course, health trials threaten us with literal death. These threats of death force us to see our own weakness, and "falling into utter despair,"[8] we no longer consider our power up to the task and so turn to God. The Apostle Paul noted the effectiveness of the threat of death to drive him from self-reliance to rely upon the power of God: "Indeed, we felt that we had received the sentence of death. But that was to make us rely not on ourselves but on God who raises the dead (2 Cor 1:9).

Forced by the suffering of the cross to see ourselves as we truly are, sinful and helpless, we gain part of the twofold knowledge of God and ourselves, seeing ourselves as weak and God as our powerful savior. This knowledge transforms us, for abandoning all trust in ourselves we

---

8. Calvin, *Com.*, 2 Cor 1:9.

humbly turn to God for help.⁹ "The bearing of the cross is a genuine proof of our obedience, since by doing this, we renounce the guidance of our own affections and submit ourselves entirely to God."¹⁰

Cross Bearing Leads Us to Seek God's Grace, Where We Find Help

Knowing now our weakness and his power, we turn to him. This is the vivifying impact of the cross. We turn from our puny reserves of self-control and endurance to his boundless stores of grace and power, offered by his ready love.

> And it is of no slight importance for you to be cleansed of your blind love of self that you may be made more nearly aware of your incapacity; to feel your own incapacity that you may learn to distrust yourself; to distrust yourself that you may transfer your trust to God; to rest with a trustful heart in God that, relying upon his help, you may persevere unconquered to the end.¹¹

Humbled, we look to our Father with confidence. Confidence that the cross comes from his love, confidence that his grace will see us through the suffering. "Our most merciful Father consoles us also in this respect when he asserts that in the very act of afflicting us with the cross he is providing for our salvation."¹²

Having been driven from our blind self-confidence to seek help from God, he abundantly supplies us with help. He extends to us grace and mercy. "Let us then with confidence draw near to the throne of grace, that we may receive mercy and find grace to help in time of need" (Heb 4:16). He works through his Holy Spirit to change us more and more into the likeness of Jesus Christ (2 Cor 3:18). His grace works to produce in us more faith, by which we are strengthened, encouraged, and transformed to believe in and rely more on him (Rom 1:17). We are trained by the cross and his grace to walk in the ways of the Lord, in the obedience of faith (Rom 1:5). His grace leads us to a place of quiet and rest, knowing that our Father is at work transforming us by the power of his cross into grains of wheat, that having died, will now bear much fruit (John 12:24).

---

9. Zachman, "Deny Yourself," 475.
10. Calvin, *Com.*, Psalms, xxxix.
11. Calvin, *Institutes*, 3.8.3.
12. Calvin, *Institutes*, 3.8.11.

Perhaps a personal example will help make this dynamic more clear. Please recall from the last chapter the failure of the Church Planting Center which I led in 1991. The public failure, the loss of reputation and respect, the loss of income, all combined to create one unbearable cross for my ambitious younger self. But this failure was a heaven-sent cross. I was humbled to the dust. I prayed long, hard, and tearfully. I came to know Christ in new and deeper ways. I lost confidence in my flesh and instead wanted to rely more deeply on his power. God's grace, found in that failure, and the six months of wilderness which followed, shaped me into a new man.

In 2016 I was asked to launch a new Center for Church Planting. Twenty-five years, and several more crosses later, my approach was entirely different. My wife, Ann, summed it up nicely. "The first Center you *had* to do, this one you are *willing* to do." Amen. Calvin extols the power of the cross in our lives.

> It is indeed a singular consolation, calculated to mitigate the bitterness of the cross, when the faithful hear, that by sorrows and tribulations they are sanctified for glory as Christ himself was; and hence they see a sufficient reason why they should lovingly kiss the cross rather than dread it. And when this is the case, then doubtless the reproach of the cross of Christ immediately disappears, and its glory shines forth; for who can despise what is sacred, nay, what God sanctifies?[13]

The cross then brings us low, giving us a true understanding of our sin and weakness, which invites us to look upward to God, where seeing his power and loving grace, we seek and find his help.

How We Are to Bear the Cross for Our Growth in Grace

Recognize Crosses as Providential Trials, Rather Than Accidents

We must first come to a deep theological and spiritual understanding of God's sovereign rule of the universe through his providence. The Westminster Shorter Catechism, answer 11, says: "God's works of providence are his most holy, wise, and powerful preserving and governing all his creatures, and all their actions." Simply put, every aspect of our lives, our

---

13. Calvin, *Com.*, Heb 2:10.

bodies, health, family, friends, work, finances, homes, etc., are all governed by God's providence. "Are not two sparrows sold for a penny? And not one of them will fall to the ground apart from your Father" (Matt 10:29).

God ordains and orders all things such that there is no room for such a thing as an accident. "First, then, we ought to acknowledge the hand of God which strikes us, and not to imagine that our distresses arise from a blind impetuosity of fortune."[14] God does achieve his ordained ends using secondary causes, such as: the human will, the seemingly random blowing of the wind, the growth of a cancer cell, the hatred of an enemy, but it is his will that is the primary cause.

God not only orders all things within his providence, he does so always for our benefit, not our ease or comfort—but our good—which is finally our holiness. "And we know that for those who love God all things work together for good, for those who are called according to his purpose" (Rom 8:28).

Should we fail to recognize that it is God's hand with which we are dealing then we may lower our sights and think we fight against disease, weather, chance, or people. Those forces, blind and hateful, we may rightly resist. But knowing that whoever, or whatever, delivered the cross to us, that it was ultimately sent by God, transforms our experience and helps us to embrace the cross rather than rejecting it. "He has surely benefited greatly who has so learned to meditate upon God's providence that he can always recall his mind to this point: the Lord has willed it; therefore it must be borne."[15]

This single perspective, this single fact, transforms the way we must understand and embrace trials in our lives. When we suffer it is not because of the misfortune of genetics, the variabilities of the stock market, the fickleness of friends, or the hatred of enemies, it is the loving providence of God. Knowing that crosses are from God's good providence helps us to more readily submit to God in them.

Submit to God's Crosses, Rather Than Resisting Them

Our natural tendency when faced with anything unpleasant is to either avoid it or bring it to an end as quickly as possible. We look for the way

---

14. Calvin, *Com.*, John 5:14.
15. Calvin, *Institutes*, 1.17.8.

around the cross, we do not look for the handles by which we may heft and bear it. In a word, we resist the cross, we do not embrace it.

God, however, calls us in humility to bear the crosses he sends our way for our benefit. "Whoever does not bear his own cross and come after me cannot be my disciple" (Luke 14:27).

Rather than avoiding the difficult providences of God we are to bear them, that is, submit to them fully. When we submit to the crosses of God we do not seek to escape them but to faithfully carry them as did our Lord. If the Lord should bring us cancer, we do not complain, "Lord I hate this, just make it go away!" But rather, we pray, "For now Lord you have ordained for me to have cancer, ok, now how do I faithfully follow you while I bear this cross."

This is not to say that we cannot pray for relief from our crosses, our Lord did: "My Father, if it be possible, let this cup pass from me." God wants us to cry out to him in this way, but we must always conclude as did our Lord. "Nevertheless, not as I will, but as you will" (Matt 26:39). It is precisely this submission, that prayer, that heartfelt bowing before the will of the Father, that is required for us to most benefit from the crosses we bear. Indeed, our trials are transformed through our submission to God. Even while we ask for relief from the disease, the heartache, the financial ruin, with sincere tears before God, who welcomes such prayers, we do so with a final submission to his will. "Thus at the funerals of our dear ones we shall weep the tears that are owed to our nature. But the conclusion will always be: the Lord so willed, therefore let us follow his will."[16]

It would be easy for us if we always understood the "why" behind the crosses that we suffer. Then we could simply agree with God that this is a good idea. Submission, to actually qualify as submissive, requires that we do not agree with the thing to which we are being asked to submit. If we agree with it then we are simply getting what we want. So, generally, our submission is rendered without our understanding or approval. Recall Calvin's submission to God in his return to Geneva after his exile, mentioned in the last chapter. Although he did not want it or agree with it he concluded: "I submit my will and my affections, subdued and held-fast, to the obedience of God."[17]

This submitting to God in his difficult providences entails a deep trust on our part. Our natural response to suffering is to doubt God, to

---

16. Calvin, *Institutes*, 3.8.10.
17. Beveridge and Bonnet, *Tracts and Letters*, 4:280–81.

mistrust and question him. "Why me?" we complain. Submission leads us to trust rather than doubt God. We must trust that he providentially sent us this trial, that he intends the trial for our ultimate good, and that he knows best. Submission bares the back to receive the rod from God, trusting that he will redeem through those very stripes. We must trust his Word rather than our emotions which bid us to rebel, or the devil who tempts us to see this trial as a sign that God either has forgotten us or hates us. "Trust in the LORD with all your heart, and do not lean on your own understanding" (Prov 3:5). This trust is growth in faith, key to our holiness.

To properly and most profitably bear the cross, which leads to our sanctification, we must with trust and faith, submit to God in difficult providences.

Endure the Cross for as Long as It Lasts, Rather Than Quitting

Part of the difficulty of the crosses we bear is their temporal nature. The crosses come at inconvenient moments and linger for inordinate lengths of time, requiring perseverance. The Apostle Paul prayed repeatedly for the thorn in his flesh to be removed, but the Lord was pleased rather to leave it longer than Paul desired, to shape his heart into one of greater dependence and humility, as Paul put it, "to keep me from becoming conceited" (2 Cor 12:7).

It is in part the bad timing and the lengthy stay of the crosses which define them as suffering. We would prefer to swallow one simple bitter pill and be cured, but the Lord, the ever wise physician, gives us a long prescription for the medicine that will heal us, which we may need to take for months, even years. "When we have prayed to him, he often delays his assistance, either that he may increase still more our ardor in prayer, or that he may exercise our patience, and, at the same time, accustom us to obedience."[18]

Because the very nature of the cross is long-suffering we must submit to the Lord's timing and duration of the cross, persevering, confident that he knows best how long we need this cross to work upon us for our good.

---

18. Calvin, *Com.*, John 11:5.

Kiss the Cross, Embracing It with Joy, Rather Than Resenting It

Finally, submission to the cross requires that we embrace it with joy. "Count it all joy, my brothers, when you meet trials of various kinds" (Jas 1:2). Since the cross conforms us more and more into the very image of Christ, we "should lovingly kiss the cross rather than dread it."[19]

We can welcome the cross, rejoicing in our sufferings, not for the sake of the suffering itself, but for the result that it brings to those who are trained by it. "Not only that, but we rejoice in our sufferings, knowing that suffering produces endurance . . . character and . . . hope, and hope does not put us to shame, because God's love has been poured into our hearts through the Holy Spirit who has been given to us" (Rom 5:3-5).

Thomas à Kempis enthusiastically endorsed the joyful embrace of the cross.

> In the cross is salvation, in the cross is life, in the cross is protection from enemies, in the cross is infusion of heavenly sweetness, in the cross is strength of mind, in the cross is joy of spirit, in the cross is highest virtue, in the cross is perfect holiness. . . . Take up your cross, therefore, and follow Jesus, and you shall enter eternal life.[20]

This kissing of the cross is essential to being trained by the cross for only then do we fully submit to its lessons. To kiss the cross we must live by faith. We must believe that the cross is from God, for our good, and guided by his love and wisdom.

Instruction in cross bearing was essential to Calvin's pastoral counsel, as I have found it to be in mine. The gentle words, "My friend, God calls you now to submit to his difficult providence, do so and it will transform your life," have become a staple of my pastoral counsel.

Submitting to God in difficult providences was such a constant part of Calvin's life that his protégé, Theodore Beza, wrote upon the death of his beloved mentor, Calvin. "I would also have profited very little from his teaching . . . if I had not learnt through all these means to submit to God's providence and be completely satisfied and content."[21]

---

19. Calvin, *Com.*, Heb 2:10.
20. Thomas à Kempis, *The Imitation of Christ*, 2:12.
21. Beza, *The Life of John Calvin*, 12.

Helpful Reminders as We Bear the Cross

1. Remember. When trials come remind yourself of these simple biblical truths.

    God is sovereign and directs all things through his providence. It does not matter how the cross arrived, friend, foe, natural calamity, or a computer virus, God sent it. "And we know that for those who love God all things work together for good, for those who are called according to his purpose" (Rom 8:28).

    God has sent the cross, not to destroy you but to develop and bless you that you might know him and his love more fully and grow in character and hope. "Not only that, but we rejoice in our sufferings, knowing that suffering produces endurance ... character and ... hope, and hope does not put us to shame, because God's love has been poured into our hearts through the Holy Spirit who has been given to us" (Rom 5:3–5).

    God calls you to submit to the cross he has sent your way, with perseverance, hope, and joy, knowing he is actively at work. "Shall we not much more be subject to the Father of spirits and live?" (Heb 12:9).

2. Watch out! Be aware that your flesh will naturally rebel in the face of suffering, looking for any way to flee the cross. You will tend to doubt God's providence, and his goodness. When you feel these doubts rising repent of them. "Whoever does not take his cross and follow me is not worthy of me" (Matt 10:38).

3. Pray. Feel free to submissively ask the Lord to remove the cross, all the while, yielding to his will. Ask him for faith and strength to endure. Ask him for guidance. "Lord, for now you wish for me to bear this cross, ok, I will. What does it look like for me to do so faithfully?"

4. Submit. Submit to the Lord in this difficult providence, remember that this is his desire for you. Take up your cross and follow Jesus.

5. Examine. While not every cross comes as discipline for sin, some do. Any time we are under the cross it is a good opportunity to use the trial to examine oneself for sin.

6. Hope. It is helpful to think about how God might use this to bless you and train you. How might this trial protect you from danger,

direct you on new paths, develop your faith, hope, and love? Think specifically about what God might be doing.

7. Rejoice. God brings crosses to his children to train them and develop them, never to destroy them. This new trial is yet new evidence that God loves you. "Count it all joy, my brothers, when you meet trials of various kinds" (Jas 1:2).

Further Resources

Study Questions

1. How would you define cross bearing?
2. What four types of crosses may we bear in this life?
3. In what ways does cross bearing help to make us holy?
4. How can we best bear the crosses God sends our way?
5. Why is submission to God in difficult providences the key to our cross bearing?
6. What cross is God asking you to bear at this time?
7. What could you do to submit even more joyfully to the crosses he has for you?

For Further Study

Timothy Keller, *Walking with God through Pain and Suffering* (New York: Dutton, 2013).

John Piper and Justin Taylor, eds., *Suffering and the Sovereignty of God* (Wheaton, IL: Crossway, 2006).

R. C. Sproul, *Surprised by Suffering: The Role of Pain and Death in the Christian Life* (Lake Mary, FL: Reformation, 2009).

11

Contemplate Heaven

"Don't be so heavenly minded that you are no earthly good," the old warning goes. I have never known anyone like that. But I have met many Christians who were, "so earthly minded that they are no heavenly good." This is a serious problem because we are built by God to find our highest joy in heaven, not in this life. Yet, we keep trying, futilely, to make heaven out of Earth. "For we undertake all things as if we were establishing immortality for ourselves on earth."[1]

As long as we think that this life is our ultimate existence we will live wrongly. We will expect too much from this life—demanding that it satisfy our deepest longings—and find ourselves disappointed when it fails to deliver. For example, trying to have heaven on Earth, we may try to turn our houses into eternal homes. We decorate and landscape—not wrong in itself, of course—but in a desperate attempt to create heaven for ourselves. "But if you examine the plans, the efforts, the deeds, of anyone, there you will find nothing else but earth. . . . The whole soul, enmeshed in the allurements of the flesh, seeks its happiness on earth."[2]

When we do not contemplate heaven rightly we overinvest our hopes in this life. While family is clearly a biblical priority, we may make our children earthly idols. We groom them for worldly success, making sure they have it all, from elite sports clubs, to the best college prep schools, to polished resumes. Then we are surprised when, as young adults, they live out the worldliness we taught them and drop out of church.

---

1. Calvin, *Institutes*, 3.9.2.
2. Calvin, *Institutes*, 3.9.1.

When we do not contemplate heaven rightly we discover that Earth cannot bear the weight of heavenly expectations. Our homes constantly decay and need repair. Children grow up and move away. Jobs don't deliver the hoped significance. Friends leave us feeling unloved. Efforts at fitness produce injuries. Vacations leave us tired.

Our solution is not, however, to stop longing for more, that is a recipe for despair. We should keep our longings, but aim them toward the place of their fulfillment: heaven.

Scripture is clear that we should long for heaven to find our fullest joy. "Set your minds on things that are above, not on things that are on earth" (Col 3:2). Those who desire a heavenly country are our examples. "They desire a better country, that is, a heavenly one. Therefore God is not ashamed to be called their God, for he has prepared for them a city" (Heb 11:16). We are told that as citizens of another world we should look expectantly there. "But our citizenship is in heaven, and from it we await a Savior, the Lord Jesus Christ" (Phil 3:20).

God not only instructs us to long for heaven, but he paints a very compelling picture of heaven to increase our longing. There will be no pain in heaven. "He will swallow up death forever; and the Lord GOD will wipe away tears from all faces" (Isa 25:8). Heaven will be filled with great splendor and beauty (Rev 22:1). There will be material abundance (Isa 25:6). In heaven we will finally know relational wholeness with God. "Behold, the dwelling place of God is with man" (Rev 21:2). There we find relational wholeness with people, too (Luke 13:29).

Our bodies will be strong, glorious, and immortal. "It is sown in dishonor; it is raised in glory. It is sown in weakness; it is raised in power" (1 Cor 15:43). Heaven will be a place for unending joy, resulting in ceaseless praise for God. "Then I heard what seemed to be the voice of a great multitude, like the roar of many waters and like the sound of mighty peals of thunder, crying out, 'Hallelujah! For the Lord our God the Almighty reigns'" (Rev 19:6). Heaven will be, in a word, paradise. "Truly, I say to you, today you will be with me in Paradise" (Luke 23:43).

Rightly longing for heaven is a key to a life that is both happy and holy. In this chapter we will discuss what it means to contemplate heaven, how contemplating heaven helps us to grow more holy, and finally, how we should practice a right contemplation of heaven.

The Contemplation of Heaven

Contemplating heaven is thinking about and longing for heaven, which produces a relative disdain for this life. Jesus was clear about setting our hearts on heaven. "Do not lay up for yourselves treasures on earth, where moth and rust destroy and where thieves break in and steal, but lay up for yourselves treasures in heaven" (Matt 6:19–20). He told the disciples to find their chief joy, not in their service for him on Earth, but in their assurance of heaven. "Rejoice that your names are written in heaven" (Luke 10:20).

Scripture invites us to look upward, to see and long for the glories of heaven "For behold, I create new heavens and a new earth, and the former things shall not be remembered or come into mind" (Isa 65:17). We are beckoned to seek this heavenly home. "For here we have no lasting city, but we seek the city that is to come" (Heb 13:14). We are bidden to wait for the joys of heaven. "But according to his promise we are waiting for new heavens and a new earth in which righteousness dwells" (2 Pet 3:13).

We are to contemplate heaven, to think of it often. Usually, we fill our days with dreams of this life: our next vacation, an upcoming family gathering, a promotion at work, or even retirement. If we can contemplate these lesser joys, we should spend even more time contemplating the greatest joy possible. God wants us to raise our sights higher, to look beyond those small joys, and look forward to the greatest joy of all, being with him in glory.

Contemplating heaven also means longing for heaven. Like the child who cannot wait for Christmas morning, the Christian is to be bursting with anticipation of heaven and Christ's return. "My soul longs, yes, faints for the courts of the LORD" (Ps 84:2). If heaven is home, then we sojourn now in a place that is a kind of exile and we rightly long for our return home.[3]

This longing is to be so deep that we experience it as a kind of inward groaning. "We ourselves, who have the firstfruits of the Spirit, groan inwardly as we wait eagerly for adoption as sons, the redemption of our bodies" (Rom 8:23). Martin Bucer explained that Christians long so much because heaven is so glorious. "He heightens the effect of the groaning with which the sons of God long for glory, so that he may show how great this longing of the saints is, and from this, how great is that glory of theirs for which they groan and sigh so much."[4]

---

3. Calvin, *Institutes*, 3.9.4.
4. Bucer, *Metaphrasis et Enarratio*, 390.

Rightly contemplating heaven leads to a necessary corollary, we have a *relative* disdain or contempt for this life. When we compare the joys of heaven with the tribulations here we rightly discount this life and long more for heaven.[5] "For this light momentary affliction is preparing for us an eternal weight of glory beyond all comparison" (2 Cor 4:17). This is not to say that we are ungrateful to God for putting us in this world or for his blessings here, but rather that we rightly disdain this life *by comparison* with the life to come.[6]

This contempt for the world is further fuel for our contemplation and longing for the life to come. Every difficulty we endure here transfers our hope from this world to heaven. "It is indeed right that those who do not find their delight in things present should here rejoice in the remembrance of things to come."[7] Noticing the disappointments and heartaches in this life, and allowing ourselves to experience and feel them fully, is a part of the spiritual discipline of contemplating heaven. For each blow we feel here causes us to groan evermore for the world to come.

For example, when I was twelve I saved my paper-route money to buy a toy, Robby the Robot, from the television series, *Lost in Space*. As I saved, I anticipated the endless hours I would enjoy playing with his battery powered arms, legs, and lights. The very day I bought Robby—the very day—he broke. I realized at that moment, as a young non-Christian, the futility of putting hope in material things and coined a lifelong maxim: "Stuff breaks."

Stuff breaks, and so knowing this we should comparatively disdain the stuff of Earth and long all the more for the glories of heaven, "where neither moth nor rust destroys and where thieves do not break in and steal" (Matt 6:20). We should allow the trials in this life to inspire us to long for the next and better life. "Whatever kind of tribulation presses upon us, we must ever look to this end: to accustom ourselves to contempt for the present life and to be aroused thereby to meditate upon the future life."[8]

Our right contempt for this life in comparison to the next does not, however, lead us to ignore this life. Rather, it equips us to serve all the more effectively—sacrificially and joyfully. Since we do not have to find

5. Calvin, *Institutes*, 3.9.4.
6. Calvin, *Institutes*, 3.9.3.
7. Bernard, *Love of God*, 17.
8. Calvin, *Institutes*, 3.9.1.

all our happiness from this life, we can endure and serve patiently in this life, confident that a better day awaits.

Contemplation of heaven includes both a daily thinking about and longing for the glory of heaven along with a relative disdain for this life, due to its hardships. Together, this longing for heaven and the disdain for this life leads us, paradoxically, to engage all the more actively and joyfully in this world, assured of the eventual reward and fulfillment in the life to come.

How Contemplation of Heaven Helps Us to Grow More Holy

Contemplating Heaven Increases Our Faith

The more we contemplate the promise of heaven, the more our faith grows, since faith is assurance in that promise. The more our faith grows, the more our holiness grows. We see in Hebrews how longing for heaven led Abraham to grow in faith and holiness.

> By faith Abraham obeyed when he was called to go out to a place that he was to receive as an inheritance. And he went out, not knowing where he was going. By faith he went to live in the land of promise, as in a foreign land, living in tents with Isaac and Jacob, heirs with him of the same promise. For he was looking forward to the city that has foundations, whose designer and builder is God. (Heb 11:8–10)

What was it that Abraham believed which encouraged him to strike out to an unknown land on Earth? "For he was looking forward to a city . . . whose designer and builder is God." It was precisely his confidence in heaven that gave him the faith he needed to obey God in a great adventure upon Earth. This hope was not just theoretical; it was a passionate longing for him. Abraham was "looking forward to," that is, he was expectantly longing for the day he would inhabit the City of God. Because he was waiting for that day, confidently believing that it would come, he was willing to live as a sojourner for the present, in a place he did not know.

Contemplating heaven increases our faith and therefore our ability to live by faith in this life—one key aspect to our growth in holiness.

Contemplating Heaven Leads to Repentance

Contemplating heaven is repentance. "The doctrine of repentance . . . requires the . . . meditating upon the heavenly life."[9] Our sinful, earthly nature loves this life and wants to make heaven out of it. Contemplating heaven leads us to repent from loving this life too much, and from trying to create heaven on Earth. When we turn from an inordinate love for this world to think of heaven, that is repentance. "Do not love the world or the things in the world. . . . The world is passing away along with its desires, but whoever does the will of God abides forever" (1 John 2:15–17).

Repenting, we accept the truth that this life is hard, fleeting, and ends with death, but we also turn to embrace the reality that God will fill all our longings in heaven in the presence of Christ. Thus contemplating heaven is repentance, a key to growth in holiness.

Contemplating Heaven Quickens the New Nature and Kills off the Old Nature

Thoughts of heaven bring the new nature to life. Heaven is the food that feeds the new creation in Christ and gives rise to the spiritual nature (Rom 8:5). Everything about heaven is designed to grow the new nature. Heaven holds forth reward for the righteous, joy in fellowship with the saints, and worship of Christ, all elements that encourage the spiritual nature.

Thoughts of heaven guide us to do good here for heavenly, not earthly, reward. "Beware of practicing your righteousness before other people in order to be seen by them, for then you will have no reward from your Father who is in heaven" (Matt 6:1). Thoughts of heaven lead us to serve humbly here for greatness there. "Whoever humbles himself like this child is the greatest in the kingdom of heaven" (Matt 18:4). Thoughts of heaven convince us to lay up treasures there, not on Earth (Matt 6:19–20). It is as we look upward that God advances in us the new nature, a nature more suited for heaven than for this world, so we should think all the more readily of heaven.

Contemplating heaven also starves the old sinful nature to death, mortifying it. Contemplating heaven kills our desire for material gain on Earth, making us see that building bigger barns is fleeting vanity. "Fool!

---

9. Calvin, *Com.*, Acts 20:21.

This night your soul is required of you, and the things you have prepared, whose will they be?" (Luke 12:20). Contemplating heaven kills our passion for fame in the world, helping us to work for reward from Christ. "For we must all appear before the judgment seat of Christ" (2 Cor 5:10). Contemplating heaven puts to death our sexual lusts, since heaven has no place for the sexually immoral (Eph 5:5).

With our hearts and thoughts focused on heaven, heaven itself becomes the medicine that destroys the cancer of sin in our lives. This is why we are instructed to set our minds on things above, for it puts to death those things in us of the Earth (Col 3:2). Thinking of heaven with Christ greatly aids our sanctification. "To conclude in a word: if believers' eyes are turned to the power of the resurrection, in their hearts the cross of Christ will at last triumph over the devil, flesh, sin, and wicked men."[10]

Contemplating Heaven Helps Us Deny Ourselves

Thinking of heaven helps our self-denial. It is the very thought of heaven—future rewards for our present self-denial—which makes self-denial possible, even desirable. If a person knows they are going to a rich banquet in a few hours, they can more easily pass up a greasy snack, confident that greater delicacies await. If we doubt heaven then naturally we will want to live so as to maximize our joy here and now. "For where there is no promise of any eternal inheritance implanted in our hearts, we shall never be torn away from this world."[11]

When we are confident that the best is yet to come—and comes in some measure in accordance with what we forgo here for Christ—we are far more willing to pass up a fleeting joy in exchange for a permanent one. When self-denial suggests that we should serve another person, thoughts of heavenly reward greatly assist our self-denial. Here the well-known quote of Jim Elliot, who gave his life on the mission field, applies: "He is no fool who gives up what he cannot keep to gain what he cannot lose."

Contemplating Heaven Helps Us to Bear the Cross

When we are confident that relief and joy are just around the corner, we can patiently endure any trial. When we doubt that eternal good waits for

---

10. Calvin, *Institutes*, 3.9.6.
11. Calvin, *Com.*, Dan 3:19.

us in heaven, then we are less willing to suffer here. Tell a man he must run forever and he will quickly tire. Tell him he must run a marathon and that great reward awaits him at the finish, and watch him make the finish line, even if he must crawl.

Knowing that Christ waits to reward our suffering—even our deaths—with a crown of glory, makes our endurance, even joy, in suffering possible. "Blessed is the man who remains steadfast under trial, for when he has stood the test he will receive the crown of life" (Jas 1:12). We are enabled to endure all trials when we are confident that there is a great reward waiting. "For you have need of endurance, so that when you have done the will of God you may receive what is promised" (Heb 10:36).

Jesus was willing to endure his own cross, and all its horror, by looking past the cross to the reward which awaited. "Who for the joy that was set before him endured the cross, despising the shame, and is seated at the right hand of the throne of God" (Heb 12:2). Like Jesus, we are to endure all trials in this world knowing that there is a better place waiting for us. "Therefore let us go to him outside the camp and bear the reproach he endured. For here we have no lasting city, but we seek the city that is to come" (Heb 13:13–14).

Because contemplating heaven is so useful to our patient, even joyful endurance of crosses, Calvin would often pastorally instruct those who were suffering to recall that their ultimate hope was in heaven. For example, in his February 27, 1559, letter to Madame de Coligny, worried over her husband's long imprisonment, Calvin wrote: "Whatever difficulties we may have to encounter, the promise given us that God will provide for us . . . teach[es] us to think more wisely, fixing our hearts, upon that life which is in heaven, so that the world shall seem nothing to us."[12] Contemplating heaven was a doctrine that Calvin, as a faithful pastor, found frequently useful for his suffering flock. "The usefulness of this teaching to us is apparent, by its inducing us to bear it patiently whenever we are often thrown prostrate on the ground."[13] Contemplating heaven while suffering will prove useful for us as well.

---

12. Beveridge and Bonnet, *Tracts and Letters*, 7:30–31.
13. Calvin, *Com.*, Dan 8:10.

Contemplating Heaven Helps Us Live the Christian Life

Contemplating heaven reminds us that in the final judgment good and evil will gain their just ends, motivating us to do good and avoid evil. "We must all appear before the judgment seat of Christ, so that each one may receive what is due for what he has done in the body, whether good or evil" (2 Cor 5:10). Confidence in heavenly reward becomes fuel for our good works here.

Contemplating heaven removes our fear of death which lends a fearlessness to our service. "It is when we turn our eyes to the glory of the life that is to come that our dread of death is vanquished."[14] When we know we cannot be finally killed our hearts are filled with desire to boldly serve the Lord, as the history of Christian martyrdom reminds us.

Meditation on the future life helps us to value heaven such that we are willing to give our time, talent, and treasure to seek the kingdom of heaven. "The kingdom of heaven is like treasure hidden in a field, which a man found and covered up. Then in his joy he goes and sells all that he has and buys that field" (Matt 13:44). Such devotion to God is the essence of holiness.

Having seen the ways in which contemplating heaven advances our holiness, we now will explore how to effectively think of heaven.

How to Contemplate Heaven for Growth in Holiness

Make a Real Disciplined Effort to Think of Heaven

Contemplating heaven requires thoughtful and disciplined effort, so we must "strive with all our heart to meditate upon the life to come."[15] "Set your minds on things that are above" (Col 3:2). Setting our minds on heaven means that we intentionally take time, each day, to consider heaven, that we teach on it, and remind one another of it. "Commendation of the future and eternal life is a theme worthy to be sounded in our ears by day and by night . . . and made the subject of ceaseless meditation."[16]

As we contemplate heaven we should focus our thoughts on its blessings and benefits. Heaven will be a place where there is no evil, sorrow, or hardship (Rev 21:27). We should contemplate the beauty of heaven. "The

---

14. Wallace, *Christian Life*, 267.
15. Calvin, *Institutes*, 3.9.2.
16. Reid, *Treatises*, 228.

wall was built of jasper, while the city was pure gold, like clear glass" (Rev 21:18). There will be abundance there: food, drink, and feasting mark our heavenly life (Matt 8:11). We should recall that there awaits for us a glorious inheritance with Christ (Rom 8:17). Heaven contains all the good that we so long for, and none of the bad that we eagerly wish to be free from, so there is great encouragement as we think about heaven.

Chiefly though we should focus our thoughts on being with Christ in heaven, as he is the highest good that waits for us. "My desire is to depart and be with Christ, for that is far better" (Phil 1:23). We are to look forward to Christ's return and all the goodness that he brings with him. "Seek the things that are above, where Christ is, seated at the right hand of God" (Col 3:1).

Let Difficulties in This Life Lead You to Thoughts of Heaven

God reminds us during trials here that our lives are not circumscribed by this world, but extend to eternity. "So we do not lose heart.... For this light momentary affliction is preparing for us an eternal weight of glory beyond all comparison" (2 Cor 4:16–17). During trials we must always remember: there is actually an eternal glory waiting for us!

Trials here are useful to loosen our grip on this world and tighten our grip on the world to come. A friend's two-year-old daughter died after a long illness. The trial of losing her, and the knowledge that she had gone before him into heaven, lifted my friend's thoughts from this world to the next. He said: "Heaven used to seem a strange place to me. Now it is where my daughter lives and therefore so much more desirable and near." When sorrow overtakes us we should use that sorrow to lift our thoughts to the time when every tear is dried. "I will turn their mourning into joy; I will comfort them, and give them gladness for sorrow" (Jer 31:13).

As we see and experience the injustice of the wicked, we are right to think of the day when God will bring justice for the godly. "The Lord knows how to rescue the godly from trials, and to keep the unrighteous under punishment until the day of judgment" (2 Pet 2:9).

The various bodily problems we face—genetic imperfections, diseases, and injuries—should help us to appropriately despise this life and look forward to the next. I love to run but can no longer do so because of arthritis in my knees. When I think of heaven, I do imagine among other greater joys, going out for a long run, where I will run and not be weary.

Each time illness or injury sidelines us we are right to think of that place where injury and illness will be no more. "What is sown is perishable; what is raised is imperishable" (1 Cor 15:42).

When it seems we have no place in this world—that we simply do not fit in or belong here—we should remember that Christ is preparing a place just for us. "And if I go and prepare a place for you, I will come again and will take you to myself, that where I am you may be also" (John 14:3). When we suffer from relational strains we are right to long for the day when all of our relationships are filled with *shalom* (Rev 7:9). When the burden of our own sin weighs us down we should look forward to the day when our hearts are light and free (Jer 31:33). When death threatens us, or those we love, we rightly hope for the place beyond all dying. "He will swallow up death forever; and the Lord GOD will wipe away tears from all faces" (Isa 25:8).

Whenever, therefore, God in his providence allows trials and suffering in our lives we should benefit from them by deepening our thoughts of heaven. "Whatever kind of tribulation presses upon us, we must ever look to this end: to accustom ourselves to contempt for the present life and to be aroused thereby to meditate upon the future life."[17] Trials here become springboards, to lift our thoughts to heaven where all trials will cease. This not only gives us courage to face those trials, but changes us into those whose hope is in heaven, that is, into those who look more and more like Jesus.

Let Blessings in This Life Lift Your Thoughts up to Heaven

God, who delights to bless us, blesses us in this life in part to help us look forward to an eternity of his blessings. The provision of the promised land was always meant to point us toward a better place. "But as it is, they desire a better country, that is, a heavenly one" (Heb 11:16). Therefore, as we experience his blessings here we should let them remind us of heavenly blessings yet to come (2 Pet 3:13).

Jesus promised his disciples blessing in this life, along with troubles, but in the world to come, nothing but blessings. "Who will . . . receive a hundredfold now . . . and in the age to come eternal life" (Mark 10:29–30). Even the Holy Spirit is given as "the guarantee of our inheritance" yet to

---

17. Calvin, *Institutes*, 3.9.1.

come (Eph 1:13–14). The word "guarantee" ἀρραβών (*arrabon*) means a deposit, or a down payment, assuring us that the rest is yet to come.

When God blesses us in this life, we should remember that they are a deposit, a foretaste, of the blessings that he holds in store for us. In this way we do not try to extract from them our final and highest joy, but rather let them, while truly a joy for us now, draw our hearts upward to Christ.

The church is meant to be a foretaste of heaven which whets our appetite for even more of heaven. When we worship joyfully in the church our hearts are prepared for the even greater joy of worship in heaven (Rev 19:1). The fellowship we know on Earth is also a foretaste—imperfect yet still satisfying—of the rich fellowship that we will know in heaven (Heb 12:22–23). The Lord's Supper draws our attention not only back to the cross, but forward to the great wedding feast of the Lamb. "Blessed are those who are invited to the marriage supper of the Lamb" (Rev 19:9). Let us remind ourselves at each Lord's Supper: "Someday I will eat this meal in person with Christ!"

The Sabbath Day is a present blessing, designed to remind us weekly that there waits for us a more satisfying Sabbath rest. "There remains a Sabbath rest for the people of God" (Heb 4:9). As we rest from our work and gather for worship, fellowship, the preaching of the Word, and sacraments, God means to open a window in our worlds to show us a bit of what the world to come will be like. "By this means he wants to lead them higher, that is, to the hope of this immortality which he has promised."[18]

As God blesses us in this life with foretastes of heaven—whether materially or spiritually—we should let each blessing prompt us to contemplate the greater joy which Christ holds for us in heaven.

Contemplate Heaven by Laying up Treasures in Heaven

We are to anticipate heaven by laying up treasures there. "Do not lay up for yourselves treasures on earth ... but lay up for yourselves treasures in heaven.... For where your treasure is, there your heart will be also" (Matt 6:19–21). When, for example, we give—tithing to the church, helping the poor—each dollar given away, invested in heaven as it were, loosens our heart from Earth and fixes it in heaven. "But if we believe heaven is our country, it is better to transmit our possessions thither than to keep them

---

18. Calvin, *Sermons on the Ten Commandments*, 286.

here where upon our sudden migration they would be lost to us. But how shall we transmit them? Surely, by providing for the needs of the poor; whatever is paid out to them, the Lord reckons as given to himself."[19]

Of course, laying up treasures in heaven is more than just giving money. We are to set our hopes, dreams, and goals on heaven as well. To make it our task to populate heaven through evangelism. To make it our calling to prepare others for heaven through discipleship. To treasure up the fellowship with Christ that we will have in heaven. "If in Christ we have hope in this life only, we are of all people most to be pitied" (1 Cor 15:19). We lay up treasure in heaven by investing everything in the life to come, rather than life here.

In all these ways then we are to contemplate heaven, and in doing so, we will be transformed more into the very image of the man from heaven. "Just as we have borne the image of the man of dust, we shall also bear the image of the man of heaven" (1 Cor 15:49).

Summary of How to Contemplate Heaven

1. Make a real disciplined effort to think of heaven. During your devotional time and at other points in the day, think about heaven, its glory and rewards, but even more, think about being with Jesus. The world pressures us to think about it, we must cultivate the new habit of thinking on heaven. Plan cues to make you think of heaven. For example, whenever you see a bird fly by, think of angels in flight; or whenever you brew a cup of coffee think of how wonderful the smells and tastes of heaven will be.

2. Let trials in this life encourage thoughts of heaven. Whenever you face suffering, small or large, use this to remind you that heaven will be a place without any suffering. Facing an injured knee? Think about heaven where you will run and not be weary.

3. Let your blessings here lift your thoughts to heaven. When some particular joy occurs in your life, use it to remind yourself that it is a small foretaste of greater blessings to come. Enjoying a birthday party with family and friends? Think of a birthday party in heaven with all those family members you have lost, where age does not matter, gifts are always just right, and your joy will be complete.

19. Calvin, *Institutes*, 3.18.6.

4. Let the joys of church life lift your heart to heaven. When worship, fellowship, preaching, or sacraments touch you, think about the greater joy of heaven to which they point.

5. Every Sabbath Day, enjoy your Sabbath and spend some of the time thinking of, or reading biblical passages about, the greater Sabbath rest of heaven.

6. Contemplate heaven by laying up treasures there. Tithe and give generously to those who have needs or who serve in ministry, laying up treasure in heaven. Treasure thoughts of reuniting with those saints who have gone before you, and most of all, of embracing Christ.

Further Resources

Study Questions

1. In what ways have you noticed that people try to create heaven for themselves on Earth?
2. Why is it not a good idea to try to find heaven on Earth?
3. Why is a disdain for this world, in comparison to heaven, healthy?
4. Contemplating heaven helps us to grow holy by: increasing our faith in the reality of heaven, leading us to repentance for loving this world too much, killing off the old nature, quickening the new, helping us to deny ourselves, enabling us to bear our cross, and living all our lives as Christians. Which of these benefits from contemplating heaven have you experienced?
5. Of the four ways to contemplate heaven (putting out real disciplined effort, letting trials here make you think of heaven, letting blessings here make you think of heaven, and laying up treasures in heaven) which have you found most helpful and why?
6. How much do you think of and long for heaven?
7. When you do think of heaven, which aspects of heaven bring you the most joy?
8. What practical steps might you take to contemplate heaven more regularly?

For Further Study

Randy Alcorn, *Heaven* (Carol Stream, IL: Tyndale, 2004).

Jonathan Edwards, "Heaven, a World of Love," in *Charity and its Fruits* (Carlisle, PA: Banner of Truth, 2005).

David Jeremiah, *Answers to Your Questions About Heaven* (Carol Stream, IL: Tyndale, 2015).

Joni Eareckson Tada, *Heaven: Your Real Home . . . From a Higher Perspective* (Grand Rapids: Zondervan, 1995).

12

Properly Use This Life

To live well as Christians in this world we must make the best use of our present lives. We make the best use of this present life as we enjoy life as sojourners who, called to a specific vocation, moderately use all things as stewards who care for the needs of others. These are six aspects of the right use of this life that we must keep before us daily. We will explain each briefly.

First, we should see that this life, despite its many struggles, is offered to us as a good gift that we should enjoy from God, "who richly provides us with everything to enjoy" (1 Tim 6:17). God blesses us here and now that we may know joy—joy surely that points forward to heaven—but real joy to relish today. "I brought you into a plentiful land to enjoy its fruits and its good things" (Jer 2:7). Creation is beautiful—even while it groans waiting for its full redemption—and is to be enjoyed. So too may we enjoy the beauty that humankind creates: art, architecture, gardens, music, and the like. "Sing praises to the LORD with the lyre, with the lyre and the sound of melody!" (Ps 98:5).

Second, while we should enjoy all of life, we should do so always conscience of the reality that we are sojourners here. Therefore, we do not hold too tightly to the blessings of this life, turning them from good gifts into idols. "This is what I mean, brothers: the appointed time has grown very short. From now on, let those who have wives live as though they had none, and those who mourn as though they were not mourning and those who rejoice as though they were not rejoicing, and those who buy as though they had no goods" (1 Cor 7:29–30).

Third, we must also understand and follow our vocation, God's call on us as individuals to certain duties and stations in life. "Only let each person lead the life that the Lord has assigned to him, and to which God has called him" (1 Cor 7:17). When we understand our particular calling in life—in terms of the work that we do, social status, economic levels, fame, usefulness for the Lord—we can more readily embrace what God wants for us in life and cooperate with him.

Fourth, moderation guides us within our individual vocations, as to how we are to use our resources. What is moderate for a king may be grossly luxurious for a pastor. Commenting on Rom 13:14, "But put on the Lord Jesus Christ, and make no provision for the flesh, to gratify its desires," Calvin writes:

> Paul, setting a bridle on our desires, reminds us, that the cause of all intemperance is, that no one is content with a moderate or lawful use of things: he has therefore laid down this rule—that we are to provide for the wants of our flesh, but not to indulge its lusts. It is in this way that we shall use this world without abusing it.[1]

Fifth, within our callings God assigns us as stewards of all that he has given us: time, talent, and treasure. "As each has received a gift, use it to serve one another, as good stewards of God's varied grace" (1 Pet 4:10).

Sixth, we steward all that God gives us by serving our neighbor. "But if anyone has the world's goods and sees his brother in need, yet closes his heart against him, how does God's love abide in him?" (1 John 3:17).

These six ideas we will combine into three principles by which we are to use the present life for the greater glory of God and good of others, and thus grow in holiness day by day.

1. Enjoying this life thankfully, we hold things loosely as sojourners.
2. Accepting our own vocation from God, we use all things moderately.
3. Living as stewards, we use everything to serve others.

We will now explain how to properly use this present life given these three principles, then we will show how the proper use of the present life advances our holiness, and finally, we will summarize how best to use this present life for the greatest growth in holiness.

---

1. Calvin, *Com.*, Rom 13:14.

How We Are to Properly Use This Present Life

Enjoying This Life Thankfully, We Hold Things Loosely as Sojourners

We must maintain these two realities in tension: while we thankfully enjoy this life as a good gift from God, yet since we are sojourners, we hold this world loosely.

First, we must understand that though fallen and imperfect, this life is offered to us as a gift from God which we should receive gratefully. "The earth is the LORD's and the fullness thereof, the world and those who dwell therein" (Ps 24:1). While fallen, beauty still exists on the earth, and beauty is an extravagance of God's love which goes beyond necessity for our joy.

> We find that the earth is full of beautiful and delightful things with qualities which can bring a richness and exhilaration to our earthly life far beyond the dictates of pure necessity. It is obviously the natural order of things that we should indulge in taking pleasure from those things which God has given us liberally to enjoy.[2]

We accept and enjoy all that God provides for us in this life with thanks (Eph 5:20).

There is to be no Platonic dualism in the Christian life, where we consider the material world bad and only the spiritual good. Bread can be as holy as prayer. "Give us each day our daily bread" (Luke 11:3). Every good gift is ours to use, for our needs, for the sake of the kingdom, and for the good of our neighbors. Even some measure of luxury is permitted to the Christian, as governed by his calling. "A rich man's wealth is his strong city" (Prov 18:11). We thankfully embrace all that God allots us in this life, to use for our own enjoyment and for the benefit of others.

Second, while we thankfully enjoy this life, we must hold it loosely as sojourners. "Beloved, I urge you as sojourners and exiles to abstain from the passions of the flesh" (1 Pet 2:11–18). We are a sojourning people: *in* this world—fully so—but never *of* this world. "They are not of the world, just as I am not of the world" (John 17:16). The Lord does not yet want to take us out of the world, he wants us here. He does want, however, to take the worldliness out of us. "I do not ask that you take them out of the world, but that you keep them from the evil one" (John 17:15).

2. Wallace, *Christian Life*, 137–38.

Part of the worldliness that he is removing from us is an ungodly love for the world, not at all meaning an appreciation of his blessings in this life. When God tells us to not love the world he means the *sinful world system* that denies God and only values the material, power, and sinful pleasures. "Do not love the world or the things in the world. If anyone loves the world, the love of the Father is not in him. For all that is in the world—the desires of the flesh and the desires of the eyes and pride of life—is not from the Father but is from the world" (1 John 2:15–16).

We are to live, then, with an eternal perspective, so that even as we enjoy and use the temporary, we hold it loosely, ready to surrender anything whenever God sees fit. The Lord might see fit in our calling to bless us with a new car. But then we may have it wrecked in an accident. What is our attitude? Are we angry and upset, or do we easily allow it to be towed to the junk yard? Our attitude upon losing anything tells us something about our heart concerning it. When we take pride in a nice car, considering ourselves worthy because we own it, then we have gone from appreciating creation to loving the world. We must remain willing to give anything, anyone, over to God the moment he requires it, or else, "whoever carries his attachment to the present life beyond this limit, *destroys his life*."[3]

This is a delicate balance, a difficult tension in which to live, but it is a very important one. If we go too far in one direction—detaching ourselves from God's good creation—we fall into the Platonic dualism which robs us of the joys God offers. If we hold too tightly to the world—desperate to derive all our joy from this life now—we become worldly and idolatrous, which also destroys joy. "You adulterous people! Do you not know that friendship with the world is enmity with God?" (Jas 4:4).

We must strive in faith to find this balance. "In short, to love this life is not in itself wrong, provided that we only pass through it as pilgrims, keeping our eyes always fixed on our object."[4] We must always keep our eyes fixed on our object: Christ, the kingdom of heaven, the glory of God, and service to others.

We see this right balance struck in the early church where believers held and enjoyed private lands, until they were needed by others, and then they readily parted with them. "There was not a needy person among them, for as many as were owners of lands or houses sold them

---

3. Calvin, *Com.*, John 12:25.
4. Calvin, *Com.*, John 12:25.

and brought the proceeds of what was sold and laid it at the apostles' feet, and it was distributed to each as any had need" (Acts 4:34–35). Here we find the example we are to emulate.

> So whether believers are rich, or in robust health, or wonderfully endowed with the Spirit's gifts, they acknowledge that God's favor is its only source. Their joy is real, and so is their thanksgiving. That is how they will use the good things of this present life. Nevertheless, while life for believers may be easy today, they will be ready tomorrow to endure whatever afflictions God may send them. He may, perhaps, take from them the goods he has given. They are prepared to surrender them, since they know they received them on one condition—that they should hand them back whenever God should choose.[5]

In part to help maintain this balance of living in the world but not holding it too tightly God created the Sabbath Day. "Observe the Sabbath day, to keep it holy" (Deut 5:12). By setting apart one day in seven, God demonstrates the reality that we are in, but not of the world. He draws us aside for twenty-four hours from our usual pursuits in this world to attend to him and the things which are above. On that day, while still residing on Earth, we practice not being of the world. The world rushes ahead pursuing its ends, thinking: "If we work the seventh day we will have a seventh more wealth." The Christian, however, knows that all his wealth comes not from his restless striving but from the Lord, so he can rest on the Sabbath.

In giving us the Sabbath Day, God trains us to hold this life loosely. The day of rest helps us to maintain the balance of living in the world but not being of the world by setting a definite schedule each week for us to focus on the things above. This benefit carries over into the other six days, where we can live a perpetual Sabbath rest, a constant focus heavenward, even as we conduct business in the world. "We must not limit ourselves to a single day of the week to submit ourselves to God, but it must be one uninterrupted day for the rest of our lives."[6]

We receive all of this life thankfully, but as the Sabbath reminds us, we are sojourners here, who hold all things loosely, always ready to joyfully hand them over for God's service.

---

5. Calvin, *Sermons on the Beatitudes*, 77–78.
6. Calvin, *Sermons on Genesis*, 132–33.

Accepting Our Own Vocation from God, We Use All Things Moderately

To live rightly in this world we must understand and accept God's particular calling for our lives, and within that call, use moderately the resources he provides. "The Lord bids each one of us in all life's actions to look to his calling."[7] Each calling is unique, each journey we take, even though we walk next to others, is specially appointed by God, so we are to take all that he has given us and made us, and use this toward his ends. "Having gifts that differ according to the grace given to us, let us use them" (Rom 12:6). Serving God in accordance with our individual calling is the only path to success and joy in the kingdom of God.

Each unique calling offers us guidelines on how to use the resources of life to advance God's purposes. There is no "one size fits all" description of how we are to use things in this world, since each calling is different. There is no square foot limit on how large a Christian's home may be, how large their bank account may grow, or how nice their clothing may be, since each calling is unique.

We have in our church many successful people whose cars, homes, and clothes are all substantially nicer than mine. However, these things suit their calling well. One of those successful families offered to give me one of their used luxury cars. I demurred, because it seemed to me that the car was nicer than a pastor of a missions-oriented church should drive. The car was moderate, given their calling in life, but excessive, given mine. Hence the importance of understanding and following our calling in order to know how we each are to use wealth in this life properly.

Vocation circumscribes for us how much wealth we may have. Striving to obtain more, or other, than God wants for us—is a root of all kinds of evil. "May we be content with our humble station."[8] When we strive for those things God has not included in our calling, we use ungodly means to fulfill ungodly passions and so abuse the present life that God has given us.

Following our vocation we also know what duties to take up—those within our calling—and which to decline—those outside of our calling. We know as well, or at least have some guidance, on how we are to use the things that God supplies us in life: the time, talent, and treasure, to serve God in our vocation. It is within our individual calling

---

7. Calvin, *Institutes*, 3.10.6.
8. Calvin, *Com.*, Dan 6:7.

that our obedience to God is proven in gray areas such as wealth. "Let us note that we must undertake nothing outside of our vocation. For what may seem to be virtue to us will be considered vice before God if we go beyond our limits."[9]

Our success should not be measured against one another in terms of results. Rather, we are to be measured against our faithfulness to our particular calling from God. One person may be called to start a small business to employ five people, another to run a company with 100,000. The world will quickly judge the latter as the more successful. But in the plan of God it may well be that the former, for reasons invisible to us, was the one more faithful to his calling. "For we are his workmanship, created in Christ Jesus for good works, which God prepared beforehand, that we should walk in them" (Eph 2:10).

Rather than seeking to break the bounds of our vocation, we should seek to faithfully follow our calling at each stage of life. "Godliness with contentment is great gain" (1 Tim 6:6). This does not mean that our status in this world may never change. God may well have different callings for us at different times. The seminary where I teach has many former business leaders who have been called into ministry, and now have a more modest material standard for their faithfulness. Yet at each stage we are to contently embrace the calling of God and prove faithful within that call. "Clearly, no one can raise a finger's breadth above his calling without God's hand immediately being against him."[10]

Once we understand our calling and God's design for us to contentedly work within its bounds then we may use all things in moderation, in accordance with our vocation. This moderation calls us again to a fine balance: joyful use without sinful abuse. Within our individual callings, each one should be guided by their own conscience before Scripture as to what constitutes moderation. "This freedom is not to be restrained by any limitation but to be left to every man's conscience to use as far as seems lawful to him."[11]

Moderation does not dictate that we only have the bare necessities, but includes the rich enjoyment of what God provides. "Wine to gladden the heart of man, oil to make his face shine and bread to strengthen man's heart" (Ps 104:15). Yet, even as we celebrate and enjoy God's goodness to

---

9. Calvin, *Sermons on 2 Samuel*, 246.
10. Calvin, *Sermons on the Nativity*, 52.
11. Calvin, *Institutes*, 3.10.1.

us, moderation remains our rule, not gluttony or drunkenness. "But put on the Lord Jesus Christ, and make no provision for the flesh, to gratify its desires" (Rom 13:14).

We should be moderate in our food and drink. "Be not among drunkards or among gluttonous eaters of meat" (Prov 23:20). While we may enjoy a good meal, overindulging is destructive to our bodies which are temples of the Holy Spirit (1 Cor 6:19–20). Wine is good and a right source of delight, but we should not drink to excess. "Do not get drunk with wine, for that is debauchery" (Eph 5:18).

While clothing is for both protection and ornamentation, again our rule should be moderation. While Solomon rightly admires his bride's adornment, "Your cheeks are lovely with ornaments, your neck with strings of jewels" (Song 1:10), yet we are warned to not make the external the primary adornment of our lives: "Do not let your adorning be external—the braiding of hair and the putting on of gold jewelry, or the clothing you wear" (1 Pet 3:3).

We should be moderate in our finances, neither loving money ("For the love of money is a root of all kinds of evils." [1 Tim 6:10]) nor failing to be good stewards of the finances entrusted to us. "If then you have not been faithful in the unrighteous wealth, who will entrust to you the true riches?" (Luke 16:11).

We should be moderate in our emotional life as well. "An essential element in the ordered Christian life is the moderation of all passions, appetites, and even zeal."[12] Rather than following our emotions and giving them full vent, the Bible bids us to rein them in, keeping them in check for the glory of God and for the good of others. We do not allow our anger to rage. "For the anger of man does not produce the righteousness of God" (Jas 1:20). Our anxiety should not be indulged, either, but turned over to the Lord to eradicate. "Do not be anxious about anything, but in everything by prayer and supplication with thanksgiving let your requests be made known to God" (Phil 4:6). Nor should fear be allowed to dominate us. "In God I trust; I shall not be afraid. What can man do to me?" (Ps 56:11).

Even joy and sorrow should be under control to the point that we may: "Rejoice with those who rejoice, weep with those who weep" (Rom 12:15). Our sorrow should not be so excessive that we forget God's goodness. "That you may not grieve as others do who have no hope" (1 Thess

---

12. Wallace, *Christian Life*, 170.

4:13). Nor should joy be so excessive that "your heart be lifted up, and you forget the LORD your God" (Deut 8:14).

This is not to say that we pretend to feel other than we feel. Rather, we take our current emotions as an accurate indicator of our current reaction to the world, not as the final word on how we should respond. Then we take our emotions to the Lord, that he might help regulate and guide them under his Spirit. "Seeing, also, that our affections are completely unstable, and that our lack of stability always entails some excess and vice . . . let us learn to turn ourselves over to God."[13]

Moderation within our particular vocation, as guided by the Word, the Spirit, and our consciences, helps us to use this present life so as to please the Lord.

Living as Stewards, We Use Everything to Serve Others

To live wisely and well in this life we must live as good stewards, making the best use of all that God has made us and given us, to benefit others. "As each has received a gift, use it to serve one another, as good stewards of God's varied grace" (1 Pet 4:10).

We must live as stewards, since it is not only the wisest way to live, but also because we must give an account of our faithfulness as God's servants. "Moreover, it is required of stewards that they be found faithful" (1 Cor 4:2). This new paradigm—living as stewards—is directly contrary to the old worldly way where each person looks out for themselves at the expense of others. "No one should live for himself, because God created all things so that they might contribute not to their own good but to that of others."[14]

This living for the sake of others begins with a real love for others, hence the second great commandment: "You shall love your neighbor as yourself" (Matt 22:39). Loving our neighbors we are naturally concerned for their interests, along with our own. "Let each of you look not only to his own interests, but also to the interests of others" (Phil 2:4). As we love others we naturally steward ourselves and our assets for their benefit.

This love and concern is not only for those with whom we are close relationally, where our concerns naturally fall, but with all of our neighbors, taking the Samaritan, who helped the unknown Jew, as our model

---

13. Calvin, *Sermons on 2 Samuel*, 659.
14. Bucer, *Christian Love*, 28–29.

(Luke 10:33–37). This love and concern extends even beyond strangers to the most difficult class of people to love: our enemies. "Love your enemies, do good to those who hate you" (Luke 6:27). Our love for our enemies should include care for their souls. "We are much more obliged to procure the salvation of [our enemy's] soul, since the soul is more precious than the body."[15]

Obviously this love and service to our neighbors should include caring for their physical needs. "But if anyone has the world's goods and sees his brother in need, yet closes his heart against him, how does God's love abide in him?" (1 John 3:17). We must, however, go beyond the physical needs of others and care for their spiritual needs. "God does not stretch forth his hand to us to lead each of us to follow his own course, but to assist others and to advance their spiritual progress."[16]

Loving our neighbors also means that we work to actively promote justice and fairness for them, defending them "when unjustly oppressed."[17] Doing justice for our neighbors includes offering them a fair wage and good working conditions when we employ them.[18]

Of course, we do not live as stewards to earn God's love, for this we have already in Christ. Rather, we live as good stewards for others because God's love fills us, and because we believe God blesses those who walk in obedience to his commands, now and forever.

We see then how we are to use this life rightly by stewarding all that we have and are to love our neighbors, body and soul. Having explained the three principles of the right use of this present life, we will now show how using this life properly helps with the advance of our holiness.

How the Proper Use of This Present Life Helps Our Holiness

The Right Use of This Present Life Is the Daily Practice of Faith That Makes Us More Like Christ

We practice faith as we recognize that we are sojourners who must hold loosely to this world. The devil, the world, and our unbelieving flesh all

---

15. Viret, *Du Devoir et du Besoing*, A2b.
16. Calvin, *Com.*, Dan 11:34.
17. Calvin, *Com.*, Ezek 18:5.
18. Calvin, *Com.*, Jer 2:13.

say to us: "This world—this life, this time—is all you will ever have, so you had better get everything you can, now." But God speaks a better word to us, telling us that this world will pass away, while heaven will last forever. "We look not to the things that are seen but to the things that are unseen. For the things that are seen are transient, but the things that are unseen are eternal" (2 Cor 4:18). As we struggle for faith, God's Word to us, that this life is transient and heaven eternal, works to strengthen our faith.

Accepting our vocation while moderately using all that God has given us, is also the daily practice of faith. Our unbelief leads us to consume more than God would give us and to pridefully seek a greater vocation. When by faith we accept that moderation within our vocation is actually God's intended blessing for us, this brings us a Christ-like contentment. "But godliness with contentment is great gain, for we brought nothing into the world, and we cannot take anything out of the world" (1 Tim 6:6–7). We must come to believe that the moderate use of the things of this world will be more satisfying than riches. "As for the rich in this present age, charge them not to be haughty, nor to set their hopes on the uncertainty of riches, but on God, who richly provides us with everything to enjoy" (1Tim 6:17).

Being stewards for the sake of others is also the daily practice of faith, as we wrestle between faith and unbelief. Unbelief tells us that we do not have enough for ourselves, so we should not give to others, while faith tells us to be confident in God's supply. "But if God so clothes the grass of the field, which today is alive and tomorrow is thrown into the oven, will he not much more clothe you, O you of little faith?" (Matt 6:30). Only growing faith convinces us that stewardship—and not the accumulation of wealth—is the path to God's joy in this life . . . and the next. "For the love of money is a root of all kinds of evils. It is through this craving that some have wandered away from the faith and pierced themselves with many pangs" (1 Tim 6:10).

As we grow in faith by living as stewards for others, we are transformed into God's design for us—those who love others—precisely because we believe that God will provide for us.[19] To live as stewards who serve others requires this growth in faith, which makes us more and more like Christ, the definition of holiness. "From this we may gather a brief definition of true Christianity—that it is a faith that is lively and full of vigor, so that it spares no labor, when assistance is to be given to

19. Bucer, *Christian Love*, 48.

one's neighbors, but, on the contrary, all the pious employ themselves diligently in offices of love."[20]

The Right Use of This Present Life Is the Daily Practice of Repentance That Makes Us More like Christ

In order to hold things loosely as sojourners we must daily practice repentance, since our sinful nature would hold tightly to the world. "Since all these things are thus to be dissolved, what sort of people ought you to be in lives of holiness and godliness" (2 Pet 3:11). As we repent of holding the world tightly, God frees us from this inordinate love of the world and we love his heavenly blessings more, and so holiness grows in us.

We practice repentance every time we use the things of this world in moderation, rather than yielding to avarice and gluttony. "Keep your life free from love of money, and be content with what you have, for he has said, 'I will never leave you nor forsake you'" (Heb 13:5). God meets us in our repentance, putting to death the desire for more and teaching us contentment. "I have learned in whatever situation I am to be content. I know how to be brought low, and I know how to abound" (Phil 4:11–12a). Repenting of our immoderate desires, God transforms us into those who find joy in moderation, for his glory.

We practice repentance daily when we are accountable stewards for the benefit of others. Sin drives us to desire more for ourselves. "You desire and do not have, so you murder. You covet and cannot obtain, so you fight and quarrel" (Jas 4:2). As we repent of this desire, seeking instead to be good stewards for others, God's grace transforms us more and more into those who will live for the good of others, as did Timothy. "For I have no one like him, who will be genuinely concerned for your welfare" (Phil 2:20).

Turning from the world to Christ in faith and repentance, we are transformed into stewards and sojourners who, content with moderation within our vocations, find our joy in serving Christ and our neighbor. That is, we become more like Jesus.

---

20. Calvin, *Com.*, 1 Thess 1:3.

Summary of How to Use This Present Life

1. Practice daily thankfulness for all that God has given you in this life, this helps our faith and confidence in God grow, so that seeing how he has blessed us, we may bless others. "I will give thanks to the LORD with my whole heart; I will recount all of your wonderful deeds" (Ps 9:1).

2. Keep your sojourner status always before you so that you hold loosely to the things of this world. This is a challenging balance to maintain, we are to plan wisely for life in this world, but at the same time, not to plan for this life as though it were our eternal home. We should daily remind ourselves that our great hope is not here, but in heaven. "These all died in faith, not having received the things promised, but having seen them and greeted them from afar, and having acknowledged that they were strangers and exiles on the earth" (Heb 11:13). Reminders such as, "I am not home yet," are helpful. Let each Sabbath Day serve to remind us, that we yet look for a greater Sabbath rest to come.

3. Joyfully accept God's calling for you in this life. Accept by faith that God is in charge of your vocation—including your career, your family and marital status, your health, your gifting, and your finances. Rather than complaining about his vocation for you, give thanks for his calling on your life, this helps us to be content and find joy in what he provides. When we first bought our present home I was unhappy with how quiet our neighborhood was, preferring more social action. When I stopped complaining to God about it and starting thanking him, I came to realize that, with the busy social life of a pastor, a quiet neighborhood was what he wanted for us.

4. Practice moderation in your use of the stuff of this world. Enjoy what he has given you but do not overindulge. Don't buy more clothes than you really need, don't overeat, do not drink enough alcohol to be drunk, spend less on yourself than you can afford, buy a more modest home than you can afford, decorate it beautifully, but not lavishly. Seek in all this to honor the Lord who lived at a very simple economic level, despite his ability to have anything he wanted. Make it a regular practice to deny yourself in various ways and use this to supply the needs of others.

5. Practice stewardship of all you have and are, confident that one day you will give an account for it all. Do not only ask, "Can I afford it?" Ask also: "Is this the best kingdom use of these funds?" Ask as well: "How might I grow in useful service to the Lord?" It was in answering that question at fifty years of age that I decided to go back to school for a PhD. It was an odd calling; I was by far the oldest one in my program. But it was God's calling for me to steward who I was, and it has yielded good benefit for his service.

6. Live to serve others in love. Our stewardship always has this as its end: to love our neighbors as ourselves. Each day ask something like this, "Whom may I better serve today? How?" It may be as simple as giving a prompt response to an email inquiry rather than postponing it, or as relational as asking someone how they are doing, and actually listening, or as financial as seeing a need and meeting it. We have a pastor on staff who had struggled to pay off an old business debt. Hearing of the need, a small group of leaders in the church decided to pay it. What a joy it was for this young pastor to find himself suddenly free of that debt. And what a joy it was for the givers as well. "One's life does not consist in the abundance of his possessions" (Luke 12:15).

As we use this present life well, practicing on a daily basis the faith and repentance that God calls us to, we are transformed more and more into the very image of Christ, thanking God for all his gifts, embracing his vocation in our lives, as we steward all we have for the love of others.

Further Resources

Study Questions

1. How well are you thankfully accepting all of this life as a good gift? Where might you be more thankful for the good gifts God has given you? What would you need to believe and what would you need to repent of to grow here?

2. How well are you holding this life loosely as a sojourner? Where might you let go some part of your life even more? What would you need to believe and what would you need to repent of to grow here?

3. How well are you joyfully accepting God's calling for you in this life, without lusting for more or other? Where could you grow in contentment with God's calling in your life? What would you need to believe and what would you need to repent of to grow here?

4. How well are you practicing moderation in your use of the stuff of this world? Are there areas of your life where you are too lavish, and should grow in moderation? What would you need to believe and what would you need to repent of to grow here?

5. How well are you practicing stewardship of all you have and are? Are there areas in your life—time, talent, or treasure—where you could especially grow as a steward? What would you need to believe and what would you need to repent of to grow here?

6. How well are you living a life of loving service for others? What could you do, practically speaking to grow in loving service of someone in your life today? What would you need to believe and what would you need to repent of to grow here?

For Further Study

Randy Alcorn, *Money, Possessions, and Eternity: A Comprehensive Guide to What the Bible Says about Financial Stewardship, Generosity, Materialism, Retirement, Financial Planning, Gambling, Debt, and More* (Carol Stream, IL: Tyndale, 2012).

Craig L. Blomberg, *Christians in an Age of Wealth: A Biblical Theology of Stewardship* (Grand Rapids: Zondervan, 2013).

Timothy Keller, *Every Good Endeavor: Connecting Your Work to God's Work* (New York: Penguin, 2016).

William C. Placher, *Callings: Twenty Centuries of Christian Wisdom on Vocation* (Grand Rapids: Eerdmans, 2005).

13

Engage the Church

The Importance of Engaging the Church

ALL OVER THE US church attendance is declining in part due to the rise of a new tendency among believers to go it alone. The Bible, however, knows nothing of a Christian apart from the church. "Now you are the body of Christ and individually members of it" (1 Cor 12:27). Throughout the New Testament the phrase "in Christ" is typically used to describe one as a Christian, who is in community. "To all the saints in Christ Jesus who are at Philippi" (Phil 1:1).

Full participation in the life of the local church is essential to the healthy growth of the Christian because God only sanctifies the church. "Christ loved the church and gave himself up for her, that he might sanctify her" (Eph 5:25b–26a). It is only to the church that God has given leaders to build up her members in holiness. "And he gave the apostles, the prophets, the evangelists, the shepherds and teachers, to equip the saints for the work of ministry, for building up the body of Christ" (Eph 4:11–12). Throughout the Bible the promises of God are given to us collectively as the people of God, not just as individuals. "I will put my laws into *their* minds, and write them on *their* hearts, and I will be *their* God, and *they* shall be my *people*" (Heb 8:10, emphasis added).

It is within the church that God has embedded the means of grace that we might grow in holiness. To the church is given the authoritative preaching of the Word. "Declare these things; exhort and rebuke with all authority" (Titus 2:15). It is to the church that God has entrusted the discipline and care of his people. "If he refuses to listen to them, tell it to the church" (Matt 18:17). To the church are given the sacraments which work to sanctify us (John 6:56). Within the church, corporate worship lifts us into the presence of God (1 Cor 14:26). It is within the church that we find fellowship (Rom 12:10). It is within the church that we find the grace to be transformed into the image of Christ. "The church is the means by which the exalted Christ accomplishes His work among men."[1] All of this leads the *Westminster Confession* to rightly declare: "The visible church . . . is the kingdom of the Lord Jesus Christ, the house and family of God, out of which there is no ordinary possibility of salvation."[2]

While many self-professed "Christians" remain detached from the local church body—often because they judge the local church unworthy—they do so at their own peril, and to the detriment of other believers. "Someone who separates himself from the body certainly alienates himself from God and from our Lord Jesus Christ."[3] When we do not give ourselves to the local communion of Christ, our faith inevitably atrophies. "When people are lax about church practices there is to be found weakness in their Christian lives."[4] We should remain in the church, even when we recognize her painful imperfections. "Let us prefer the state of the Church, which may be yet sad and deformed, and such as we would shun, were we to follow our own inclinations. . . . Let us embrace the miseries common to the godly."[5]

Since Christ loves the church, we are called not only to participate in, but to give ourselves in love to the church as well. "The church of Christ where I am . . . I ought to esteem and hold as precious, as being that through which the Lord wishes to grant me his word and spirit, forgiveness of sins and all good. I am to give myself wholly to such a congregation."[6] We must give ourselves wholly to the church to build her up. "Strive to excel in building up the church" (1 Cor 14:12b).

Sanctification is a communal operation, uniquely effective to those within the body of Christ; therefore, we need Christ's church to become like Christ.[7] We will explain here four aspects of Christ's sanctifying work

---

1. Niesel, *Theology of Calvin*, 185.
2. *Westminster Confession of Faith*, 124; Chapter 25.2.
3. Calvin, *Sermons on 2 Samuel*, 389.
4. Bucer, *True Care of Souls*, 168.
5. Calvin, *Com.*, Jer 51:50.
6. Stephens, *Theology of Bucer*, 161.
7. Wallace, *Christian Life*, 198.

though the church: the Word preached, church discipline, the sacraments, and worship.

The Word of God Taught Authoritatively within the Church Helps Us to Grow Holy

Understanding the Authority of the Word within the Church

As was mentioned earlier in this book, while all reading and study of the Bible is helpful, the church uniquely brings to bear God's authority in the preaching of the Bible to the people of God. "It is this Word, that is the ministry of the Church, by which his voice has always been heard in the Church since the commencement of the World."[8]

While anyone may teach the Bible, the officers of the church are especially imbued with God's authority (Eph 4:11–12) so that their proclamation of the Word builds up the church.[9] This is why the apostles were unwilling to give up preaching. "It is not right that we should give up preaching the word of God to serve tables" (Acts 6:2). This is why Paul exhorted young pastor Timothy to keep on preaching. "Preach the word; be ready in season and out of season; reprove, rebuke, and exhort, with complete patience and teaching" (2 Tim 4:2).

God sends his Spirit into his church to enliven his Word preached by his leaders in order that the Word may powerfully change the lives of his people. Through the authoritative ministry of preaching the lost are saved. "It pleased God through the folly of what we preach to save those who believe" (1 Cor 1:21). Through the ministry of the Word, Christians grow in holiness. "Him we proclaim, warning everyone and teaching everyone with all wisdom, that we may present everyone mature in Christ" (Col 1:28).

When God delivers his Word through one of his duly ordained modern prophets, that is, when a pastor preaches to us, we can truthfully say that we have heard the Word of God. "'The grass withers, and the flower falls, but the word of the Lord remains forever.' And this word is the good news that was preached to you" (1 Pet 1:24–25). Jesus declared this as he sent out the seventy-two to preach. "The one who hears you hears me, and the one who rejects you rejects me" (Luke 10:16).

---

8. Viret, *La Parolle de Dieu*, 7–8.
9. Calvin, *Institutes*, 4.2.1.

The Bible preached by God's chosen representatives has all the authority and power needed to build up the church. "We must hold to what we have quoted from Paul—that the church is built up solely by outward preaching."[10] Therefore, if we are to grow in holiness we must take full advantage of God's design to teach us his Word through the pastors of his church.

How the Word Preached in the Church Helps Us Become More Holy

First, the Word preached works to increase our faith. "So faith comes from hearing, and hearing through the word of Christ" (Rom 10:17). Our personal study helps our faith, of course, but even more powerfully, God works faith in our hearts when his Word is preached authoritatively to us in the church.[11] "God rises to invite us, and also to receive us, whenever his word is proclaimed among us, by which he testifies to us his paternal love."[12] The Word preached always reminds us of the mercy and the promises of God in Christ for us, and this more than any other portion of the Word, creates faith in us. "We see here which is the true manner of preaching the gospel: namely to give knowledge of God's love towards us."[13]

It is the common experience of pastors to have church members declare that a sermon struck them as God speaking directly to them. One member wrote me: "It never ceases to amaze me how every sermon over the past six months seems tailored specifically to me." This regular occurrence is neither due to the pastor's intentional targeting of an individual, nor to the pastor's great insights. Rather it is the ordinary working of the Spirit through the Word preached, speaking directly and powerfully to the heart of his people to engender faith in them. This is why preaching is so very helpful to our growth in holiness: through it God uniquely speaks to us to help our faith.

Second, the Word preached helps to produce repentance, so that turning to God we are transformed by his grace. While personal study may convict us, God has so designed preaching that his voice is more clearly heard to convince us of sin and bring us to repentance. While

---

10. Calvin, *Institutes*, 4.1.5.
11. Viret, *L'Interim Fait par Dialogues*, 247.
12. Calvin, *Com.*, Jer 7:23.
13. Calvin, *Sermons on Galatians*, 313.

we may excuse ourselves, or ignore difficult passages, in our personal study, the Word preached confronts us in ways that leave us consistently uncomfortable with our sin, as were the people of Nineveh. "The men of Nineveh will rise up at the judgment with this generation and condemn it, for they repented at the preaching of Jonah" (Matt 12:41).

Effective preaching will apply the Law of God to the people of God to remind them of their sin and call them to repentance, to seek yet more of God's grace. "When God appoints us to proclaim his word, it is as if he were assigning us to be his attorneys to explain his rights. We must daily point out vices and transgressions, for which we are responsible before God. Each individual must be rebuked."[14] For this reason the pastor is not to quarrel but to teach, with clarity and with conviction, so that his hearers may understand it is ultimately God, and not the preacher, who calls them to repentance. "The Lord's servant must not be quarrelsome but kind to everyone, able to teach, patiently enduring evil, correcting his opponents with gentleness. God may perhaps grant them repentance leading to a knowledge of the truth" (2 Tim 2:24–25).

Third, the Word preached helps us to grow in holiness by guiding our grace-enabled hearts in the path of God's commandments. "Blessed is the man who walks not in the counsel of the wicked . . . but his delight is in the law of the LORD, and on his law he meditates day and night" (Ps 1:1–2). The Word instructs us to follow our love for God with our obedience to him. "If you love me, you will keep my commandments" (John 14:15). Having our hearts transformed by God's Word preached to us, we love Christ more and are ready to submit to his rule over us, which he exercises through the preaching of the Word. "For since God has willed to govern his church by the outward preaching of his Word, let us each submit to it, being diligent to listen to the sermons, holding the system of being taught by the mouth of mortal men as sacred and holy."[15] Since this is Christ's plan, we should come eagerly to the preaching of the Word, to discover his commands that we might lovingly obey our Savior.

Engaging the church in the Word preached we grow in faith and repentance and are helped to walk in obedience to God's commands, that is, we are conformed more and more into the image of Christ.

---

14. Calvin, *Sermons on Genesis*, 545.
15. Calvin, *Sermons on the Ten Commandments*, 268–69.

How to Practice Engaging the Word within the Church

Since we covered this at length in a prior chapter on engaging the Word, we will only emphasize a few ways in which we are to engage the Word preached in the church. 1) Attend to the preaching of the Word regularly. To grow strong in grace, we must include the Sabbath Day sermon as the cornerstone of a healthy spiritual diet. 2) Attend to the preaching of the Word expectantly. We should go expecting that God will speak to us through his Word preached. The Scriptures, designed by the Holy Spirit to be preached, transmit to us the Word of God in such a way that when we listen with open hearts, we may hear, through human instruments, the very voice of God. 3) Attend to the preaching of the Word submissively. The Word preached will confront our sins and we will not enjoy that. With humble hearts, desiring to learn of our sins, we should come ready to repent and find even more grace.

Pastoral Care and Discipline Help Us to Grow More Holy

Understanding Pastoral Care and Discipline within the Church

In order to make real progress in holiness we must have the help of others because we cannot accurately see our sin. "Because we are all too fond of ourselves, we are not able to recognize or judge our own needs properly."[16]

We discount our sins because sin contains within itself a blinding agent that hides its presence. Much like the mosquito that, when it draws blood, first administers a small dose of anesthetic so we cannot notice that we are bitten, sin masks to us its presence in our hearts. "Whoever hates his brother is in the darkness and walks in the darkness, and does not know where he is going, because the darkness has blinded his eyes" (1 John 2:11). Since none of us can accurately see our sin, the only way to be informed about our sin is to have outside help. In 1999 I wrote in my journal regarding this "dark side:"

> Each of us possesses at the core of his being a dark and destructive side. This is our old sinful nature made manifest. Just as the lighted moon hides its darker half by outshining it, our shadow side is not easily discernable. . . . Though we all have it, we live intentionally to not see this darkness. The dark side so enmeshes our soul that our soul cannot on its own accurately see the depth

---

16. Bucer, *True Care of Souls*, 203–4.

and breadth of its darkness. The shadow contains in its very genetic makeup a gene that spins illusions and lies and smoke, all to cover itself from the view of the one it occupies.

Pastoral care and church discipline are designed precisely to give us the feedback we must have in order to see our sin clearly, so that we may fight it. "Exhort one another every day, as long as it is called 'today,' that none of you may be hardened by the deceitfulness of sin" (Heb 3:13).

This accountability, church discipline, comes both informally through brotherly admonitions among church members, and more formally through the church officers. When we refuse to yield to milder forms of correction, it is necessary for our sin to be confronted with authority, by those who can tell us "No," and make it stick. This authority lies with the church's governing body, to which Jesus has given the keys of the kingdom (Matt 16:19).

We find the biblical practice of church discipline in the teaching of Christ, beginning with the informal exhortation to turn from sin, and concluding—in the case of an unrepentant person—with the church moving to excommunicate.

> If your brother sins against you, go and tell him his fault, between you and him alone. If he listens to you, you have gained your brother. But if he does not listen, take one or two others along with you, that every charge may be established by the evidence of two or three witnesses. If he refuses to listen to them, tell it to the church. And if he refuses to listen even to the church, let him be to you as a Gentile and a tax collector. (Matt 18:15–17)

This work of church discipline begins informally, with the duty that every Christian has toward another. "The Holy Spirit wants us to engage neither in flattery . . . nor promoting our neighbor's vices, rather he wants us to strive to correct their vices as much as we possibly can and, at the same time, to support them without discouraging those who have erred."[17] This we do with gentleness in the hope of convincing the wayward of their error by using a tone they can better receive. "Brothers, if anyone is caught in any transgression, you who are spiritual should restore him in a spirit of gentleness" (Gal 6:1).

In accord with Christ's admonition to remove the log from our own eye before addressing the speck in our neighbor's eyes we should examine our own motivation before correcting others (Matt 7:3–5). However, if

---

17. Calvin, *Sermons on the Ten Commandments*, 208–9.

the person refuses our gentle rebukes, then our tone and intensity may rise in order to wake them from their slumber. "When I see that Satan has hardened him to the extent that only great hammer blows can awaken him, I can proceed with such vehemence, which is also why I strive to enumerate his faults."[18]

If then they do not respond to our informal admonitions we are to "tell it to the church," that is, to ask the governing body of the church to take up the matter, thus entering formal discipline. But even here the hope of formal discipline is still repentance and restoration.

Of course all the discipline of the church, informal and formal, only takes Scripture, never pet peeves or personal opinions, as the source for deciding what must be confronted. "Let us only judge of the character of each man's works by the law of the Lord."[19]

This formal church discipline is backed by the threat of formal sanctions—such as admonition, suspension from the sacraments, and finally, excommunication. These sanctions are essential to the holiness of members and the health of the church, for if we do not deal with sin, it overruns the church. Thus, Paul complained to the Corinthian church that they had failed to discipline sin in their midst. "It is actually reported that there is sexual immorality among you, and of a kind that is not tolerated even among pagans, for a man has his father's wife. And you are arrogant! Ought you not rather to mourn? Let him who has done this be removed from among you" (1 Cor 5:1–2).

To function as the church, to help each of its members grow up in Christ, a church and all of its members must provide church discipline, or else they silently condone sin and destroy the church. "Where discipline is dormant, men are asleep and the devil sows tares."[20] Should a church fail to discipline its members it risks failing to be a true church. "This discipline is one of the principle marks of the true church."[21] It is a grave dereliction of duty—unfortunately very common in our day—when the leadership of a church demurs from calling its members to repent of particular sins. "As Churches have this mode of punishment put into their hands, those commit sin . . . that do not make use of it, when it is required."[22]

---

18. Calvin, *Sermons on the Ten Commandments*, 213.
19. Calvin, *Institutes*, 4.12.9.
20. Engelsma, "Martin Bucer," 54.
21. Schnetzler et al., *Pierre Viret*, 293.
22. Calvin, *Com.*, 1 Cor 5:2.

Within Presbyterianism the authority to bring discipline lies with the elders of the church. "I exhort the elders among you ... shepherd the flock of God that is among you, exercising oversight" (1 Pet 5:1–2). These godly men are responsible to see to the holiness of the people of God and intervene when needed. "Their office is to have oversight of the life of everyone, to admonish amicably those whom they see to be erring or to be living a disordered life, and, where it is required, to enjoin paternal corrections themselves and along with others."[23]

The sanctifying impact that formal discipline has within the body of a church is astounding, not only for the one disciplined, but for those who are properly made aware of that discipline. Discipline has three broad aims: 1) upholding the glory of God by declaring that he does not countenance sin, 2) purifying the body of Christ by demonstrating that sin is not tolerated, and 3) restoring the wayward Christian. Regarding point two, purifying the church, it is remarkable to see the response of individual members to formal discipline at congregational meetings. I recall, for example, when a man was excommunicated for abandoning his wife. I watched the men of the church pull their wives close and humbly vow in their hearts, "Lord please, by your grace, let me be faithful!"

To truly grow in holiness we must have the pastoral care and spiritual discipline found only within the church, for without it we would remain blind to our sin. With it, we are helped by others to see our sin, and, leaving it behind, turn to the Lord for greater growth in grace.

How Discipline in the Church Helps Us to Grow More Holy

Church discipline is remarkably effective at waking us from our stupor and calling us to repent, so helping us to grow in holiness. Confronting us with sin we would rather not see, discipline is the bridle which checks our headlong plunge into sin and returns us to fellowship with God.

Church discipline also helps our faith to increase, by leading us back into God's Word, from which our sin had drawn us. Repenting under discipline we experience freshly the grace of God in Christ in his forgiveness and love, which increases our faith. Church discipline humbles us in repentant prostration before God while also lifting us up in the exaltation of God, conforming us to the image of Christ.

---

23. Reid, *Treatises*, 63.

This growth in humility and faith are seen in David's psalm of repentance as he declares the glory of God, after undergoing "church discipline" at the hands of Nathan and God. "O Lord, open my lips, and my mouth will declare your praise. . . . The sacrifices of God are a broken spirit; a broken and contrite heart, O God, you will not despise" (Ps 51:15–17). When we imagine what might have become of David had he not been called to repent, we may see from David's repentance the vital role church discipline serves to our advance in holiness. "Discipline serve[s] as [the church's] sinews, through which the members of the body hold together, each in its own place."[24]

How to Engage in Pastoral Care and Church Discipline to Grow in Holiness

Have Accountability Relationships in the Church and Heed Their Counsel

Christian growth is a group activity which only works when we are deeply interconnected in church community. "And let us consider how to stir up one another to love and good works, not neglecting to meet together" (Heb 10:24–25).

These relationships may happen within various settings, but we encourage them at our church through one primary structure: prayer triads, groups of three men, or three women, who meet for long-term accountability and encouragement. Often in these groups members will air their more serious issues and struggles, asking for counsel, accountability, and prayers.

When my current prayer triad began more than twenty-five years ago, we pledged to confess our worst sins to each other. Driving to the meeting, however, I had decided to not tell them the very worst of my sins, fearing they might lose respect for me. Fortunately, I did not confess first, and the one who did said, "Well, I was not going to tell you my really worst sins, but I am convicted by the Spirit that I should." With that prompting, I plunged in as well and found great help in fighting against sin.

Being able to confess our sins to one another and receive prayer is vital to our growth in Christ. "Therefore, confess your sins to one another and pray for one another, that you may be healed" (Jas 5:16). Sin and the devil keep us under control, in part, by trying to convince us that we must

---

24. Calvin, *Institutes*, 4.12.1.

hide our sins in order to preserve ourselves. However, concealing sins actually only traps us in them, while confessing sin is a way to turn to Christ and find help and freedom. "Whoever conceals his transgressions will not prosper, but he who confesses and forsakes them will obtain mercy" (Prov 28:13).

The Reformers understood this need for mutual accountability. "Let us learn to love one another in such a way that . . . instead of friends flattering one another so that they abet one another in their vice and entertain each other with it, they will admonish one another to withdraw from it, and follow the good."[25] Humanly speaking, few things have been as helpful for my turn from sin to Christ as these intimate accountability relationships.

Be in Relationship with Your Pastors and Elders

The Lord provides the shepherds of his church to serve as the overseers of our souls (1 Pet 5:1–2). Therefore, make it a point to get to know those who watch over your soul on God's behalf. And as you do, express your desire to be open to their insights about your life and your doctrine. One of my favorite questions to ask is this: "Do you see something that you think I might be missing?" Then sit back and listen carefully, taking it to heart. Let them know your prayer needs and seek them out for counsel. God means to help us through the officers of his church.

Hold Others in the Church Accountable in Relationship

While we receive encouragement and accountability we are also to offer that for others. "Brothers, if anyone is caught in any transgression, you who are spiritual should restore him in a spirit of gentleness" (Gal 6:1). We are faithful as friends when we wound them somewhat that they might be greatly healed. "Faithful are the wounds of a friend" (Prov 27:6). This responsibility is for all believers with one another. "But exhort one another every day, as long as it is called 'today,' that none of you may be hardened by the deceitfulness of sin" (Heb 3:13).

Calvin implored his congregation to take this mutual responsibility seriously. "If I see a friend of mine stumble in some vice, I will not be so mean as to let it pass from my sight without pointing out to him how it

---

25. Calvin, *Sermons on 2 Samuel*, 621.

will cause him shame ... if I do not say a word about it, am I not a double traitor, inasmuch as he is my friend, and he trusts in me?"[26] While we may feel inadequate for the task, and may want to shrink back from fear of losing our friendship, this duty is expected of every Christian.

Submit to the Formal Discipline of the Church

While formal church discipline may only rarely touch our lives, if it does, we should be particularly careful to heed this as a correction from the Lord. God has invested the leaders of his church with the authority to hold members of the church accountable for their sin, calling them to repent and return to Christ. "Exhort and rebuke with all authority" (Titus 2:15).

When a church calls us to submit to its discipline we should recognize in ourselves the natural sinful tendency to want to disparage those who are disciplining us. Accept the fact that it is extremely unpleasant to be corrected, but resist the urge to flee. "Let us receive [discipline] with a compliant spirit. Why? Because we will have nothing to gain by being stiff-necked and rebellious."[27] Instead, take the uncommon approach of submitting to the church. "Obey your leaders and submit to them, for they are keeping watch over your souls, as those who will have to give an account" (Heb 13:17).

Be aware as well that submission begins when we disagree with those in authority over us. As long as we are in agreement, we are simply getting what we want. It is precisely when we disagree that our willingness to actually submit is tested, and it is at this point, that our submission becomes helpful to produce repentance.

Let us consider ourselves, when under church discipline, as someone who is trapped in a house on fire and filled with smoke. Blinded by the smoke, we cannot see the way out. Consider those church leaders who speak to us as the firefighters who are there to help rescue us. Listen to them and follow their voices out of the fire to the safety of repentance and obedience. When we are trapped and in danger we do not think clearly. Listening to God's rescue workers is the best choice. We are wise to humbly receive their correction as though the Lord himself were rebuking us.

---

26. Calvin, *Sermons on 2 Samuel*, 621.
27. Calvin, *Sermons on Genesis*, 548.

Sacraments within the Church Help Us to Grow More Holy

Understanding the Sacraments

There are two sacraments which Christ has given to the church to help us: baptism and the Lord's Supper. A sacrament is "an outward sign by which the Lord seals on our consciences the promises of his good will toward us."[28] God provides the sacraments to us because in our weakness, in addition to the Word heard, we need the Word seen, in the physical elements of the sacraments.[29]

In baptism, as the entrance sign into the covenant people of God, the person, coming for the first time to be identified with the church, is shown to be within the covenant family. "For as many of you as were baptized into Christ have put on Christ" (Gal 3:27). With the Lord's Supper we have the sacrament which is intended to sustain us in the Lord by helping our faith to grow strong.[30] "Do this, as often as you drink it, in remembrance of me" (1 Cor 11:25).

More than mere symbols which only remind of us God's promises, the sacraments are the "efficacy and fulfillment of the promises which belong to them."[31] Through these visible signs, but only by faith, we partake of the power and life of Christ, such that we grow in faith and so in holiness.[32]

How the Sacraments Help Us Grow in Holiness

It is God's grace we need, and the sacraments, when worthily received through faith, act as channels for God's grace to flow to us. The sacraments' primary benefit to us is "to establish and increase faith."[33] By increasing our faith in Christ, the sacraments unite us more fully with him, who transforms us by this union through the Holy Spirit.[34]

---

28. Calvin, *Institutes*, 4.14.1.
29. Gerrish, *Grace and Gratitude*, 61.
30. Wright, *Common Places*, 433.
31. Calvin, *Com.*, Rom 2:25.
32. Baird, *Theodore Beza*, 92.
33. Calvin, *Institutes*, 4.14.9.
34. Wright, *Common Places*, 262.

In the Lord's Supper we are spiritually united to Christ's human body[35] such that his life flows into us and transforms us into his image.[36] Yet, while it is from the actual body of Christ that the life of Christ flows to us, we are not united to his flesh by a physical act—even the act of eating and drinking—such that our substance is commingled with his.[37] Rather, the Holy Spirit unites us to Christ spiritually, while we partake of the elements by faith. It is by faith, through the sacraments, that we "draw near to our Lord Jesus Christ," and "we are so joined to Him there is nothing of Himself that He is not willing to communicate to us."[38]

The union with Christ's death and resurrection in baptism increases our faith by confirming our place in Christ, showing us visibly that God has a good will toward us.[39] "Having been buried with him in baptism, in which you were also raised with him through faith in the powerful working of God, who raised him from the dead" (Col 2:12).

The sacraments work to give us assurance that we are adopted children of God. The Supper shows that, "God declares that we are His children and that we can claim Him openly as our Father."[40] The sacraments further assure us that if God has declared that we are his children, he will also care for us.[41]

Finally, the sacraments help our holiness by increasing a desire for holiness within us, for the sacraments demand that we turn from sin. "Let a person examine himself, then, and so eat of the bread and drink of the cup" (1 Cor 11:28). Helped by the sacraments we want to be more like Christ and this very desire leads us to find more of him and to follow him more closely.

35. Wallace, *Christian Life*, 18.
36. Reid, *Treatises*, 267.
37. Calvin, *Com.*, 1 Cor 11:24.
38. Calvin, *Ioannis Calvini Opera*, 46:955–68.
39. Calvin, *Institutes*, 4.15.6.
40. Calvin, *Ioannis Calvini Opera*, 46:833–46.
41. Reid, *Treatises*, 141.

How to Use the Sacraments for Growth in Holiness

Use Them Regularly

To be helpful we must avail ourselves of these means of grace. If you have not been baptized, be baptized into a local congregation. When your church offers the Lord's Supper, partake of it in a worthy manner.

During the Baptism of Others Consider Your Own Baptism

We should reflect upon the fact that God has covenanted to make us his people and set us aside as his holy ones through this sign and seal. This should give us both a sense of security in him and responsibility to live for him.

Prepare Yourself for the Lord's Supper by Self-Examination

We should examine ourselves to see that we truly have faith in Christ. "Examine yourselves, to see whether you are in the faith. Test yourselves" (2 Cor 13:5). We should examine ourselves for unconfessed sin and if we find any, confess it appropriately. "Search me, O God, and know my heart! Try me and know my thoughts! And see if there be any grievous way in me, and lead me in the way everlasting!" (Ps 139:23–24). Having done this we are ready to receive the Supper with all its benefits.

Prepare Yourself for the Lord's Supper by Recognizing Your Deep Need for Grace

Beyond faith, the single most important characteristic we bring to the table of Christ is humility. "This is the worthiness—the best and only kind we can bring to God . . . to despair in ourselves so that we may be comforted in him; to abase ourselves so that we may be lifted up by him; to accuse ourselves so that we may be justified by him."[42] As we partake of the sacraments by faith we grow more and more like Christ.

---

42. Calvin, *Institutes*, 4.17.42.

Worship within the Church Helps Us to Grow More Holy

Understanding Worship in the Church

In many ways our sanctification in relationship with God culminates in corporate worship. "Ascribe to the LORD the glory due his name; bring an offering, and come into his courts" (Ps 96:8). Because sin silences the worship of God, God's ultimate plan in redemption is to have all nations assembled before him in worship (Ps 86:9).

We are summoned by the glory and the grace of God to gather before him as his children and offer him praise. "Oh come, let us worship and bow down; let us kneel before the LORD, our Maker!" (Ps 95:6). Our worship brings joy—for us and for God. "Let us make a joyful noise to him with songs of praise!" (Ps 95:2).

In corporate worship we are helped by one another's worship to bring praise to God. "When you come together, each one has a hymn, a lesson, a revelation, a tongue, or an interpretation" (1 Cor 14:26). Our corporate worship, therefore, aids our sanctification by helping us render to God his due, drawing our hearts up to him in worship.

The joy of the Lord in our worship may be likened to that of parents whose grown children return over a holiday to assemble for dinner. The parents delight in their children, who also bask in the glow of their loving parents, so that love and joy are reflected all around. God rejoices when his children gather before him in worship. "The LORD your God is in your midst, a mighty one who will save; he will rejoice over you with gladness; he will quiet you by his love; he will exult over you with loud singing" (Zeph 3:17).

The only worship that is profitable, however, is that which is regulated by God's Word. "If we sincerely want to adopt the true order of worship that pleases God, then we have to pay heed to what God has commanded us."[43] We see how much God despises unbiblical worship from the example of the priests, Nadab and Abihu, who offered an extra and unauthorized round of incense to God. "And fire came out from before the LORD and consumed them" (Lev 10:2). To help us grow closer to God, we should worship God, in conformity to his Word.

---

43. Calvin, *Sermons on Micah*, 36.

How Corporate Worship Helps Us to Grow in Holiness

Worship is the ultimate reversal of our fall into sin, such that we no longer ignore or despise God, but, prostrating ourselves before him, we lift our hearts up to him in exaltation.

Worship demands that we prostrate ourselves before God, jettisoning pride and clothing ourselves in humility, that we might worship him as the Exalted One. "The haughtiness of man shall be humbled, and the lofty pride of men shall be brought low, and the LORD alone will be exalted in that day" (Isa 2:17). This very move toward humility is a work of God's grace, which is holiness.

Worship leads us to exalt in God, to see and proclaim his worth as King, Creator, Lord, and Redeemer. "Oh, magnify the LORD with me, and let us exalt his name together!" (Ps 34:3). Since the sanctified heart is one that praises God for his glory, thanks him for his goodness, and seeks his help always, our corporate worship leads us to this deeper relationship of gratitude, which is relational holiness with God. "Oh give thanks to the LORD, for he is good; for his steadfast love endures forever!" (Ps 118:1).

The Holy Spirit works in the midst of our worship to conform us individually and corporately to the image of Christ. "You yourselves like living stones are being built up as a spiritual house, to be a holy priesthood, to offer spiritual sacrifices acceptable to God through Jesus Christ" (1 Pet 2:5). Corporate worship therefore makes us holy in humility, in gratitude, and by building us into Christ's spiritual house.

How to Use Corporate Worship for Growth in Holiness

Prepare for Worship Seriously

Worshipping well takes preparation. If we exhaust ourselves with chores, sports, and late nights on Saturday, we may show up Sunday with bodies so tired and minds so preoccupied that our worship is half-hearted at best. However, when we anticipate corporate worship during the week—studying the text, singing the songs, praying for the service, resting properly on Saturday—then we can come with hearts ready to worship God.

Attend Worship Faithfully

Particularly on the Lord's Day we should avail ourselves of the privilege of assembling with God's people to worship. Far too often Christians only worship when there is nothing better to do on the Sabbath, no pressing sports, work, or family visits. In doing so we rob ourselves of the very medicine that would cure our apathy and draw praise from our hearts: the assembly of the saints in worship. Wherever you are on the Sabbath Day, gather with God's people to praise him.

Participate in Worship Fully

Is the congregation singing? Sing, mindful of the words, pouring out your heart to God. Do not allow yourself to be distracted by your neighbor's monotone or restless children. Is the congregation being led in prayer? Agree consciously with the prayer. Is the congregation confessing sin? Search your heart and confess all that the Holy Spirit brings to light. Is the congregation listening to the Word preached? Listen as though God were speaking. Is the congregation partaking of the sacraments? Recognize the sacredness of this act and give yourself fully to it. God is seeking your worship, give him all you have! "The Father is seeking such people to worship him" (John 4:23).

Summary of Engaging the Church

1. Remember that God sanctifies us within his church, and so, be a vital member of a local church.
2. Attend to the preaching of the Word regularly, coming with an expectant and submissive heart to hear from God through the sermon, and then, make deliberate application of it to your life.
3. Have accountability relationships in the church and heed their counsel, along with that of pastors and elders. Submit to the formal and informal discipline of the church in your life.
4. Hold others accountable, too, by speaking the truth in love.
5. Partake of the sacraments, be baptized if you are a Christian and have not been. Remember your baptism when others are being baptized, that you are set apart from the world for God. Come to the

Lord's Supper having repented of sin and with a desire for his grace and your faith to grow.

6. Come to corporate worship regularly and well prepared. Fully give yourself to God as you exalt and thank him, pouring your heart out to him in adoration.

7. Take part only in worship which is done in conformity with God's Word.

Further Resources

Study Questions

1. Why should one remain involved in the local church in order to grow in holiness?

2. How should we attend to the Word preached to gain the greatest benefit for our growth in grace?

3. How are accountability relationships within the church helpful to our growth in holiness? What is it about our sin that makes them necessary for us?

4. Why is it so important to submit to both formal and informal church discipline?

5. How well do you in your church hold others accountable to live a holy life, speaking the truth in love?

6. What could you do to better partake of the Lord's Supper next time?

7. What are your worship practices? Is there some aspect of your worship—preparation, attendance, or participation—where you could grow?

8. Overall, what is the first step you could take to improve your engagement with Christ's church for your growth in holiness?

For Further Study

B. A. Gerrish, *Grace and Gratitude: The Eucharistic Theology of John Calvin* (Eugene, OR: Wipf and Stock, 2002).

Keith and Kristyn Getty, *Sing!: How Worship Transforms Your Life, Family, and Church* (Nashville: B&H, 2017).

Ken Ramey, *Expository Listening: A Practical Handbook for Hearing and Doing God's Word* (The Woodlands, TX: Kress, 2010).

Robert Rayburn, *O Come, Let Us Worship: Corporate Worship in the Evangelical Church* (Eugene, OR: Wipf and Stock, 2010).

R. C. Sproul, *What is the Lord's Supper?* (Orlando, FL: Reformation Trust, 2013).

Bibliography

Alcorn, Randy. *Heaven: Biblical Answers to Common Questions*. Carol Stream, IL: Tyndale, 2004.

———. *Money, Possessions, and Eternity: A Comprehensive Guide to What the Bible Says about Financial Stewardship, Generosity, Materialism, Retirement, Financial Planning, Gambling, Debt, and More*. Carol Stream, IL: Tyndale, 2012.

Anselm. *Cur Deus Homo*. Translated by S. N. Deane. Fort Worth, TX: RDMc, 2005.

Augustine, St. *The Retractions*. Translated by M. Inez Bogan, RSM. Fathers of the Church Patristic Series 60. Washington, DC: Catholic University of America Press, 1968.

Bainton, Roland. *Here I Stand: A Life of Martin Luther*. New York: Abingdon-Cokesbury, 1950.

Baird, Henry Martyn. *Theodore Beza the Counsellor of the French Reformation, 1519–1605*. Reprint, London: Forgotten Books, 2016.

Balserak, Jon. "The God of Love and Weakness: Calvin's Understanding of God's Accommodating Relationship With His People." *Westminster Theological Journal* 62 (2000) 177–95.

Battles, Ford Lewis. *Interpreting John Calvin*. Edited by Robert Benedetto. Grand Rapids: Baker, 1996.

———, ed. *The Piety of John Calvin: An Anthology Illustrative of the Spirituality of the Reformer of Geneva*. Grand Rapids: Baker, 1978.

Beeke, Joel R. "Does Assurance Belong to the Essence of Faith? Calvin and the Calvinists." *The Master's Seminary Journal* 5 (1994) 43–71.

———. *The Family at Church: Listening to Sermons and Attending Prayer Meetings*. Family Guidance. Grand Rapids: Reformation Heritage, 2008.

Bernard of Clairvaux. *On the Love of God*. Translated by Terence L. Connolly. New York: Spiritual, 1937.

Beveridge, Henry, and Jules Bonnet, eds. *John Calvin: Tracts and Letters*. 7 vols. Edinburgh: Banner of Truth, 2009.

Beza, Theodore. *The Life of John Calvin*. Durham, UK: Evangelical, 1997.

Blomberg, Craig L. *Christians in an Age of Wealth: A Biblical Theology of Stewardship*. Bibilical Theology for Life. Grand Rapids: Zondervan, 2013.

Bucer, Martin. *Concerning the True Care of Souls*. Translated by Peter Beale. Edinburgh: Banner of Truth, 2009.

———. *In Sacra Quatuor Evangelia Enarrationes Perpetuae Secundum Recognitae*. Basel: Johann Herwagen, 1536.

———. *Instruction in Christian Love*. 1523. Translated by Paul Traugott Fuhrmann. Reprint, Eugene, OR: Wipf and Stock, 2008.

———. *Metaphrasis et Enarratio in Epistolam D. Pauli Apostoli ad Romanos.* Basel: Peter Perna, 1562.

Burroughs, Jeremiah. *Moses' Self-Denial.* Grand Rapids: Soli Deo Gloria, 2010.

Calvin, John. *The Bondage and Liberation of the Will.* Edited by A. N. S. Lane. Translated by G. I. Davies. Grand Rapids: Baker, 2002.

———. *Calvin's Commentaries.* The Calvin Translation Society. 22 vols. Grand Rapids: Baker, 2005.

———. *Institutes of the Christian Religion.* Edited by John T. McNeill. Translated by Ford Lewis Battles. Philadelphia: Westminster, 1960.

———. *Instruction in Faith (1537).* Edited and translated by Paul Traugott Fuhrmann. Louisville: Westminster John Knox, 1977.

———. *Ioannis Calvini Opera Quae Supersunt Omnia.* Edited by Johann-Wilhelm Baum et al. 59 vols. Brunswick, Germany: Schwetschke, 1863–1900.

———. *Sermons on 2 Samuel Chapters 1–13.* Edited by Douglas Kelly. Edinburgh: Banner of Truth, 1992.

———. *Sermons on the Beatitudes.* Translated by Robert White. Edinburgh: Banner of Truth, 2006.

———. *Sermons on the Book of Micah.* Edited and translated by Benjamin W. Farley. Phillipsburg, NJ: P&R, 2003.

———. *Sermons on Election and Reprobation.* Translated by John Fielde. Willowstreet, PA: Old Paths, 1996.

———. *Sermons on Galatians.* Translated by Arthur Golding. Audubon, NJ: Old Paths, 1995.

———. *Sermons on Genesis Chapters 1–11.* Translated by Rob Roy McGregor. Edinburgh: Banner of Truth, 2009.

———. *Sermons on Job.* Translated by Arthur Golding. Edinburgh: Banner of Truth, 1993.

———. *Sermons on the Ten Commandments.* Edited and translated by Benjamin W. Farley. Reprint, Eugene, OR: Wipf and Stock, 2019.

———. *Songs of the Nativity: Selected Sermons on Luke 1 and 2.* Translated by Robert White. Edinburgh: Banner of Truth, 2008.

Carson, D. A. "God's Love and God's Wrath." *Bibliotheca Sacra* 156, no. 624 (1999) 387–98.

Dowey, Edward A., Jr. *The Knowledge of God in Calvin's Theology.* New York: Columbia University Press, 1965.

Edwards, Jonathan. *Charity and its Fruits.* Edinburgh: Banner of Truth, 2013.

———. *The Religious Affections.* Mineola, NY: Dover, 2013.

Engelsma, David J. "Martin Bucer: Reformed Pastor of Strasbourg." *Mid-America Journal of Theology* 3 (1987) 35–63.

Ferguson, Sinclair. *Devoted to God: Blueprints for Sanctification.* Edinburgh: Banner of Truth, 2016.

———. *The Grace of Repentance.* Today's Issues. Redesign ed. Wheaton, IL: Crossway, 2010.

Fitzpatrick, Elyse M. *Idols of the Heart: Learning to Long for God Alone.* Rev. ed. Phillipsburg, NJ: P&R, 2016.

Foster, Richard J., and James B. Smith, eds. *Devotional Classics: Selected Readings for Individuals and Groups.* New York: HarperCollins, 1993.

Franklin, Benjamin. *The Autobiography of Benjamin Franklin.* 1793. Edited by Frank Woodworth Pine. https://www.gutenberg.org/files/20203/20203-h/20203-h.htm.

Gaffin, Richard B., Jr. "Calvin's Soteriology: The Structure of the Application of Redemption in Book Three of the *Institutes*." *Ordained Servant* 18 (2009) 68–77.

Gerrish, B. A. "Calvin's Eucharistic Piety." In *Calvin and Spirituality*, edited by David Foxgrover, 52–65. Grand Rapids: CRC, 1998.

———. *Grace and Gratitude: The Eucharistic Theology of John Calvin*. Eugene, OR: Wipf and Stock, 2002.

Getty, Keith and Kristyn. *Sing!: How Worship Transforms Your Life, Family, and Church*. Nashville: B&H, 2017.

Gilbert, A. H. "Martin Bucer on Education." *The Journal of English and Germanic Philology* 18 (1919) 321–45.

Godfrey, W. Robert. "Faith Formed by Love or Faith Alone? The Instrument of Justification." In *Covenant, Justification, and Pastoral Ministry: Essays by the Faculty of Westminster Seminary California*, edited by R. Scott Clark, 267–84. Phillipsburg, NJ: P&R, 2007.

Gordon, T. David. *Why Johnny Can't Preach: The Media Have Shaped the Messengers*. Phillipsburg, NJ: P&R, 2009.

Gregory the Great. *Pastoral Care*. Edited and translated by Henry Davis. New York: Newman, 1950.

Hildebrand, Dietrich von. *Humility: Wellspring of Virtue*. Manchester, NH: Sophia Institute, 1997.

Holder, R. Ward. "Calvin's Exegetical Understanding of the Office of Pastor." In *Calvin and the Company of Pastors*, edited by David Foxgrover, 179–209. Grand Rapids: CRC, 2004.

Jeremiah, David. *Answers to Your Questions About Heaven*. Carol Stream, IL: Tyndale, 2015.

Jones, Mark. *Antinomianism: Reformed Theology's Unwelcome Guest?* Phillipsburg, NJ: P&R, 2013.

Keller, Timothy. *Every Good Endeavor: Connecting Your Work to God's Work*. New York: Penguin, 2016.

———. *Walking with God through Pain and Suffering*. New York: Dutton, 2013.

Kraan, E. D. "Le Péché et la Repentance." *La Revue Reformée* 48 (1997) 39–49.

Lane, A. N. S. "Calvin's Doctrine of Assurance." *Vox Evangelica* 11 (1979) 32–54.

Lane, Timothy S., and Paul David Tripp. *How People Change*. Greensboro, NC: New Growth, 2006.

Lobstein, Paul. *Die Ethik Calvins in Ihren Grundzügen Entworfen*. Strasbourg: C. F. Schmidt's, 1877.

Luther, Martin. *Commentary on Galatians*. Translated by Erasmus Middleton. Grand Rapids: Kregel, 1979.

———. "Disputation on the Power and Efficacy of Indulgences." In *Luther's Works, American Edition*, edited by Jaroslav J. Pelikan and Helmut T. Lehmann, 55 vols., 31:25–33. Philadelphia: Fortress, 1957.

MacArthur, John. *How to Study the Bible*. Chicago: Moody, 2009.

Manton, Thomas. *A Treatise of Self-Denial*. Christian Classics. Pensacola, FL: Chapel Library, 2014.

Marshall, Walter. *The Gospel Mystery of Sanctification*. Grand Rapids: Reformation Heritage, 1999.

McMahon, C. Matthew. *John Calvin's View of God's Love and the Doctrine of Reprobation*. Crossville, TN: Puritan, 2015.

Muller, Richard A. *Calvin and the Reformed Tradition: On The Work Of Christ And The Order Of Salvation*. Grand Rapids: Baker Academic, 2012.

Murray, Andrew. *Humility: The Beauty of Holiness*. Abbotsford, WI: Aneko, 2016.

Murray, John. "Definitive Sanctification." *Calvin Theological Journal* 2 (1967) 5–21.

———. *Redemption Accomplished and Applied*. 1955. Reprint, Grand Rapids: Eerdmans, 2015.

Niesel, Wilhelm *The Theology of Calvin*. Translated by Harold Knight. Philadelphia: Westminster, 1956.

Official Report of the Fifteenth International Christian Endeavor Convention. Boston, MA: United Society of Christian Endeavor, 1896.

Ortlund, Dane. *Edwards on the Christian Life: Alive to the Beauty of God*. Wheaton, IL: Crossway, 2014.

Owen, John. *The Mortification of Sin*. Edinburgh: Banner of Truth, 2009.

Packer, J. I. *Rediscovering Holiness: Know the Fullness of Life with God*. Grand Rapids: Baker, 2009.

Parker, T. H. L. *John Calvin: A Biography*. Philadelphia: Westminster, 1975.

Piper, John, and Justin Taylor, eds. *Suffering and the Sovereignty of God*. Wheaton, IL: Crossway, 2006.

Placher, William C. *Callings: Twenty Centuries of Christian Wisdom on Vocation*. Grand Rapids: Eerdmans, 2005.

Ramey, Ken. *Expository Listening: A Practical Handbook for Hearing and Doing God's Word*. The Woodlands, TX: Kress, 2010.

Rayburn, Robert. *O Come, Let Us Worship: Corporate Worship in the Evangelical Church*. Eugene, OR: Wipf and Stock, 2010.

Reid, J. K. S., ed. *Calvin: Theological Treatises*. Louisville: Westminster John Knox, 2006.

Roberts, Alexander, and James Donaldson, eds. *The Ante-Nicene Fathers*. 10 vols. Peabody, MA: Hendrickson, 1994.

Ryle, J. C. *Holiness*. Louisville: GLH, 2015. Kindle.

Schaff, Philip, ed. *The Creeds of Christendom*. 3 vols. Grand Rapids: Baker, 1977.

———. *The Nicene and Post-Nicene Fathers*. 28 vols. Peabody, MA: Hendrickson, 1994.

Schnetzler, Charles, et al., eds. *Pierre Viret d'après lui-même*. Lausanne: Georges Bridel, 1911.

Schreiner, Susan. "Calvin's Concern with Certainty in the Context of the Sixteenth Century." In *Calvin, Beza and Later Calvinism*, edited by David Foxgrover, 113–31. Grand Rapids: CRC, 2006.

Selderhuis, Herman J. "Faith Between God and the Devil: Calvin's Doctrine of Faith as Reflected in his Commentary on the Psalms." In *John Calvin and the Interpretation of Scripture*, edited by Charles Raynal, 188–205. Grand Rapids: CRC, 2006.

———. *John Calvin: A Pilgrim's Life*. Downers Grove, IL: InterVarsity, 2009.

Sproul, R. C. *Surprised by Suffering: The Role of Pain and Death in the Christian Life*. Lake Mary, FL: Reformation, 2009.

———. *What is Repentance?* Sanford, FL: Reformation, 2014.

———. *What is the Lord's Supper?* Crucial Questions. Orlando, FL: Reformation Trust, 2013.

Stephens, W. P. *The Holy Spirit in the Theology of Martin Bucer*. Cambridge: Cambridge University Press, 1970.

Stuart, Douglas, and Gordon Fee. *How to Read the Bible for All Its Worth*. 4th ed. Grand Rapids: Zondervan, 2014.

Bibliography

Tada, Joni Eareckson. *Heaven: Your Real Home . . . From a Higher Perspective*. Grand Rapids: Zondervan, 1995.
Tamburello, Dennis E. *Union with Christ: John Calvin and the Mysticism of St. Bernard*. Louisville: Westminster John Knox, 1994.
Ten Boom, Corrie. *The Hiding Place*. Peabody, MA: Hendrickson, 2015.
Thomas à Kempis. *The Imitation of Christ*. Translated by Aloysius Croft and Harold F. Bolton. Milwaukee, WI: Bruce, 1962.
Timmerman, Daniel. "Martin Bucer as Interpreter of the Old Testament: A Re-examination of Previous Scholarship in Light of Bucer's *Enarrationes in Librum Iudicum* (ca. 1540)." *Reformation and Renaissance Review* 9 (2007) 27–44.
Torrance, Thomas F. *Calvin's Doctrine of Man*. Westport, CT: Greenwood, 1997.
Viret, Pierre. *Catechism of 1541*. http://www.pierreviret.org/theology-catechetical.php.
———. *Du Devoir et du Besoing qu'ont les Hommes à s'Enquerir de la Volonté de Dieu par sa Parole*. Geneva: Jean Girard, 1551.
———. *Instruction Chrétienne*. Lausanne: L'Age d'Homme, 2008.
———. *La Vertu et Usage du Ministère la Parolle de Dieu*. Geneva: Jean Girard, 1548.
———. *L'Interim Fait par Dialogues*. New York: Peter Lang, 1985.
Wallace, Ronald S. *Calvin's Doctrine of the Christian Life*. Edinburgh: Oliver and Boyd, 1959.
Warren, Rick. *Rick Warren's Bible Study Methods*. Grand Rapids: Zondervan, 2006.
Watson, Thomas. *A Body of Divinity*. Edinburgh: Banner of Truth, 2015.
———. *The Doctrine of Repentance*. Carlisle, PA: Banner of Truth, 1988.
———. *The Duty of Self-Denial and Ten Other Sermons*. Morgan, PA: Soli Deo Gloria, 2004.
Wendel, Francois. *Calvin: Origins and Development of His Religious Thought*. Translated by Philip Mairet. New York: Harper & Row, 1963.
Westminster Confession of Faith. Lawrenceville, GA: Christian Education and Publications, 2007.
The Westminster Shorter Catechism, With Scripture Proofs. Carlisle, PA: Banner of Truth, 1989.
Winecoff, David K. "Calvin's Doctrine of Mortification." *Presbyterion* 13 (1987) 85–101.
Wright, David F., ed. and trans. *Common Places of Martin Bucer*. Abingdon, UK: Sutton Courtenay, 1972.
Zachman, Randall C. "'Deny Yourself and Take up Your Cross': John Calvin on the Christian Life." *International Journal of Systematic Theology* 11 (2009) 466–82.

www.ingramcontent.com/pod-product-compliance
Lightning Source LLC
Chambersburg PA
CBHW070245230426
43664CB00014B/2409